Creation and Beauty in Tolkien's Catholic Vision

Creation and Beauty in Tolkien's Catholic Vision

A Study in the Influence of Neoplatonism in
J. R. R. Tolkien's Philosophy of Life as "Being and Gift"

Michael John Halsall

Foreword by
Alison Grant Milbank

◥PICKWICK *Publications* • Eugene, Oregon

CREATION AND BEAUTY IN TOLKIEN'S CATHOLIC VISION
A Study in the Influence of Neoplatonism in J. R. R. Tolkien's Philosophy of Life as "Being and Gift"

Copyright © 2020 Michael John Halsall. All rights reserved. Except for brief quotations in critical publications or reviews, no part of this book may be reproduced in any manner without prior written permission from the publisher. Write: Permissions, Wipf and Stock Publishers, 199 W. 8th Ave., Suite 3, Eugene, OR 97401.

Pickwick Publications
An Imprint of Wipf and Stock Publishers
199 W. 8th Ave., Suite 3
Eugene, OR 97401

www.wipfandstock.com

PAPERBACK ISBN: 978-1-5326-4110-7
HARDCOVER ISBN: 978-1-5326-4111-4
EBOOK ISBN: 978-1-5326-4112-1

Cataloguing-in-Publication data:

Names: Halsall, Michael John, author. | Milbank, Alison Grant, foreword.

Title: Creation and beauty in Tolkien's Catholic vision : a study in the influence of Neoplatonism in J. R. R. Tolkien's philosophy of life as "being and gift" / by Michael John Halsall ; foreword by Alison Grant Milbank.

Description: Eugene, OR: Pickwick Publications, 2020 | Includes bibliographical references.

Identifiers: ISBN 978-1-5326-4110-7 (paperback) | ISBN 978-1-5326-4111-4 (hardcover) | ISBN 978-1-5326-4112-1 (ebook)

Subjects: LCSH: Tolkein, J. R. R.—(John Ronald Reuel),—1892–1973—Criticism and interpretation. | Fantasy literature, English—History and criticism. | Neoplatonism | Catholic Tradition | Fiction—Religious aspects—Christianity | Theology in literature.

Classification: PR6039 H15 2020 (print) | PR6039 (ebook)

Manufactured in the U.S.A.   01/02/20

This book is dedicated to my mother, and the loving memory of my father.

Throughout life my parents have been a supreme source of encouragement and support, and without clear demonstrations of their love, moral courage, and many sacrifices, I would not be the man I am today.

Contents

Foreword by Alison Grant Milbank | xi
Author's Preface | xv
Acknowledgments | xvii
List of Abbreviations | xix

Chapter 1
Prolegomenon to the Sub-Creative Genius of Tolkien amongst His Contemporaries | 3

    1.1 Tolkien and the Edwardian Legacy   3

    1.2 The Current Status of Tolkien Studies   8

    1.3 Influences and Inspiration   10

    1.4 Structure of the Book   16

Chapter 2
Creation and the Metaphysics of Music: Tolkien's Philosophy of Createdness as 'Gift' | 21

    2.1 *Creatio Sub Specie Aeternitatis*   21

    2.2 The Metaphysics of Music: Tolkien's Creative Symphony   36

    2.3 Creation and Fall in the *Ainulindalë*   52

    2.4 Music, Vision, and Reality in Creation   62

    2.5 The Thomist Revision under the Influence of Jacques Maritain   73

Chapter 3

The Concept of Life as 'Being and Gift' in Tolkien's Literary Corpus | 105

    3.1. Towards a Mythology for England   105

    3.2 *Beowulf* as an Anglo-Saxon Paradigm of Myth-as-Truth   114

    3.3 Freedom's Optimistic Turn in an Anglo-Saxon World   127

    3.4 Grace in Human Realization and Destiny   143

Chapter 4

Tolkien, Eriugena, and the Conjoining of Borrowed Traditions | 167

    4.1 Tolkien's Neoplatonism, and the Mystical Paths of Christian Mythology   168

    4.2 Eriugena's Defence of Freedom   189

    4.3 Siewers' Celtic Otherworld Interpretation of Tolkien's 'Strange Beauty'   195

Chapter 5

A Diversion towards Mutability and the Possibility of Evil | 213

    5.1 Life as Gift and Variety: Augustine's Optimistic Neoplatonism   213

    5.2 Evil as the 'Embodiment of Non-Being' from the Perspective of Being   215

    5.3 The Good and Grotesque as Expressions of *Omnis Natura Bonum Est*   222

    5.4 A Critique of Augustine's 'Free Will' and 'Aesthetic' Theodicies   228

Chapter 6

Concluding Comments: There and Back Again | 235

Appendices

Appendix A: Michelangelo's Statues in the Accademia, Florence | 243

Appendix B: A Synopsis of *The Tale of Tinúviel: Of Beren and Luthien* | 251

Appendix C: Three Crosses in the Churchyard of Whalley Abbey, Lancashire | 254

Appendix D: The Standard of the King of Gondor | 258

Appendix E: Iconography in the *Book of Kells* | 259

Bibliography | 263

Foreword

In the last ten years or so, Tolkien criticism has enjoyed a new flowering, gathering professional status through the academic journal *Tolkien Studies* and a number of fine monographs. Bizarrely, *The Lord of the Rings* has finally achieved the respectability in university English departments it has long been denied through the Peter Jackson films, so that Tolkien can now be studied as an example of popular culture. Some of the most insightful critical work has attended, as Michael Halsall does in this volume, to Tolkien's religious and philosophical ideas, as exemplified in his fiction. Tolkien often spoke of his main creative work as the construction of languages, and to invent a tongue, one has to embrace an entire worldview and create syntax and grammar. In moving to create actual other worlds and cultures in which these languages are spoken, Tolkien cannot help but engage in metaphysics: his cosmos not only has to have geography, history, and culture but a consistency and a meaning which introduces the need for metaphysics. Much of the power of Tolkien's writing comes from a sense that you can go all the way down in his world, and its conception will not fail you: there will always be more to learn. It is the complete opposite of the coding of the computer game, which always comes up against the limits of its design.

Metaphysics is therefore built into the fantasy genre, as the author imagines the categories of experience, the ontology, epistemology, and ethics of his or her creation. What I find particularly compelling about Michael Halsall's claim for a Christian Neoplatonism as structuring Tolkien's metaphysics is that it accounts for another important aspect of the reading experience: its mixture of joy and melancholy. All Tolkien's writing is shot through with a sense of the sadness of life, its mutability and loss. Typically, the Jackson film balked at narrating the harrowing of the Shire, when the return of the hobbits to their homeland leads to no triumphant welcome but to the discovery of catastrophe and ruin. In Tolkien's essay *On Fairy-stories*, every happy ending has poignant grief as well as joy, and is achieved only after the worst has transpired. And yet, the actual writing trusts in words as good things. Tolkien writes in a manner that gives every object described a kind of radiance. As G. K. Chesterton writes, "The goodness of the fairy tale was not affected by the fact that there might be more dragons than princesses; it was good to be in a fairy tale."[1] Similarly, it is always good to be in a novel by Tolkien, so that even the Orcs, perverted elves though they may be, have a zany energy, and the mere objects are so valued that he grants them their own index at the end of *Return of the King*.

All this is made sense of in a Neoplatonic ontology, in which being is good, and evil has none being, but a lack or loss of being. Beyond the One, and especially in the realm of the material, there is mutability, change, and loss. In Michael's scholarly investigation, he finds this Neoplatonic metaphysics structuring Middle-earth and the mythology that undergirds it. In particular, viewed through this lens, much of what is assumed to be determinist in Anglo-Saxon fashion is shown to leave the will much freer. Michael demonstrates that the way in which Tolkien conceives of his status as sub-creator under God owes much to Aquinas's perception that we are made in the image of God, who gives life and freedom, so that we too may give life and freedom to the things that we make. More speculatively, he suggests a possible and mediated influence of John Scotus Eriugena on Tolkien's story of Beren and Lúthien, where that creaturely freedom includes the capacity to shape-shift, to craft and change one's own form.

Another powerful element of the Tolkien reading experience is the way the text opens to pull the reader in, so that for most readers who make it to the end of the three volumes of *The Lord of the Rings*, the novel is now part of their life, and cannot be forgotten. As Erich Auerbach described the Bible, so Tolkien's is an omnivorous text. The reader responds and is called into the act of interpretation, holding together, for example, the two discrete endings of the novel, with Frodo in the Undying Lands and Sam at home in the Shire. As the audience of a Greek tragedy experienced both pity and fear in the cathartic effect, so the reader of Tolkien holds joy and loss, and in this way participates in the story through a kind of Neoplatonic contemplation. Michael has a great deal to say about *theosis*, philosophically, which is where the Christian version of participation is important, since it valorizes the material realm more strongly than Plotinus, and takes everything back to its source in God, where it is most itself. The amazing thing about Tolkien's Middle-earth is that everything participates in the splendid array of creation, and is drawn to its source. We see this most clearly in the unalienated

---

1. G. K. Chesterton, "The Ethics of Elfland," *Orthodoxy* (London: Bodley Head, 1957 [1908]), 66–102 (82).

labour of the Lothlórien elves; they put their whole selves into their work, and the result is rope that can untie itself and has an element of agency. It is more rope-like than any rope in our world, because it participates fully in being. Its created nature, to use Michael's terminology, is received as gift, as is the creativity of the elves who make it, and thus it is united to its source, and wholly radiant in pointing beyond itself to its origin.

Michael refers to Augustine quite frequently, and it is to Book 10 of Augustine's *Confessions* that I would point for an analogy with the way the world of Tolkien is marked by participation. In a celebrated rhetorical passage, Augustine questions the natural world:

> I asked the sea and the deeps, and the creeping things that lived, and they replied, "We are not thy God, seek higher than we." I asked the breezy air, and the universal air with its inhabitants answered, "Anaximenes was deceived, I am not God." I asked the heavens, the sun, moon, and stars: "Neither," say they, "are we the God whom thou seekest." And I answered unto all these things which stand about the door of my flesh, "Ye have told me concerning my God, that ye are not He; tell me something about Him." And with a loud voice they exclaimed, "He made us." My questioning was my observing of them; and their beauty was their reply.[2]

In the same way, the reader of Tolkien questions the origin and meaning of the ents or hobbits, the flowers and trees of his Middle-earth, and is enabled to move back through the Neoplatonic triad to the Creator himself, not just by the knowledge of the creation myth of the 'Ainulindalë' but by the reading experience itself. Fragile and lovely, the things of Tolkien's world always show that they did not make themselves, but point beyond themselves to another world, a deeper reality. Like Augustine in his mystical ascent, they take us back to the mysterious source, and that mark of 'madeness' is the beginning of relation and participation. With the most delicate color palette of green, heathery blue, silver, and gold Tolkien evokes a cosmos that we would all like to live in, but one that is never an end in itself. Its beauty awakens in the reader a hungering for something beyond the material, which is symbolized by the worlds beyond worlds of Tolkien's legendarium. It awakens that natural desire for the supernatural about which a Catholic theologian of Tolkien's own day, Henri de Lubac, wrote about in *Surnaturel* in 1946, which seems to breathe the air of Middle-earth.

---

2. Augustine of Hippo, *Confessions*, trans. J. G. Pilkington, in *Select Library of Nicene and Post-Nicene Fathers*, series 1, vol. 1, ed. Philip Schraff (Edinburgh: T. & T. Clark, 2001), Book 10, 6, 9, 144.

I commend Michael's book to all readers of Tolkien, whether they be philosophers or not. They will find in the sturdiness of his texts under philosophical scrutiny even more to admire, and in Michael's intertextual research, original and exciting insights into Tolkien's thought. Michael has worked on a range of manuscript material, including notes for the medieval poem *Pearl*. He compares Boethius to King Alfred's own translation, and suggests a Celtic overlaying of worlds. This is a rich engagement at all levels with Tolkien, full of suggestive comparisons with the tradition of the music of the spheres and with the modernist music of his own time. It is deeply scholarly but clear and accessible. And it is both Catholic in relating Tolkien to Catholic theology, including Maritain, and the Thomism of the early twentieth century, but also in its range of reference, which does full justice to Tolkien's intellectual background and his generosity of spirit, which had room for wild-men and oliphants, wereworms and Barliman's best bitter, all with the mark of createdness upon them, gifted to his readers.

Alison Grant Milbank

November 2017

Author's Preface

Amidst themes of discordance, order, and harmony, Tolkien sought to juxtapose beauty and ugliness, unity and difference, perfection in God and a lapse from that transcendent ideal, in order to offer a philosophy of creation in a carefully crafted narrative. Tolkien begins his entire corpus with a cosmogonic drama, Neoplatonic in its stylizing of whirling stars in planetary motions, producing cycles of 'awareness' from eternity to finitude. There is here an ideal in God's unity and simplicity, but much is lost as temporality proceeds from the cosmic drama into reality and experience.

The cultural interplay between Tolkien and contemporaries such as Eliot, Britten and Chesterton, alongside his well-documented literary interchange with his friends in The Inklings, sets Tolkien amongst an intellectual and cultural *milieu* which was striving to bring meaning, enchantment, and wonder out of the mythology and biblical imagery of the English literary canon on the one hand, and the horror and disillusion caused by the Great War on the other.

Tolkien has been included as one of a number of those 'traumatised authors' writing fantasy, but voicing in that fantasy "the most pressing and immediate relevant issues of the whole monstrous twentieth century."[1] One might ask, why can't Tolkien's Middle-earth writings be simply what they are—fantasy—a story of journey and quest, of brotherhood and friendships forged in the face of adversity? The answer is quite straight forward: for the author, written into that fantasy are things which are, at an altogether different level, very real. Tolkien utilizes a variety of resources with which he constructs a world of imagination, enchantment, *and* reality. This reality points to what things are in their relation to God: being and gift. Things are what they are/are not (ontologically and meontologically)

---

1. Tom Shippey, *Road to Middle Earth*, xix.

precisely because something has willed that they be so, and are ordered hierarchically in a great chain of being.

This book explores these themes, alongside the challenges of evil and suffering, in the face of a wide-ranging breadth of scholarship, which finds its origins in Plato and his contemporaries, but also in how their ideas were absorbed in the Christian Neoplatonic tradition. This study offers original insights into previously unpublished Middle-earth texts of Tolkien, available in print for the first time, alongside his own unpublished textual notes on Anglo-Saxon poems such as *Beowulf* and *Pearl*. I have sought to keep in mind Tolkien's original project, in creating a mythology for England, but imbued also with the Catholic mindset of his generation.

Acknowledgements

A number of people deserve particular acknowledgment, as having had a significant role to play in the inspiration, inception, and completion of this book which, like many of its kind, is a reworked PhD thesis. The first of whom is one of my Junior School teachers—Miss Poole—who encouraged me in my reading generally, and introduced me to Tolkien's *The Hobbit* in particular. Due to her inspiration, I have never stopped reading.

Further formation in theology and philosophy would not have been possible without opportunities afforded by the Church of England's ministerial theological programme at Wycliffe Hall, Oxford. As a science graduate, they gave me the necessary skills in the study of humanities, an excellent grounding in the study of sacred Scripture and historical theology, and have been kind enough to provide me with bed and board during several trips to Oxford for research. Since my reception into the Catholic Church, my philosophical formation owes much to two highly talented scholars—Professors Johannes Hoff and Simon Oliver—who, whilst at the University of Wales (Lampeter), encouraged me in the research aspects of my Masters' Degree, and set me on a path to further research.

In addition, the librarians at the British Library, and the Special Collections Department of the Bodleian Library, Oxford, have shown both kindness and patience in my search for obscure and unpublished materials, as well as currently available titles—sometimes at short notice.

To my wife Jane, who has endured many evenings, days and weekends alone, listened to the various doings of Hobbits, and shown at least a modicum of interest in a subject on which she is entirely agnostic, I am eternally grateful for her patience and sense of humour (usually at my expense). During these periods of research I was (evidently) not easy to live with at times.

Furthermore, to my former students of Religious Studies at Westcliff High School for Boys, Essex, I hope that my research has enriched their lives also. A special mention goes to the modest *WHSB Tolkien Society*, for together we explored many avenues of enquiry, and they did at times shown genuine interest in my own studies.

The final acknowledgment, and fittingly with most profound thanks, I offer to my PhD Supervisor—Professor Alison Milbank—who was (and still is) a constant source of encouragement, friendly critic, and someone whose understanding of Tolkien's philosophical and literary influences and associations is encyclopaedic. She gave much of her personal time at weekends to provide excellent supervision; gave clear direction when I felt myself lost in 'the bogs and arid places' of confusion; and most of all encouraged me to continue my studies when I almost gave up at the first hurdle. Alison has always been a friendly voice at the end of the telephone, often at the end of a long working day for both of us.

This book is not so much the culmination of a course of study and research, but a life-long journey in faith and change along the way. To all of those who have gone before me, or shared that journey I say, "Thank you".

List of Abbreviations

J. R. R. Tolkien

Biography	*J. R. R. Tolkien: A Biography* (Carpenter (ed.), 1977)
Bodleian SC–MSS	The unpublished notes, drawings, and papers of J. R. R. Tolkien in the Special Collections Department of the Bodleian Library, Oxford
Tree and Leaf	*Tree and Leaf* (containing *On Fairy Stories, Mythopoeia, Leaf By Niggle*)
Letters	*The Letters of J. R. R. Tolkien* (Carpenter (ed.), 2006)
LOTR	*The Lord of the Rings*
Monsters	*The Monsters and the Critics and Other Essays*

Saint Augustine Of Hippo

Civ Dei	*De Civitate Dei*	City of God
Conf	*Confessiones*	Confessions
De DocChr	*De Doctrina Christiana*	On Christian Instruction
De Gen ad Lit	*De Genesi ad Litteram Libri Duodecim*	Twelve Books on the Literal Sense of Genesis
De Gen c. Man	*De Genesi contra Manichaeos*	Genesis: Against Manichaeans
De lib arb	*De Libero Arbitrio*	On Free Choice of the Will

De Mus	De Musica	On Music
De nat. boni c. Man	De Natura Boni contra Manichaeos	On the Nature of the Good against the Manichaeans
De Trin	De Trinitate	On the Trinity
EnPs	Enarrationes in Psalmos	On Psalms
Enchr	Enchiridion	The Handbook on Faith, Hope, and Love

Saint Thomas Aquinas

QDP	Quaestiones Disputatae De Potentia Dei	Disputed Questions on the Power of God
QDV	Questiones Disputatae de Veritate	Disputed Questions on Truth
SBT	Super Boethium de Trinitate	Commentary on Boethius' On the Trinity
SCG	Summa Contra Gentiles	Treatise on the Truth of the Catholic Faith against Unbelievers
ST	Summa Theologiae	Summary of Theology

Others

AS-D	Anglo-Saxon Dictionary
CCC	Catechism of the Catholic Church
Consolations	Consolations of Philosophy (Boethius)
Enneads	The Six Enneads (Plotinus)
DivNom	On the Divine Names (Pseudo-Dionysius))
DivPre	Treatise on Divine Predestination (Eriugena)

All references from sacred Scripture are taken from the Revised Standard Version, unless otherwise stated.

O perpetual revolution of configured stars,
O perpetual recurrence of determined seasons,
O world of spring and autumn, birth and dying!
The endless cycle of idea and action,
Endless invention, endless experiment,
Brings knowledge of motion, but not of stillness;
Knowledge of speech, but not of silence;
Knowledge of words, and ignorance of the Word.
All our knowledge brings us nearer to our ignorance,
All our ignorance brings us nearer to death,
But nearness to death no nearer to God [. . .]
The cycles of heaven in twenty centuries
Bring us farther from God and nearer to the Dust.[1]

---

1. Eliot, *Complete Poems*, 147.

1

Prolegomenon to the Sub-Creative Genius of Tolkien and His Contemporaries

1.1 Tolkien and the Edwardian Legacy

The opening stanza of T. S. Eliot's "Choruses from the Rock" (above), originated in a 1934 pageant called *The Rock*, which was commissioned in order to raise funds for building churches in the new suburbs in the diocese of north London between the wars. The building projects were aimed at creating sacred spaces in the expanding 'waste lands,' where Eliot perceives London as a 'time kept city' of commerce and shipping trade: hallmarks of early-mid-twentieth-century secularism. In this problem of secularized loss of transcendent meaning, Frank Sawyer notes that Eliot uses words where composers of the day might have used musical notation, in that "all his poems play with intellectually discordant thoughts, discordant sounds, and unexpected juxtapositions, often depending on word-plays and half-hidden meanings or pointers."[1]

It is these themes of discordance amidst order and harmony that contemporaries of Eliot, such as Tolkien and Britten, used in order to juxtapose beauty and ugliness, unity and difference, perfection in God and a lapse from that transcendent ideal. Eliot was writing at the same time that Tolkien was redrafting elements of his own cosmo-genesis and, like Tolkien, begins the above work with a cosmogonic drama, Neoplatonic in its stylizing of whirling stars in planetary motions, producing cycles of 'awareness' from eternity to finitude. There is here an ideal in God's unity and simplicity, but much is lost as temporality proceeds from the cosmic drama into reality and experience.

---

1. Sawyer, "The Rock," 1.

We know that Tolkien was aware of, and read Eliot, and that Britten put Eliot's words to music, in particular, those with a religious theme.² This cultural interplay, therefore, alongside his well-documented literary interchange with his friends in the TCBS and the Inklings, sets Tolkien amongst an intellectual and cultural *milieu*, which is striving to bring meaning, enchantment, and wonder out of the mythology and biblical imagery of the English literary canon on the one hand, and the horror and disillusion caused by the Great War on the other.³ There is no evidence that Eliot was a direct influence on Tolkien, but I make the point that they had a similar literary intention, as presented to an English-speaking audience.⁴ In the foreword to *The Book of Lost Tales*, Christopher Tolkien explains that his father's writings originated in 1916–17, during convalescence from his sickness and combat experiences during the Battle of the Somme, and left incomplete several years later.⁵ During this hiatus, he turned to composing the long poems of *The Tale of Tinúviel* and *The Children of Hurin* in alliterative verse. However, over many revisions and compilations, they existed and were still being edited in early versions of *The Silmarillion* in 1937. It was in this decade that Eliot wrote and first performed *The Rock* (1934). Tom Shippey includes Tolkien as one of a number of "traumatised authors" writing fantasy, but voicing in that fantasy "the most pressing and immediate relevant issues of the whole monstrous twentieth century."⁶ One might ask why can't Tolkien's Middle-earth writings be simply what they are—fantasy—a story of journey and quest, of brotherhood and friendships forged in the face of adversity? The answer is quite straight forward: for the author, written into that fantasy are things which are, at an altogether different level, very real. Tolkien utilizes a variety of resources with which he constructs a world of imagination, enchantment, *and* reality. This reality points to what things are in their relation to God: being and gift. Things are what they are/are not (ontologically and meontologically) precisely because something has willed that they be so, and are ordered hierarchically in a great chain of being.

In his 1992 Encyclical Letter *Fides Et Ratio*, Pope (now Saint) John Paul II recognized that:

---

2. Evans, *Music of Benjamin Britten*, 411–14. It wasn't until 1971, however, that Britten composed and performed the setting for Eliot's *Journey of the Magi*, and 1975, two years after Tolkien's death, that he composed the setting for *The Death of Narcissus*.

3. The Tea Club, Barovian Society was a literary club, comprising Tolkien and several friends from King Edward's School in Birmingham. The Inklings were a similarly disposed group of Oxford scholars.

4. Carpenter, *Letters*, 350, 353.

5. Tolkien, *Book of Lost Tales 1*, 8.

6. Shippey, *Road to Middle Earth*, xix.

Men and women have at their disposal an array of resources for generating greater knowledge of truth so that their lives may be ever more human. Among those is *philosophy*, which is directly concerned with asking the question of life's meaning and sketching an answer to it.[7]

This investigation is partly in response to that quest towards meaning in terms of life's createdness and giftedness, as it may be discerned from the complex linguistic strands of Tolkien's entire *corpus*. It is also in part to St John Paul II's appeal to

> *philosophers* and to all *teachers of philosophy*, asking them to have courage to recover, in the flow of an enduringly valid philosophical tradition, the range of authentic wisdom and truth—metaphysical truth included—which is proper to philosophical enquiry.[8]

The extent to which Tolkien was working towards that end in his own time will be explored here. As a Catholic, Tolkien believed in the *Fidei Depositum*—a body of faith, based on right reason and revelation, but based also upon the writings of Christian scholars who utilized in a variety of ways the philosophy of Plato. Tolkien's belief in an objective truth about life and the world rises out of his own faith and life-experience, and St John Paul II sums up what I am postulating concerning Tolkien's entire project: "Only within this horizon of truth will people understand their freedom in its fullness and their call to know and love God as the supreme realization of their true self."[9] The claim of human freedom, constituted as 'being and gift,' is supported throughout this investigation in both their physical and metaphysical aspects.

Tolkien's genuine ambition was to create a 'mythology for England' using ancient literary sources, devices and idioms.[10] Consistent with classical and Neoplatonic method, Tolkien introduced his mythological world through the agency of music—divine music, to create and evolve a landscape, and people it with a plenitude of (apparently) substantially good creatures. He was not alone in this project. In a different and yet equally very English manner, his later contemporary Benjamin Britten wrote:"One of my chief aims is to try and restore to the musical setting of the English

---

7. John Paul II, *Fides et Ratio*, para 3.
8. Ibid., para 106.
9. Ibid., para 107.
10 Carpenter, *Letters*, 144–45.

language a brilliance, freedom and vitality that have been curiously rare since the death of Purcell."[11]

For Britten, music had both a pithy and immediate quality, but conversely conveyed eternal ideas where words simply fail, and for him this was epitomized by a lifetime's struggle with the Christian faith and pacifism, amidst his own turbulent relationships. In a letter to Henry Boys, he expressed this inner and aesthetic struggle:

> It is cruel, you know, that music should be so beautiful. It has the beauty of loneliness & of pain: of strength & freedom. The beauty of disappointment & never-satisfied love. The cruel beauty of nature, and everlasting beauty of monotony. [. . .] Perhaps if I could understand some of the Indian philosophies I might approach it a little. At the moment I can do no more than bask in its heavenly light—& it is worth having lived to do that.[12]

In his 1937 work *The Company of Heaven*, he weaves into the musical text words from Gerard Manley Hopkins about the struggle between Lucifer and the 'sons of God' whereby he (Lucifer), instead of shouting for joy, crafted his own song in self-praise and in opposition to the mind and purposes of God. The Britten text reads:

> When all the sons of God shouted for joy, Lucifer would not take part, but sang his own song. This song of Lucifer's was a dwelling on its own beauty, an instressing of his own inscape, and like a performance on the organ and instrument of his own being; it was a sounding, as they say, of his own trumpet and a hymn in his own praise. Moreove [sic] it became an incantation, others were drawn in; it became a concert of voices, a concerting of selfpraise, an enchantment, a magic, by which they were dizzied, dazzled, and bewitched. They would not listen to the note which summoned each to his own place and disturbed them here and there in the liturgy of the sacrifice; they gathered rather closer and closer home under Lucifer's lead and drowned it, raising a countermusic and countertemple and altar, a counterpoint of dissonance and not of harmony.[13]

It is this dissonance, projecting itself into harmonic structures that attempt to express the inner struggles of writers and composers of the day; it is also the case within Tolkien's co-creation, expressing his own self-understanding

---

11. Brett, *Benjamin Britten: Peter Grimes*, 149.
12. Matthews, *Britten*, 22.
13. Britten, *Company of Heaven*, 6.

and inner struggles with life, and his Catholic Neoplatonic understanding of the cosmos. Britten, a pacifist, writing amidst the growing strength of Nazi Germany, was crafting a pre-existent account of "Chaos" (section I of the work above); whilst in the same year Tolkien published *The Hobbit*, commenced work on *LOTR*, and sent a complete draft of *The Silmarillion* to his publisher for consideration.[14] If Shippey is correct in his assertion above, then this fruitful period of literary and musical enterprise presented to English audiences a foil whereby they may hear in music and read in their native tongue the Neoplatonic enterprise of late Antiquity and the early medieval period. Creation and fall, restoration and return, are features of pre-modern philosophies, presented in literary genres bearing the context of their own day. Tolkien's romantic or anti-modern outlook seeks a re-enchantment which reflects the struggles of early twentieth-century Europe, but at the same time incorporates a range of philosophical themes consonant within a broad Neoplatonic account of life as 'being and gift':

> [When an author creates a believable world] what really happens is that the story-maker proves a successful 'sub-creator.' He makes a Secondary World which your mind can enter. Inside it, what he relates is 'true': it accords with the laws of that world. You therefore believe it, while you are, as it were, inside. The moment disbelief arises, the spell is broken; the magic, or rather art, has failed. You are then out in the Primary World again, looking at the little abortive Secondary World from outside.[15]

The conclusions of my study rest, therefore, upon the following postulates: First, that Tolkien was a writer of both fantasy *and* philosophy, utilizing a wide array of Christian and pre-Christian mythology and philosophy, and melding them into a complex whole: a *multiplex theoria*. Indeed, he was a writer who incorporated into his work a sophisticated and, at times, very original metaphysics of being. Secondly, that Tolkien utilized a broad Neoplatonic metaphysics of participation: life as 'being and gift' in Tolkien's co-creation subsists only insofar as it participates in something prior to itself, namely God. Thirdly, that as a skilled storyteller and gifted medievalist, Tolkien crafted into his own mythology a variety of Neoplatonic strands, and did not rely on a single source. His works have a striking dependency upon different scholars within this tradition, at different points in his literary life. Fourthly, that 'human being' containing a created free moral agency, displays a freedom of the will which originates in its source, and in its most mysterious expression demonstrates

---

14. Carpenter, *Biography*, 265; Tolkien, *Book of Lost Tales 1*, 8.
15. Tolkien, *Tree and Leaf*, 37.

a freedom from material form, independent of the narrow categories of material genus. This freedom is shared amongst all created beings in Tolkien's *legendarium*, but is never independent of the providence of God, even where there is a turn towards evil and corruption.

There is an over-arching *thema* to this investigation, in that Tolkien was never free from his lifelong belief and practice as an English Catholic, committed as he was to promoting Catholic intellectual and theological truths through his works. There is no strident polemic, such as we see in the works of his colleague and close friend C. S. Lewis, and he doubtless did not set out to systematise one: but one exists nevertheless.

1.2 The Current Status of Tolkien Studies

The significant and original contribution to Tolkien studies offered here is due largely to a dearth of scholarly material on the themes upon which I have chosen to focus. In particular, use of previously unpublished material in the Bodleian Library's Special Collection Department at the University of Oxford has opened up opportunities for original and incisive interpretations of key aspects of Tolkien's *corpus*.

Criticism and analysis in Tolkien's work is largely literary and cultural, and most of that from the perspective of 'Tolkien the medievalist.' Notable commentators along these lines are Chance, Chism, Le Guin, Luthi, Pearce, Rateliff, Shippey, and Gray, though the latter two write biography in a different manner than does Humphrey Carpenter—Tolkien's official biographer. Tolkien has been read as both modernist and postmodernist. Alison Milbank acknowledges Tolkien's modernist endeavor as a parallel to Eliot's *The Waste Land*, and asserts that, "Modernist writing reaches back to assert the influence of earlier culture on the present through the 'mythic method,' while simultaneously stressing the gap between modernity and the past through ironic juxtaposition."[16] Patrick Curry cites Tolkien as restoring to our cultural heritage a re-enchantment, realization, and 'myth-as-truth' perspective about our own real-world possibilities. Curry attempts to decry the aesthetic and environmental expressions of modernism, and posits Tolkien's writings as a postmodernist response to the demystifying 'absolutism' of its own self-confidence.[17] Curry and Luling attempt to address Tolkien's mythology in terms of ecological and anthropological responses to issues raised by modernism, as does Alfred Siewers—linking Tolkien's ecological writings to those of John Scottus Eriugena. Recent contributions from Alison

---

16. Milbank, *Chesterton and Tolkien*, ix.
17. Curry, "Tolkien and His Critics," 97–99.

Milbank, Houghton, Eden, and Flieger, take Tolkien's works as a reference for serious reflection on important philosophical themes; whereas Skögemann and O'Neil attempt a Jungian interpretation of his works. Themes that recur throughout these studies relate to his own ideas of creation and fall (in *The Silmarillion*), and the resulting growth of moral evil challenging the emergent races of Middle-earth. Tolkien's project defies simplistic interpretation and categorisation.[18] There have been particular strident efforts by some to advance the distinctively Catholic nature of the work, and Alton, Caldecott, and Coulombe champion this cause with some intellectual vigor. Notwithstanding the great acclaim that his works have received since the recent resurgence of interest, there are many dissenters still.[19]

Craig Bernthal's recent publication seeks to extrapolate a sacramental understanding in Tolkien's works, based upon the use of 'signs' in John's Gospel, and places Tolkien firmly amongst his own Catholic contemporaries. Jonathan Macintosh's 2009 doctoral thesis and book—"The Flame Imperishable: Tolkien, St. Thomas, and The Metaphysics of Faërie"—has provided several leads into the use of Aquinas' metaphysics in Tolkien's philosophy of creation, in particular his description of the 'mind-music-vision-reality' of Arda. This is supported by an influential chapter on "Music in Middle-earth," in which he proposes that a corrective is necessary when considering Tolkien's created nature, inspired as it is by Neoplatonism. Though largely undeveloped (in terms of my own investigation), it shows a clear understanding of the alleged patristic and medieval influences on Tolkien's method, in particular Aquinas' analysis of created being in terms of its distinction from the One and divine extravagance in created being.

Verlyn Flieger (1983), Bradford Eden (2003), and Kathleen Dubbs describe Tolkien's creation myth in terms of a diminution of being, largely in line with a Neoplatonic understanding of idealism: the further that things are distanced from their source, then the less that they are.

---

18. Tolkien corrects his publisher (again): "do not let (Rayner) suspect 'Allegory.' There is a 'moral,' I suppose, in any tale worth telling. But that is not the same thing. Even the struggle between darkness and light is [...] one example of its pattern [...] but not The Pattern; Of course, Allegory and Story converge, meeting somewhere in Truth [...] the only perfectly consistent allegory is a real life; and the only fully intelligible story is an allegory" (Carpenter, *Letters,* 120–21). However, three years later, Tolkien concedes that despite his dislike of direct allegory, "any attempt to purport of myth or fairytale must use allegorical language, anyway all this stuff is mainly concerned with Fall, Mortality and the Machine" (Carpenter, *Letters,* 145).

19. Curry, *Tolkien and His Critics,* 88–89, refers to criticisms which label Tolkien as sexist, racist, escapist, infantile, Marxist, nostalgic, quietist, and fascist. For a comprehensive panorama of the critical and academic reception of Tolkien's works, in both the UK and USA, see Chance, *Mythology of Power,* 18–19.

1.3 Influences and Inspiration

The primary sources of this investigation prioritize Tolkien's own published works. In addition, his posthumously published *Letters* add significantly to his own project, and provide an essential historical collection of his own commentary on how one might interpret his works. His son, Christopher Tolkien, has done much to advance Tolkien studies, by his meticulous *Introductions* and careful reconstructions of posthumously published works, as recently as June 2018. These and the unpublished manuscripts now residing in the Special Collections Department of the Bodleian Library, Oxford, shed much light on the gaps hitherto left by Tolkien's death in 1973.[20] Secondary sources which constitute scholarly commentaries on Tolkien's works are thin on the ground, and part of the originality of this book is its extensive reliance on primary texts. There is no acknowledgment in Tolkien's own works of dependency upon key scholars, and I have undertaken extensive forensic investigations in several obscure Tolkien publications, in order to tease out support for my thesis.

The sources of, and influences on, Tolkien's works are complex, and the subject of much debate and speculation. Many biographers and commentators (such as Carpenter, Shippey and Garth) rightly highlight his interest in north European legend and lore, his experiences in the First World War, his love of the countryside, and his fear and loathing of industrialization and modernism. In addition to these insightful observations, it is hard to deny that Tolkien's primary philosophical influences demonstrate a largely Augustinian outlook, whilst simultaneously drawing from other theological strands from the late patristic to the early medieval period. Given also Tolkien's professional career at Oxford, first as Rawlinson and Bosworth Professor of Anglo-Saxon (1925 to 1945) and later Merton Professor of Language and Literature (1945 to 1959), a broad Christian Neoplatonism can never be underestimated, even if it was nowhere clearly stated or supported in his published works. That Tolkien could be termed a 'medievalist' is a hypothesis in which significant Tolkien literary studies take their stand. Given his professional penchant for Early and Middle English (and Welsh), and his antipathy towards the cultural trauma of the Norman invasion, this is a bold but well-founded assumption. Tolkien, as one would expect of a

---

20. Christopher Tolkien has published twenty one books posthumously, which elucidate his earlier notes and draft works. In addition, they contain various collections of unique transcripts which are appropriate to this thesis. John Garth, *Tolkien and the Great War*, 71–88; 214–23, gives a detailed 'life setting' of the earliest of his unpublished works, clearly relating them to his experiences in the First World War, and early interest in ancient European languages. See also Carpenter, *Biography*, 102–6.

Classicist, already had a mastery of Greek and Latin before he was awarded his (minor) Exhibition to study at Oxford. What is certain, is that he soon became bored with Classics, and spent far too much time discovering Germanic languages, largely inspired by his teacher and Professor of Comparative Philology, Joe Wright.[21] In his unpublished *Notes on the Origins of the English Nation,* he remarks that the "neglectedness" of our particular linguistic history is the direct "confusion of practically all writers on Northern European history."[22] He adds a pejorative remark that this linguistic turn was 'the first French intrusion into English as an end to 850 years of 'the speakers of English.'" However, he tempers this comment by adding that "the disappearance and corruption of English literature was not only due to the Norman Conquest, but had really begun, before their arrival, under the Danish Kings."[23] Accompanying the Northern European intrusion into the English language of the early medieval period, were philosophical themes and a manner of looking at life—a *temper*—based on these invading peoples' indigenous ideas of life's origin and destiny.

Arising out of this period we encounter Boethius, whose works enfolded the core subjects of the *Quadrivium,* and his *Consolations of Philosophy* became almost a universally read text for scholars of late antiquity, developing the earlier philosophical ideas of Augustine and Pseudo-Dionysius. Tolkien scholars such as Jane Chance and Tom Shippey postulate a dependency on Boethius for such themes as chance, free-will, and the challenge of mutability and evil.[24] Shippey notes that in Old English, 'doomsday' has no sense of 'luck' or 'chance' about it, but more of 'fate'—the idea of a power sitting above mortals and ruling their lives by its sentence or by its speech alone.[25] In the dialogue with Lady Philosophy, Boethius is consoled with the hard truth of Fortune's fickle nature:

> It is the sea's right at one moment to smile indulgently with glassy waters, and at another to bristle with storms and breakers. [. . .] This power that I wield comes naturally to me; this is my perennial sport. I turn my wheel on its whirling course, and take delight in switching the base to the summit, and the summit to the base. So mount upward, if you will, but on condition

---

21. Carpenter, *Biography,* 62–64.
22. Bodleian SC–MSS A21/1, 68–79.
23. Ibid., 76
24. Shippey, *Author of the Century,* 129–31.
25. Shippey, *Road to Middle Earth,* 288.

that you do not regard yourself ill-treated if you plummet down when my humour demands and takes its course.[26]

Shippey's argument here is unduly pessimistic: God orders the fates of all and, whilst He may be transcendent in order to do so, this higher power still pervades. I shall demonstrate, however, that Tolkien adopted a far less deterministic approach to life and being in relation to God's foreknowledge of temporal events, and that Shippey's reading has more coherence with the Anglo-Saxon pre-Christian worldview. Tolkien's use of Latin sources (late antique and early medieval) in the philosophy of his mythology, includes Boethius' *Consolations*. From here, Jane Chance postulates that Tolkien may have borrowed concepts such as the reconciliation of providence, fate, and free will that help to explain the often-antithetical statements about chance and fate. Here she concedes that Tolkien was strongly influenced by Platonic and Neoplatonic philosophy.[27] To what extent Tolkien could be said to be a Neoplatonist, in light of the works of Augustine and his successors, will be the question at the heart of this investigation.

C. S. Lewis once commented that no-one ever influenced Tolkien: "you might as well try to influence a Bandersnatch."[28] Whilst this may entertain a degree of apocryphal truth, Tolkien's works are saturated with external influences, though he was reluctant to name many of them. William Gray postulates that, whilst the greatest modern influence upon Tolkien was William Morris, the greatest single influence was "the author of Beowulf."[29] Tolkien's celebrated essay, "Beowulf: The Monsters and Their Critics," being the text of his now-famous 1936 Sir Israel Gollancz Memorial Lecture to the British Academy, demonstrates the literary link between the emerging Christianization of northern Europe and Tolkien's own project: the weaving of ancient themes into a narrative which expresses both the language and 'temper' of an earlier age, and can be seen in his 'tower allegory.'[30] The use of ancient materials to build something contemporary and useful—"to see the sea"—may at first seem illogical, but on later inspection and reflection, may indeed prove a worthy and coherent project. I shall demonstrate that this

---

26. Boethius, *Consolations*, 2.2.8–10.

27. Chance, *Mythology of Power*, 16–17. She acknowledges Tolkien as a "master assimilator" of sources, but only offers a "may have borrowed" theory to what follows in her discussion. Chance relies instead on the evidence of Kathleen Dubs in "Providence, Fate and Chance," 133–42.

28. C. S. Lewis, in a letter to Charles Moorman 15 May 1959, quoted by Bratman, "Gifted Amateurs," 305. Lewis saw literature as a web of mutual influence, much more so than Tolkien, who instead preferred to "plough his own furrow."

29. Gray, *Fantasy*, 64; and Shippey, *Road to Middle Earth*, 389.

30. Tolkien, *Monsters*, 7–9.

is how Tolkien saw the intention and method of the author of *Beowulf*, and gives us a clue to his own project. Flieger summarized the importance of this tower allegory as "the desire to seek something without knowing what it is."[31] Tolkien's philological quest begins with ancient words, developed and honed into stories, influenced by their ancient usage. But here we must differentiate between 'source' and 'influence': "a source gives us something to write about; an influence prompts us to write in a certain way."[32] Tolkien supports this hypothesis, wherein he writes:

> what is I think a primary 'fact' about my work, that it is all a piece, and fundamentally linguistic in inspiration. [. . .] The invention of languages is the foundation. The 'stories' were made rather to provide a world for the languages than the reverse. To me a name comes first and the story follows.[33]

Tolkien, like others of his generation, took copies of Morris with him into the trenches in the June of 1916, but to infer any direct influence from this is highly speculative.[34] In winning the Skeat Prize at Oxford for English in the same year, Tolkien purchased several Morris volumes, including Morris' translation of the *Volsungasaga* and prose-and-verse romance, *The House of the Wolfings*.[35] As a saga, *LOTR* resembles ancient works much cherished in Tolkien's early studies. Chance notes that the correlation between the *LOTR* trilogy and both the Norse-Icelandic *Eddas* and the Finnish epic of the *Kalevala*, although its loosely episodic technique of branching journey-quests most approximates *entrelacements*, displays a late medieval romance characteristic.[36] However, it was earlier, in 1914, that he discovered words from an ancient Anglo-Saxon Christian poem, *Crist*: "*Eala Earendel engla beorhast / ofer middengeard monnum sended.*"[37] In another posthumously published work, he claimed that:

> when I came across that citation [. . .] I felt a curious thrill, as if something had stirred in me, half wakened from sleep. There

---

31. Flieger, *Splintered Light*, 50, 14–16.
32. C. S. Lewis, *Authorised Version*, 133–34.
33. Carpenter, *Letters*, 219.
34. Garth, *Great War*, 296.
35. Carpenter, *Biography*, 77. For sources and influences see also Shippey, *Road to Middle Earth*, 388–98; Gray, *Fantasy*, 64–69.
36. Chance, *Mythology of Power*, 15–16.
37. "Hail! Earendel brightest of angels / above the Middle-earth sent unto men."

was something very remote and strange and beautiful behind those words, if I could grasp it, far beyond ancient English.[38]

Later in 1914, he wrote the poem "The Voyage of Earendel the Evening Star," which opens with the line: "Earendel sprang up from the ocean's cup / in the gloom of the mid rim." In the Latin antiphons for Vespers for the last days of Advent, we read *O Oriens*: "O Rising Sun, splendour of eternal light and the sun of justice: O come and enlighten those who sit in darkness and in the shadow of death."[39] Set in a Christian context, this Antiphon clearly refers to Christ; in a pre-Christian context it appeals to a forerunner of Christ, to a Saviour whose nature was as yet unknown.[40] Tolkien later wrote this poem as the "launching of his ship" into mythology, and was to appear in the earliest of his written *legendarium*, *The Fall of Gondolin*. Mindful of his desire to exclude any explicit Christian material he adds, "the use of Earendel in [Anglo-Saxon] Christian symbolism as the herald of the rise of the true Sun in Christ is completely alien to my use."[41] Throughout his works, Tolkien is keen to avoid obvious religious rituals, prayers, and the like. This investigation demonstrates that his entire *legendarium* is, however, imbued with Catholic Christian themes, and that he does not rely on a single source only for inspiration. He melds the methodologies of scholar and author by thinking metaphorically in his published essays, and experimenting theoretically in his fiction, allowing him to scrutinize the uses and powers of both. *LOTR*, at one level, is a renunciation of mythology, and the willed return to history:

> Middle-earth unfolds, grows more intricate, more peopled, more culturally diverse, more deep as we wander through it, but it blooms forth only in the shadow of its own immanent destruction.[42]

It is no accident that the writing of this 'renunciatory' narrative occupies dark night after dark night, during a time when Germany was mobilizing and recasting heroic Germanic ideals to articulate and impose its own terrifying new world. Tolkien's writing works to recover and imaginatively re-animate past traditions, lost words, gap-ridden stories: in writing, he sought to present them in their true light.[43] Tolkien negotiates the ethical dilemma

38. Tolkien, *Sauron Defeated*, 236; and Carpenter, *Biography*, 71–72.
39. *The Divine Office*, 153.
40. Shippey, *Road to Middle Earth*, 277–81.
41. Carpenter, *Letters*, 387.
42. Chism, "Middle-earth," 64.
43. Carpenter, *Letters*, 56, 219; Shippey, *Road to Middle Earth*, 26–31, notes that

that Wagner's devotees must still negotiate: how can one separate enjoyment of the complex artistic *diagetic* world from the political and cultural uses to which its power can be put? Can the work of art remain innocent in itself, though cursed in its usage? Chism offers a resounding 'No!' on Tolkien's behalf.[44] Given how highly Tolkien regarded fantasy and sub-creation, as both an art form and foil for literary realism, it is small wonder that he offers a recasting of the Wagnerian tradition, in light of his own understanding of virtue and morality, along clearly drawn and traditional Christian lines.[45] Tolkien's own sub-creation must transcend the dull interpretation of allegory (at least in his own eyes), and offer a mythology which, whilst never neutral in its 'applicability', focused upon the good to which all ends seek. Chance introduces Tolkien's project, as a serious contribution to the catastrophe that had torn apart Europe in the first half of the twentieth century:

> *The Lord of the Rings* is generally recognized today as a powerful work of creative imagination, whose levels of understanding are dependent on the synthesis and assimilation of medieval and modern materials.[46]

Against the backdrop of the modern age, with growing industrialization, threat of nuclear holocaust, and totalitarianism, Tolkien wrote his narrative where the individual was becoming dispossessed and powerless against fate and the universal horror of evil, whether in Auschwitz, South Africa, or Eastern Europe. If there is evil in this world, whatever its source (and/or ontology), then at least for Tolkien, an attempt at a solution was pressing. For the Christian, it may appear a strange project to recast a broadly Augustinian solution into such a vast body of work. However, as I shall demonstrate, Augustine is neither the totality of Tolkien's influence and source, but one, nevertheless, whose shadow is cast over this work.

---

the 'stories' were made rather to provide a world for the languages, and not the reverse. Shippey describes how Tolkien uses the process of 'calqueing' in order to achieve his literary realism, and give places and people a historical credibility (115–16). It is in this philological sense that he can say that Middle-earth is 'our world' (Carpenter, *Letters*, 220).

44. Chism, "Middle-earth," 78.

45. Shippey, *Road to Middle Earth*, 81, argues that to attempt a justification of Tolkien's Middle earth in a literal sense as 'Realism' is being too naive, and has no sensible claim in scholarship. His worldview was to create nouns and places out of adjectives which themselves have sources in the Norse *Elder Edda*. Examples are Gandalf, Beorn, Gollum, and the dwarves in *The Hobbit*.

46. Chance, *Mythology of Power*, 1.

1.4 Structure of the Book

The opening section (chapter 2) focuses on key themes of how Tolkien may have used and adapted a variety of Neoplatonist models of creation in his own sub-creation. The strands are rich and varied and, whilst at times I have engaged in speculative investigation, I have demonstrated that Tolkien owes his methodology to a sophisticated melding of these strands in his own works, which we read in the opening section of *The Silmarillion*, and its various stages of development published by his son, Christopher. This section maps the trajectory of Platonic and Neoplatonic idealism from Plotinus, through Augustine, Boethius, Pseudo-Dionysius, to Aquinas' highly developed philosophy of 'createdness' as gift. Each in their own way will be shown to contribute to the co-creative project of Tolkien, and sets the scene for the main emphasis of this section: that creation is not a necessary emanation from an impersonal transcendent deity, but the free and unmerited gift of a gratuitous God, who shares the process of co-creation with his creatures, both incorporeal and (Middle) earthly.

There has been a marked tendency in recent Tolkien literature to read his cosmo-genesis and the 'Music of the Ainur' in terms of the emanationist logic of Neoplatonic philosophy: the later stages of the creation process, and the development of Middle-earth are seen as metaphysically inferior to, and a *lapsus*—a tragic falling away—from the supposedly more authentic divine and pure reality presented by the primeval music. I hypothesize, however, that whilst this may be one reading of Tolkien's cosmo-genesis, he intended a more orthodox reading of the text in light of what I propose is his Thomistic understanding of metaphysics and aesthetics of beauty and being. Through the combined metaphors of music and vision of the Ainur, Tolkien provides a worldview that is not so much a tragic lapse from either a Plotinian emanationist schema, nor an Augustinian ideal Eden-like state, but one which is consistent with what we shall see to be his Thomistic existential realism. The world's gift in creation is 'euchatastrophically' surpassed when it is blessed/hallowed by the Creator, and Tolkien can be seen to have successfully synthesized the *musica universalis* tradition within a Thomistic metaphysics of creation, influenced as he was by contemporary philosophers such as Jacques Maritain and David Jones.

Chapter 3 constitutes a philosophical and linguistic Case Study, based around Tolkien's favorite story, and early text—*The Tale of Tinúviel*. In this, I argue that, given the particular focus of the broader investigation, Tolkien's philosophy of life as 'being and gift' draws on later Neoplatonic writers such as Boethius from the sixth century, but is equally rooted in the Old- and Middle-English traditions of *Beowulf*, *Pearl*, *The Wanderer*, and

The Seafarer. This investigation therefore draws attention to Tolkien's use of Christian Neoplatonism constituted as multi-layered, and that he draws from a number of sources in promoting his philosophy of life. In the first instance, I have demonstrated that Tolkien's philosophy of being in *The Tale of Tinúviel* has its origins in his own personal life and marriage to Edith, and yet it borrows narrative sources from Tolkien's store of European mythology and Anglo-Saxon myth—especially *Beowulf*. Secondly, I present using Neoplatonist texts the assertion that rational beings in Tolkien's early *legendarium* are both psychologically and morally free, despite the choices of others which act as incidental 'chance' events. This is demonstrated by a comparison between Boethius' (Latin) and Alfred's (Anglo-Saxon) versions of the *Consolations*, given that Tolkien adapted a broad Augustinian and Boethian view, modified by other influences in the tradition. Thirdly, the theme of 'doom,' which has an Anglo-Saxon provenance, will be seen to have a narrower meaning than common contemporary usage, and supports an earlier (Latin) rendering of providence and fate. This section concludes with an assertion that death, when spoken of as 'doom,' is both proper to a thing's (mortal) nature, but is also subject to freedom in certain cases.

Chapter 4 introduces the recent scholarship of Alfred K. Siewers, and offers an intriguing and fresh approach to Tolkien's sub-creative vista, along the lines of those we read in Irish and Welsh legend, and from the perspective of John Scottus Eriugena.[47] I have demonstrated that Siewers' works present both a mystical and Otherworld Neoplatonist approach to Tolkien's metaphysics, one that is both distinct from the Graeco-Latin profile of Plato and his legacy, and also takes into full account the over-layering of this textual tradition. I further hypothesize that, whilst there can be no certain dependency theory; Tolkien also derived much of his philosophical framework of life—especially the life and destiny of humanity—from Eriugena. Siewers makes significant and bold claims that as a medievalist, Tolkien draws on the anthropology and eco-philosophy of Eriugena, in order to stretch beyond his Augustinian Catholicism, combining it also with a Celtic mysticism.[48] It is no surprise that Eriugena's works and popularity in the Carolingian court correlate to the commonly held dating of *Beowulf* in the mid-late ninth century AD. Eriugena's links to both Augustine and Pseudo-Dionysius, and influences from Aristotle's *Ten Categories*, point towards that subtle craft of Tolkien's mythological invention, given his reticence to systematize Christian allegory into his own fantasy genre. Human freedom is itself multi-layered,

---

47. Alfred K Siewers is presently an Associate Professor of English and an Affiliated Member in Environmental Studies at Bucknell University, Lewisburg, PA.

48. Siewers, "Tolkien's Cosmic-Christian Ecology," 140.

and involves a 'freedom from form' in corporeality and finitude, and this is seen to be evident in *The Tale of Tinúviel*, in episodes concerning shape-shifting. An examination of Eriugena's anthropology in his *Periphyseon*, as an extension to a broad Augustinian-Boethian Neoplatonism, and Eriugena's earlier presentation of the issue in his *Treatise on Divine Predestination* demonstrates that in this respect, Eriugena supports earlier forms of the tradition, in that humanity is free from the hard determinism and fatalism common to their European pagan forebears. The key concept of participation is restated, but in a more mystical and less defined manner than the later developments of Aquinas. As such, Tolkien's speculative reading of Eriugena opens the door to viewing human destiny and it's *reditus* more in the mode of a *theosis*, than a realized bodily resurrection.

The destiny of Beren and Lúthien displays a striking freedom of the mind and will, accompanied by a resultant transformation of form: from life to death (Beren) and from elf to mortal woman (Lúthien). In either respect, their *Reditus* as formulated in an Eriuganean Neoplatonic mysticism is simply a return to 'self', in terms of unfallen human nature, within the enfoldments of God—without sexual differentiation, without even a body. This cross-over of interdisciplinary study of Tolkien's works demonstrates the multi-layered appeal of his mythology. Seen on a broad canvas, the fantasy becomes the real.

Chapter 5 considers a significant theme in the Middle-earth writings: the problem of evil and suffering. Given that Tolkien's sub-creation reflects the broad Augustinian outlook on creation, that God only creates substantially good creatures and that matter is essentially good, there is the challenge of the mutability towards evil. Amongst the Ainur there is Melkor, who in his immanent form becomes Morgoth, and chooses to become corporeal like one of the Valar.[49] Amongst the Maiar is the protagonist Sauron, enemy of the free peoples of Middle-earth;[50] and Melkor's archaean spider, Ungoliant.[51] I have shown that Tolkien adopts an equally

---

49. The Valar were the fourteen powerful spirits of the race of the Ainur who entered Arda after its creation to give order to the world and combat the evils of Melkor. They dwelt originally on the Isle of Almaren, but after its destruction, long before the Awakening of the elves, they moved to Aman and founded Valinor.

50. Each of the Maiar was associated with one or more particular Vala, and were of similar stock, though less powerful. For example, Ossë and Uinen, as spirits of the sea, belonged to Ulmo, while Curumo, who came to be known in Middle-earth as Saruman, belonged to Aulë the Smith. Tolkien, *Silmarillion*, 33–35.

51. Ungoliant's origins are shrouded in mystery. It is thought that she may have been one of the Maiar, or a lesser spirit, whom Melkor corrupted long ago, but she is not listed among the Ainur. It is also said that she came from the darkness above the skies of Arda, leading some to believe that she may be an incarnation of darkness or emptiness itself.

broad Christian Neoplatonist approach to evil, in particular one reflecting Augustine's aesthetic approach to theodicy, where goodness and evil—or at least beauty and ugliness—may coexist in some kind of juxtaposed struggle for supremacy and resolution. This is linked to his adoption of Maritain's Neo-Thomist approach to the Beautiful and the Good, whereby all things within creation can be said to display those attributes temporally, and in their proper natures, where in God they exist perfectly.

But you may say, how can I know what is good and what is not good?
I may wince at the cheap seascape over the mantelpiece
but does that necessarily mean that I should go to the Tate Gallery
and worship a floor full of dyed rice?
Years ago, when I was living briefly with a stockbroker who had
a good cellar,
I asked him how I could learn about wine.
"Drink it," he said.[1]

The intellect [. . .] draws it into itself—it eats being and drinks being —so as itself to become, in a certain fashion, all things. [2]

1. Winterson, *Art Objects*, 16.
2. Maritain, *Art and Scholasticism*, 5.

2

Creation and the Metaphysics of Music

Tolkien's Philosophy of Createdness as 'Gift'

2.1 *Creatio Sub Specie Aeternitatis*

A key concept within a Christian Neoplatonist understanding of how the universe originated is *creatio ex nihilo*: matter has its origin in the free and gratuitous agency of God. Just how this creation-as-process proceeds from the One is expounded by different writers of the tradition, there being a high degree of consistency between the Latin writers, such as Augustine, Boethius, and Aquinas, all of whom have their common origin in Plato. This, therefore, provides my own platform to extrapolate how Tolkien used sources familiar to him from his studies as a medievalist, and his own Catholic faith. This opening section, however, focuses on Tolkien's use of the *musica universalis* tradition of Neoplatonism, and how this was incorporated into his own creation myth in *The Silmarillion*, giving an account as to how life is experienced via the concept of participation in the One. In addition to these classical themes, I shall consider the extent to which Tolkien was influenced by his intellectual contemporaries, and the importance of the writings of Jacques Maritain in the post-Edwardian Catholic aesthetics of life as 'being and gift'. It shall be seen that in Tolkien's own antipathy to the ambitions of the Second Vatican Council, there is in his work the influence of an emergent *rapprochement* influenced by the reforms of both Popes Leo XIII and (St) Pius X. Tolkien's dislike of modernism, and its impact upon the English landscape, projects also into his understanding of how grace is mediated via the emergent Neo-Thomism of his generation. Beauty and Goodness as transcendentals, imbue all aspects of life, and life's radical giftedness apart from, but participating in, the One who is beyond all such definition and characterisation, is central to Tolkien's metaphysics.

2.1.1 Plato as Prototype

Prior to any evaluation as to how Tolkien may have incorporated Christianized versions of Neoplatonism into his own cosmo-genesis, we need to return to the source of the tradition, in order to make sense of what follows. Plato's late dialogue the *Timaeus* (alongside his *Republic*) is the primary source in how we may understand his method of accounting for the universe, in both its transcendent and visible forms. Here, Plato pursues an analogy between the World Soul and our own soul. The universe supplies, the 'larger text' for deciphering the nature of the human soul. The *Timaeus* offers an account of—or metaphor for—the origins of the universe. A *Demiurge* or 'craftsman god,' finding "the visible universe in a state not of rest but of inharmonious and disorderly motion, reduced it to order from disorder, as he judged that order was in every way better."[1] In so doing, and wanting "everything to be good, marred by as little imperfection as possible," he took an eternal and unchanging model (Form) as his paradigm.[2] There is one universe, not many, but "a single spherical universe in circular motion, alone but because of its excellence needing no company other than itself, and satisfied to be its own acquaintance and friend."[3] The previously spasmodic, imbalanced movements of chaos, are replaced by ordered motion: "and made it move with a uniform circular motion on the same spot."[4] The reason and harmony of the universe is arranged geometrically, and consists in (or is expressed by) sets of mathematical ratios. These ratios also equate to the harmonic structure of Greek music, in that the World Soul is at the same time a kind of musical instrument. Cosmic order is ordered (and harmonious) beauty, such that

> It should come as no surprise that God, the supremely rational and perfectly wise Being, would produce a highly structured, complexly ordered universe in which everything has its proper place. It should come as no surprise either, that human beings, who are created in God's image, share this affinity for

---

1. *Timaeus*, 30a, 42.
2. Ibid., 29b.
3. Ibid., 34b.
4. Ibid., 34a.

order, and that we flourish when we order things—including ourselves—well.⁵

However, in subjects which defy internal structure these analogies break down. An apposite example, and continuing the musical theme, is found in the principle subject of Wagner's last opera *Parsifal*—the Holy Grail—the cup of Christ and beatific vision of God in the sacramental *calix*. The first five bars of the opening *Prelude* are simply a long-breathed theme. In the analysis of Barry Millington:

> on closer inspection one notices that the theme has no metre [. . .] it is impossible to tell where the bar lines are. Immediately then, we are in a sphere literally outside of time, and this [. . .] conjures an atmosphere of transcendent serenity.⁶

The effect of this timeless and unstructured music, in contrast to Platonic ideas, serves to defy the distinction between time and space; substance and accidents.⁷

In the *Timaeus*, the cosmos is investigated and described through the establishment of axioms from which emerge mathematical proportion and the "harmonic music of the heavens."⁸ Simon Oliver's study *God, Philosophy and Motion* lays clearly the Platonic foundations for later Christian Neoplatonic ideas, chief amongst them is the 'truth' that this cosmos is a realm not of static being, but of *change and becoming*, which finds its explanation only with reference to its origin, and its continuous participation in the unchanging, eternal and transcendent realm of the Forms, and ultimately and crucially in its relation to the Good.⁹ This is a foundational model within which Tolkien's own co-creation is established, in harmonic and creative participation with the divine, without using overt cross-referencing to Plato's language. The use of Plato in Augustine, Boethius and Aquinas—but especially in Aquinas' 'metaphysics of participation'—can be seen in Tolkien's carefully crafted and edited cosmo-genesis, even in his use of Middle-English poems such as *Pearl*. The *Timaeus* does not imply that truth lies within the universe but without, in the realm of the unchanging Forms. To the extent that the

---

5. Ibid., 36a; De Young et al., *Aquinas' Ethics*, 15.

6. Barry Millington, *As Though Lit from Behind*, programme notes from the 2011 English National Opera production of *Parsifal*, page 21

7. When Parsifal, the 'pure fool' is taken to see the Holy Grail unveiled, he is literally transported beyond time and space, to its sanctuary, known only to the Grail Knights: '*Du siehst, mein Sohn, zum Raum wird hier die Zeit*' ('You see, my son, time here becomes space,' Act One)

8. *Timaeus*, 35b–36c.

9. Oliver, *God, Philosophy and Motion*, 8.

visible world fails to participate in these immutable ideals, then it becomes unintelligible, and corresponds instead to a realm of mere 'opinion.' For Oliver, the cosmology presented by Plato in the *Timaeus* is not an account aimed at definitive statements,

> because there cannot be any such neutral exhaustive [...] supracosmic statements about the universe, because the universe is the visible realm of becoming: the *Timaeus* presents a mythical story about a universe which is itself 'mythical.'[10]

Plato's cosmology is an attempt to see the universe in its most fundamental being, that is, in its relation to these eternal Forms—and ultimately the Form of the Good as the source of all being.[11] In Plato's philosophy of being, the realm of becoming (or opinions), and the beings within it—this world—is an 'image' or 'likeness' of the creatures which reside in the World of the Forms, and this model can only make sense of 'being' in things insofar as it corresponds to a transcendent ideal. Just as a copy cannot be understood apart from its relation to, and origin, in the reality from which it emanates, neither can Plato's cosmology be understood independent of the model or ideal from which the universe emanates.[12] We have in Plato, therefore an aesthetic and analogical model in which the goodness and/or beauty of the universe—and by association—things contained within it, have a participatory relationship to the Form of the Good.

The transcendent (ideals) and immanent (appearances) modes of existence for Plato have their ontological origins in his postulated and logical sequence of Existence—Sameness and Difference—via the World Soul.[13] The World Soul and the body of the universe are not distinct ontological entities, which stand over and against each other, for they partake of the same being which resides in the World of the Forms and emanates from the Good. This World Soul plays an intermediary role between the realms of being and becoming, through which all things desire their own motion and are dispersed through the universe. The World Soul's composition of Existence, Sameness, and Difference, is expressed in both the realm of being (indivisible) and becoming (divisible). Existence is possessed fully by the Forms, so for a thing to exist, is to say that it partakes of existence to a lesser degree in the visible realm. Sameness refers to the positive content of a Form by virtue of what it is, always the same as

---

10. Oliver, *God, Philosophy and Motion*, 9.
11. *Timaeus*, 29a–b; *Republic*, 509b.
12. *Republic*, 597a–b
13. *Timaeus*, 35a.

itself, excluding any kind of change. With no affected change, however, no matter or visible form could arise. Therefore, the 'paradox' of Difference implies that the Forms must participate in Difference, for all Forms are distinct from each other, and therefore the realm of the visible, being subject to change, participates only partially in Sameness and Difference, and to a lesser extent than the Forms themselves. The World Soul resembles the realm of becoming, and is therefore a mediator between the invisible and indivisible realm of being, and the visible and divisible realm of becoming and change.[14] It is via this hierarchy of Existence—Sameness and Difference—that the Demiurge forms a hierarchy of motions, the cosmos is endowed with the principle of autonomous and ordered self-movement, such that "the cosmos is an ensouled living entity."[15]

Via this account of the World Soul, Plato devised the hypothesis that the characteristics which the Good bestows on the Forms (beauty, proportion, harmony, symmetry) can be expressed in mathematical language. First, the World Soul is given the most perfectly symmetrical of motions—namely, circular rotation at constant speed (and to the right in Sameness). Secondly, the Demiurge divides the World Soul according to certain mathematical proportions, such that the different parts move in consonant proportion to each other.[16] All motion originates in, and is governed by, the circle of the Same, whose motion is perfect. The circle of Difference partakes of this motion, although imperfectly, as do the planetary bodies through the circles of the Different. The motion of the stars, which is directly bestowed by the circle of the Same, and the motion of the planets, which is bestowed by the circle of the Different, is thus rendered rational via symmetrical proportion. This approximates to Boethius' music of the spheres, transmitted through the Soul of the universe.

This circular motion within the World Soul mediates to the realm of becoming a greater participation in the realm of being, as it is representative of the circular motion of time, itself being the orbiting movement of the heavenly bodies. Time for Plato is the moving image of eternity, and that is because the Living Being is eternal, and by necessity this characteristic cannot be conferred on anything temporal, so Plato believes that the Demiurge created an everlasting likeness which moves according to number, "that to which we give the name Time."[17] Oliver makes a significant point in that, to be in a situation of rest—or *stasis*—might be the greatest

14. *Timaeus*, 37d–38c; Oliver, *God, Philosophy and Motion*, 12–13.
15. *Timaeus*, 36e.
16. Ibid., 36c; Oliver, *God, Philosophy and Motion*, 15.
17. *Timaeus*, 37c–38c.

approximation to the unchanging realm of being, for this would remove the corruption of change:

> However, it is through time that the realm of becoming attains a greater approximation to the realm of being because the realm of becoming is most fully itself, just as the realm of being is always most fully realised as itself. Within the realm of becoming, stasis actually denies the very nature of that realm as a realm of movement, change and therefore of becoming.[18]

This is a crucial step in Plato's understanding of 'being' within the world of change, because the teloi of the cosmos is to be the cosmos most perfectly in relation to its source, via the physical motion of the Different.[19]

The myriad souls of the universe partake of this motion, as also does the physical realm by means of the motion of the heavenly bodies. It is via these ordered movements that in a positive and creative sense of real possibilities that we correctly distinguish the real from its image. For Plato (contrary to modern science), movements of the soul arise out of the emotions and intelligence which reside in the soul, and are the very source of motion. It is through this participatory ontology between the World Soul and the embodied souls of rational agents that we come to identify correctly the realms of being and becoming in their relation to each other. Disordered wanderings of the soul (in a rational being) produce negative confusion which misunderstands the Forms, and fails correctly to identify the realms of becoming and being. All bodies, whether alive (ensouled) or not, possess some kind of motion by virtue of their place and ordering in the universe. Bodies which are not alive are at the lowest point of the hierarchy of motions, but are subject to the World Soul by some degree. Bodies which do not possess their own soul are recipients of a disordered motion, which is at many times removed from its origin in the circle of the Different. For Plato, the motions of the soul are paramount, whilst the physical motions are dependent upon the soul.[20]

The primary purpose of the *Timaeus* arising out of these readings is to account for the *purpose* of creation, that things become the best that they can be, by the efficient cause of the divine craftsman—"the best of causes."[21] One of the features of both the Christian and Tolkien's own cosmo-genesis, is that creation is a *free action* of a deity—*The One*—who has no *need* to create, save to bring into being those things upon which he can bestow some measure of

---

18. Oliver, *God, Philosophy and Motion*, 17.

19. Ibid.

20. Oliver, *God, Philosophy and Motion*, 16.

21. *Timaeus*, 29a.

his own ineffable being. These *myths* have an affinity with Plato's mediatory and participatory ontology, but Plato cannot account for this absolute freedom to create in his own cosmogony. There is an apparent lack of freedom in that which causes into being. The distinction between what constitutes a necessary and a sufficiently causal explanation informs Plato's considerations of 'reason' and 'necessity' in the *Timaeus*. For Plato, necessity refers to the realm of chaos preceding creation by the Demiurge, and is referred to as such for two reasons: first, it is indeed a necessary cause of the existence of an ordered and visible realm of becoming. The demiurge required raw materials with which to work in fashioning the universe after the Form of the Living Creature. Secondly, this realm of necessity is one of mechanistic causes in which elements interact 'of necessity,' but with no reference to a *telos* which transcends this mechanism.[22] Plato, like Aristotle, associates necessity with 'chance'—a theme taken up by Boethius in his *Consolations*—and on this view, phenomena are the result of causes which cannot act in any other way in which they do, "which are necessary but not ordered to any transcendent end and which can therefore give rise to chance."[23]

Necessity is contrasted with purpose, and these mechanistic causes are not arranged in any particular order, and it is for this reason that this realm is properly called 'chaotic.' The realm of necessity is called the 'errant cause' for Plato, and it is a necessary and wholly insufficient cause of the universe.[24] It would appear, therefore, to lack any teleological purpose apart from being the best that it could be, given the necessary constraints of the chaotic and pre-existent matter in which it exists after being fashioned according to the eternal Forms.

If Plato's creation myth appears bleak and deterministic, then it is tempered by the suggestion that the universe was fashioned by the victory of reasonable persuasion over necessity:

> Intelligence controlled necessity by persuading it for the most part to bring about the best result, and it was by this subordination of necessity to reasonable persuasion that the universe was originally constituted as it is.[25]

Here we see a metaphor of reasoned and persuasive speech triumphing over the chaotic 'wanderings' of a necessitated mechanistic process. Reason and necessity work in co-operation, symbiotically, in such a way that the universe

---

22. Oliver, *God, Philosophy and Motion*, 19.
23. Ibid.
24. *Timaeus*, 46d.
25. Ibid., 48a.

is not the result of an arbitrary or violent imposition of the will of the Demiurge, "rather, the Demiurge 'persuades' the realm of necessity, the realm of chance and chaos, to yield to an ordered and purposeful cosmos."[26]

2.1.2 Plotinus and His Legacy (1): Deity and Freedom in Tolkien's Anti-Modern Mythology

The Platonic legacy which began to exert itself in the patristic period, did so most systematically in the life and writings of St Augustine of Hippo. Influenced as he was by the Egyptian scholar, Plotinus, we read in Augustine an evolving philosophy and theology of life as being part of the created *ordo*, using both the philosophical devices of Plato and his followers, but tempered by an emergent Christian orthodoxy also. Tolkien allies himself to this received inheritance of the Augustinian Neoplatonic tradition in terms of goodness and evil in a pre-lapsarian state (though he does not acknowledge it directly). That all in creation is essentially good is a deliberate intention of Tolkien's co-creation, wherein the chances of *doom* and *fate* are interwoven with creatures who lapse from that original state of perfection under God's omniscient gaze: "In my story I do not deal in Absolute Evil. I do not think there is such a thing, since evil is zero. I do not think that at any rate any 'rational being' is wholly evil. Satan fell. In my myth Morgoth fell before Creation of the physical world."[27] The Anglo-Saxon concept of doom becomes a significant factor in reading Tolkien's mapping of human destiny, and I argue later that this concept is (largely) free from a hard-deterministic burden.

The God-figure of Tolkien's *legendarium*, his relation to creation, and his part in the unfolding of 'creaturely' history, is embraced in this Neoplatonic phrase, 'Eru,' the One. Verlyn Flieger notes that the designation 'Eru' does not originate with any national or ethnic mythology, and is therefore assumed to be of Tolkien's own design.[28] Examinations of Tolkien's presentation of this God-figure will show its relationship to, and difference from, its Neoplatonic antecedents. For Plotinus, the manner in which the One gives rise to the universe is by 'emanation,' a concept difficult to grasp, except by metaphor. The *Timaeus* offers an account of—or metaphor for—the origins of the universe. A *demiurge* or 'craftsman god,' finding "the visible universe in a state not of rest but of inharmonious and disorderly motion, reduced it from disorder to order, as he judged that order was in every way better."[29]

26. Oliver, *God, Philosophy and Motion*, 20.
27. Carpenter, *Letters*, 243.
28. Flieger, "Naming the Unnameable," 128.
29. *Timaeus*, 30a.

For both Plato and Plotinus recognise the need for the creation by the Demiurge or the One. They differ, in that Plotinus' Demiurge (at once both craftsman and model, and not simply an efficient cause, as in Plato) creates spontaneously, with no deliberation whatsoever, with no effort and merely as a consequence of being what it is.[30] Illumination emanates from a source of light, heat emanates from a source of heat, power emanates from a source of power, etc. This central reliance on metaphor creates difficulties in reading Plotinus and, one might say, also of Tolkien. As he made not the merest suggestion upon which model he based his 'cosmo-genesis,' then we may here have a plethora of ideas, based on early medievalism (itself based on late antiquity) and north European mythology, underpinned by a distinctive Judaeo-Christian creation belief. There appears to be an absence of the later medieval development of Aquinas, whereby the creative action of God sustains every finite being in existence between generation and corruption (in the case of material substances) by participation. This might lead some to a 'deist' reading of Tolkien's creation narrative, but I shall demonstrate that this is not necessarily the case.

John Deely summarizes Plotinus' metaphor and guiding principle of origination in that "whatever is real is one," and "whatever is one is also good."[31] In the creation myth of Tolkien's *The Silmarillion*, there is a clear hierarchy of being which would initially feel entirely at home with Plotinus' own order: whatever is prior (Eru-Ilúvatar) is of greater reality than that which is subsequent (Ainur). Thus the One, as prior to all division, is supremely Good. What emanates out from the One, being Other, is divided, and so both one and other than one. As 'one,' the creature is good, but as 'other than One' it could be said to partake at the same time of evil, because it is subject to mutability. As dependent upon the One, it is a 'creature,' but as separated from the One it partakes at the same time of non-being. That creature closer to the One will have less of evil and further away from the One is 'lower' in the descent, and matter itself is the lowest of all. It is not difficult, therefore, given the self-confessed 'Catholic' origin of the work, to read out of Tolkien a Neoplatonist motif of creation, but one that is at the same time unspecific and couched in biblical and liturgical metaphor. If matter is problematic for Plotinus, then it is not so for both Augustine and Tolkien, since *omnis natura bonum est*.

In his interfaith study of monotheistic accounts of creation and freedom, David Burrell poses the question as to whether the origin of the

---

30. Puigarnau, "Creation and Freedom," 243–54; *Timaeus*, 30a; Plotinus, *Enneads*, 5.8.7; 3.2.1.

31. Deely, *Medieval Philosophy Redefined*, 64.

universe could be construed as a *necessary consequence* of the One (Plotinus) in its inner fecundity, or does the universe come forth *freely* from that One (monotheism)?[32] What is at stake here is not just a clarification of the distinction between Augustine (and Tolkien's) and a Neoplatonist understanding of 'deity,' but of the universe itself, and our place (and reason) for being in it. This distinction (emanation/creation) is presented in clear juxtaposition by Puigarnau, whereby the incompatibility of Platonist emanationism and Christian providentialism has its root in the distinction between the Platonist conception of the One, and the Judaeo-Christian concept of a personal God. In Plotinian cosmogony, the maker is in fact powerful, but does not manage to maintain a complete transcendence over the material. In defending emanation, the One eliminates transcendence, and consequently, providence. With God (in Augustinian terms), transcendence is compatible with providence.[33] In understanding the origins of the universe by *necessity* operative in the prevailing necessary emanation scheme was that of logical deduction, on which the scheme was modelled. That sort of necessity rejects the notion of a personal, free Creator. Yet the One who creates without any presuppositions whatsoever (*ex nihilo*) cannot do so amongst other free choices, as there literally are no alternatives from which to choose. The freedom associated with creating, will therefore have to be a freedom closer to accepting the determinations of divine wisdom, than choosing among alternatives. The radical alternative to create is always a possibility, yet that freedom is better described as consenting to the inherent tendency of good to overflow and diffuse itself than it is a 'free choice.'

In Plotinus' scheme, to refuse consent would be impossible to the One (in that this One is also the Good), so in this case that radical freedom would be counterfactual, as being contrary to the very nature of the One as the Good.[34] It might logically be inferred that, in rejecting the emanationist scheme, we only run up against a further barrier of 'creative determinism,' in that the One (God) selects from competing universes which may be created (in the Aristotelian sense of a 'formal cause'). This is perhaps because we (humanly) only perceive choice as 'free choice' when there are alternatives on offer. In Tolkien's music there feasibly could have been other themes and variations, arising out of the freedom of both Eru and the Ainur, and therefore a different Middle-earth arising out of the subsequent command, Eä. It seems that *if* there were no choice in the creating, then the Creator would

32. Burrell, *Faith and Freedom*, 130.

33. Puigarnau, "Creation and Freedom," 245–47, *Enneads*, 5.5.9. See also Mann, "Augustine on Evil," 41–42.

34. Flieger, "Naming the Unnameable," 128.

be thus constrained, and this universe would be the only universe possible, given the Creator it has. Once we are alerted to accepting that the universe is indeed a free gift, then the utter freedom of creation not only denies any *need* on the part of the Creator, but also any *constraints* on the part of the world. There can be no possibility preceding God's free origination, except by reference to the power of God. So there are no 'possible worlds' from which the Creator selects *this* one, as though God's action in creating were primarily a matter of will and indeed of choice. In this sense of divine freedom, 'what is' could always have been otherwise, and this operative sense of contingency distinguishes the 'what is' of 'creation-as-gift' from what might never have been at all. Aquinas developed this by clearly arguing against any creature existing by absolute necessity, for it is only on the supposition that the divine will has unchangeably decreed its preservation.[35] For, "as the production of a thing into existence depends on the will of God, so likewise it depends on His will that things should be preserved; for He does not preserve them otherwise than by ever giving them existence; hence if He took away His action from them, all things would be reduced to nothing."[36] God preserves things in existence only by perpetually giving existence to them, and to withdraw this activity would be to consign all things to nothingness.

The opening words of *The Silmarillion*, "There was Eru, the One, who in Arda is called Ilúvatar," declares at once (like Plotinus and Dionysius) the unity, pre-existence, and the limited human perception of this God-figure. Flieger postulates that:

> The first three words are striking in their simplicity, a plain declarative in the past tense singular of the verb 'to be,' coupled with no place and no time other than the indeterminate pre-present, plus a single noun with no modifier, no Dionysian superlative, no embellishment.[37]

Tolkien presents his reader with subject-predicate, the necessary minimum to put meaning into his literary opening. He simply adds the explication, "the One." In Tolkien's device, the primordial essence is Eru—a word with no prior meaning—and glossed by a name, Ilúvatar (not an 'It,' as in Plotinus and Dionysius).[38] This is suggestive of an Aristotelian God-figure as the motionless generator of motion, beyond movement (since 'all-ness,'

---

35. Burrell, *Faith and Freedom*, 78; QDV, 3.7 ad3.
36. ST 1.9.2. resp.
37. Flieger, "Naming the Unnameable," 128.
38. Ibid., 130. Flieger makes the philological link between 'Eru' and the Indo-European root '*er*'—'to set in motion'

cannot go beyond itself), but giving rise to movement: Eru, Prime Mover, is the essential nature of the One.[39]

Ilúvatar is name, not essence. It is later translated in his "Index of Names" as "Father of All."[40] This description can only ever be partial perception, a revelation of Eru perceived from the perspective of human generation. Not the One, not Prime Mover, but 'Father'—a word with generative, domestic, and with rich theological overtones (and common to many mythologies).[41] Tolkien creates, where his predecessors explain. After his opening words he adds, "and he made first the Ainur, the Holy Ones, that were the offspring of his thought, and they were with him before ought else was made."[42] Here is creation—conscious creation—beginning, the 'firstness' before which only Eru was. He also uses the term 'offspring,' suggesting progeny. As 'offspring' of Eru's thought, the Ainur are aspects of the whole mind, differentiations of Eru's undifferentiated nature. They are divided parts of that which is undivided, thought springing out from the mind, assuming a life of their own. As parts, they express, but cannot encompass the whole, "for each comprehended only that part of the mind of Ilúvatar from which he came, and in the understanding of their brethren they grew but slowly."[43] This is Plotinus' contrariety, and Dionysius' "thing rational and intellectual," the multiple products of the one mind from which arise conflict, energy, tension.[44]

If Eru Iluvatar is defined as personal, then the cosmo-genesis becomes problematic from an Augustinian perspective. Having initially ruled out an emanationist principle in favor of creation, Augustine's account (of creation) has God as its sole originator. In Tolkien's account it is the Ainur who mediate the creation of Middle-earth. They sing the plan of the Great Music, which originates in Eru, but which they are free to elaborate within the mind of Eru (hence Melkor's discord and desire to dominate). The rest of Tolkien's vast mythology is carried out without Eru—he has no further role in the action, and hence the charge of deism. He remains throughout unknowable, and unreachable in his Oneness, perceivable and approachable only to the extent by which the part can represent the whole: the Unknown

---

39. Ibid.

40. Tolkien, *Silmarillion*, 404.

41. Flieger, "Naming the Unnameable," 130. God the Father is one 'persona' of the Christian Trinity; Greek Zeus 'Pater' becomes Jupiter; Odin, chief God of the Norse pantheon has the epithet 'All Father.'

42. Tolkien, *Silmarillion*, 15.

43. Tolkien, *Silmarillion*, 15.

44. Flieger, "Naming the Unnameable," 131–32.

God.⁴⁵ Tolkien's myth of creation is not a purposeful transmutation, or a carrying over of properties from one thing to another. He himself says,

> References to these things are not causal but fundamental: they may well be fundamentally 'wrong' from the point of view of Reality (external reality). But they cannot be wrong inside this imaginary world, since that is how it is made.⁴⁶

The sub-creation is not subject to the same rules as creation; the properties of creation have not been 'carried over' to sub-creation, so as to make them coeval or correlative. To read Augustine or any other of the Christian Neoplatonists directly out of Tolkien is too simplistic, and naïve, and it would appear that once again, he has deliberately chosen a degree of independence in order to avoid a simplistic allegorical or analogical reading.

2.1.3 Plotinus and His Legacy (2): Creation in Augustine's *De Genesi Ad Litteram*

The book of Genesis held a particular fascination for Augustine, as contained within its embryonic ideas reveals a subtle refutation of the dualism of Manichaeism, and a corrective against certain aspects of Neoplatonism.⁴⁷ When Augustine treats of Genesis as having a 'literal' interpretation, we must not confuse it with contemporary expressions of biblical fundamentalism and/or creationism. John Houghton's sharp analysis draws our attention to Augustine wanting to rule out figurative, allegorical meaning from the outset precisely because the 'literal' sense he finds in the opening of Genesis is itself *expressed* figuratively.⁴⁸ Augustine calls his symbolic interpretation the 'literal sense of Genesis' because he is convinced that Moses (whom he believed to be the author) deliberately used symbols in writing about real historical events of the creation. Augustine's concern in *De Genesi ad Litteram* is not to find ways in which Moses' story prefigures later events (as

---

45. There is one notable exception, where the Ainur call upon him to put down rebellious humanity (in the destruction of Númenor), otherwise he remains above and beyond the world, working only in and through his personified aspects—the Ainur (as Valar).

46. Carpenter, *Letters*, 188.

47. The latter part of his *Confessiones*, *De Civitate Dei*, and three biblical commentaries: *De Genesi contra Manicheos*, *de Genesi ad litteram imperfectus liber* (An Incomplete Book on the Literal Sense of Genesis), and *De Genesi ad Litteram Libri Duodecim* (Twelve Books on the Literal Sense of Genesis) testify to this attention given to creation-as-creation.

48. Houghton, "Augustine," 173.

did Ambrose), but rather to explain Moses' literal historical meaning, as Moses expressed it in symbolic language.[49]

Augustine's opening move is to concern himself with the creation of 'heaven and earth,' in that spiritual creatures (i.e., angels) were created in a state of perfection, and corporeal creatures were created as unformed matter, in accordance with what follows—"The earth was invisible and formless."[50] The repetition of the phrase, "And God said, 'Let there be made' [. . .] and so it was made," is followed in that God named the thing created, and God sees that it is good. The phrase, "And God said," at least for Augustine, refers to the fact that God calls things to form through the second person of the Trinity, the Word who is the form of all creation. We see this later in his *De Musica*, where the Word is—for Augustine—the agent whereby creation is actualized. The initial reference to the creation of corporeal things as formless matter refers to the second person simply as "the Beginning," avoiding any reference to "the Word." Thus, "Let there be made" refers to the creation of things as ideas in the minds of the angels, for when God causes these spiritual beings to understand what it is that God is creating, the concept of the angelic minds is itself something that God has made. "Let light be made" refers to the creation of spiritual creatures themselves, an event that the angels experience, rather than one that is revealed to them.[51] "And God made," in turn refers to the creation of things in their own proper existence, creation in the ordinary sense of the word. Finally, "God saw that it was good" refers to the Holy Spirit brooding over creation—not passively approving of what is made, but actively holding it in being. "And so it was done" means that God creates in the angels' knowledge of what he is about to create; "There was evening" refers to the angels' direct knowledge of the created things in themselves. "There was morning" means that the angels turn back from seeing created things to contemplate, and praise the source of the creation in God, and receive revelation of further new creatures. For Augustine particularly, and Neoplatonism generally, knowledge of instantiated and corporeal being is only a sort of dim echo of knowledge of the thing as an idea in God. For Augustine, the universe is comprised fundamentally of existing realities, of natures or substances that have being. So that which truly *is*, is the source of all being: every existing nature must be either that which truly *is* or the sort of thing that depends for its being on what truly *is*. Hence, insofar as a nature exists, it has being to some extent and, if it is not that which truly *is*, then it must depend for its being on what

---

49. Ibid., 173–75.
50. *De Genesi ad Litteram*, 1.1.3.
51. Ibid., 2.8.16–19.

truly *is*.[52] There can be no existing nature that is distinct from and utterly independent of God; its existence is so in relation to its participation in God as that which truly *is*.

Augustine's analysis of these repetitions, leads him to formulate a four-stage process, one that we might think of as repeated on subsequent 'days' of creation: "Let there be made [. . .] and God made [. . .] God saw that it was good [. . .] and so it was done." The statements concerning 'evening' and 'morning' are not referred to as in the ordinary sequence of temporal days, as they only have reference to a local effect—then it is evening in one place, it is morning in another, half the world away.[53] It would be wrong to read Augustine as speaking of creation taking place over chronological days (or *eons* of whatever length), to be followed by rest on the seventh. Rather, God creates everything simultaneously, in an eternal moment. Nor does the sequence in angelic knowledge indicate a passage of time: the angels are temporal creatures, but in their direct contemplation of God they observe the simultaneity of divine action. So here we have a true six-fold repetition in the act of creation, but that repetition takes place in one single moment. Whilst this may appear to be a concept inconsistent with a 'temporal' reading of the Genesis account, Augustine says that is precisely why Moses used such terms, making the difficult simple enough for a child to understand.[54] Given that some aspects of the creation need, by their very nature, a causal relationship with past events or beings, then Augustine self-refines his ideas to include both the creation of some things in their actuality and the creation of the 'causal reasons' of other things. He likens these 'causal reasons' to seeds, and for this reason calls them 'seminal reasons' (*rationes seminales*). The concept refers to a real material element that will bring about some phenomenon at a later point in time, after a sort of dormancy.[55] The working out of the potentiality of causal reasons is subject both to the effect of secondary causes and to the explicit will of God: both the ordinary course of nature and miracles express the causal reasons. Augustine posits that God may have reserved some causal reasons in God's self, so that they are not subjected to the necessity of other causes and take effect only when God chooses, encompassed within the necessity of God's will. Miracles may surprise us, but one part of God's plan does not contradict another.[56]

52. De nat. boni c.Man, 24.26—25.27; Civ Dei, 7.29–30.
53. De Gen ad Lit, 4.30.47.
54. Ibid., 5.3.6.
55. Houghton, *Augustine*, 173–75, explains it in terms of DNA: "a child may grow to adulthood or may die in adolescence; water may become wine through the growth and fermentation of grapes or through the words of the 'Word made flesh.'"
56. De Gen ad Lit, 6.14.25–18.29, esp 6.18.29.

Augustine's analysis and presentation of creation, as a single moment of divine action may be seen as a five-part internal structure: first, God's eternal intention to create, enunciating in the Word; secondly, God's creation in the minds of the angels of a knowledge of what is to be made; thirdly, God's creation of things, some of them (like angels) in full existence, but most of them (like trees, plants, humans) in the potentiality called 'causal reasons'; fourthly, the angels' perception of the created things; and finally God's eternal support of the creation through the Holy Spirit.[57] We see, therefore, how Augustine's procession of creation, from the mind and deliberate will of God, is one of gift, and that what creation becomes is comprehended by the angels outside of what becomes time. In Tolkien's creation myth in *The Silmarillion* we see a similar fourfold procession, but in this case he can be seen to weave into his philosophy of being the musical craft of both God and his created effects—the Ainur.

2.2 The Metaphysics of Music: Tolkien's Creative Symphony

2.2.1 The Music of the Spheres in Medieval Cosmology

Tolkien's use of music to denote the agency and method of creation, from the mind and will of Iluvatar and the Ainur, has resonances with a key medieval concept. The music of the spheres, (*musica universalis*) was grounded in ancient and classical philosophy, theorized by Plato and Aristotle, through early Christian writers via the third-century philosopher Plotinus, up to its eventual standardization by Boethius in the early sixth century. Nothing in Tolkien's published works and/or *Letters*, nor his *Biography*, testifies to his incorporation of any particular philosophical model or cosmological theory in the construction of his own mythology in general, and cosmogony in particular. Bradford Eden asserts that, as both a classicist and medievalist, the music of the spheres would have been conceptually and religiously ingrained deeply into his thinking, and furthermore influenced his creative processes.[58]

---

57. *De Genesi's* twelve books deal with related themes, alongside God's external (transcendent) management of the universe. Angels are God's agent for carrying out the design of providence (8.24.45), and elsewhere are likened to gardeners—they do the work, but God gives the increase (9.18.35). Augustine even considers the proposition that angels were created in two varieties, the heavenly and the mundane, where only the latter were subject to the fall (11.17.22). He also toys with the idea that Satan lived for a while among the angels (11.26.33).

58. Eden, "Music of the Spheres," 184. This use of the *musica universalis* tradition is used by Tolkien's contemporary C. S. Lewis, in the creation of Narnia in *The Magician's*

I shall demonstrate that the creational use of music was a significant feature in his cosmogony as the means wherein created things have Being. Eden further asserts that it is the influence of Boethius here, and not primarily Augustine, that informs Tolkien's literary device in employing this music of the spheres, amidst the wider backdrop of the use of music in creation myths.[59] The cosmo-genesis of reality, through music and vision is summarized in the opening chapter of *The Silmarillion*, *The Ainulindalë* as follows:

Ilúvatar proposed musical themes to the Ainur, and they sang, individually at first, reflecting the individual parts of Ilúvatar's mind from which they came.[60] As they began to discover harmony, Ilúvatar called them together and from him issued a Great Theme, so that each of them could adorn according to their nature. The symphony began, but after some time Melkor—the mightiest of the Ainur—began to introduce discordant themes of his own invention. As others followed him, then discourse spread, until at length Ilúvatar introduced a second theme of his own. Growing ever more violent, a third theme was introduced, drawing together his earlier two. Finally, there seemed two separate musics, until Ilúvatar drew all into one final chord.[61] When the music had ended, Ilúvatar, in order to demonstrate that Melkor's discord only served his own higher purpose, gave the Ainur a vision of what, until then, had only been music.[62] He showed them a world sustained in the void: their music was its design and history. From this vision, and their memory of the music, the Ainur had foreknowledge of the world's development, but the knowledge of some things Ilúvatar reserved for himself. The Ainur were unaware that the third theme revealed the creation of elves and men, and that the world was (anthropically) designed as a home for them—his children.[63] The vision was brief and transient, and when it faded, all was enshrouded in darkness. Iluvatar then gave the world real existence, creating it with a single word, 'Eä'—"Let these things be."[64]

Nephew.

59. Ibid., 184.

60. Tolkien, *Silmarillion*, 15.

61. Ibid., 16.

62. Ibid., 18. Melkor (later referred to as Morgoth) is also spoken of as "the Dark enemy of the world," coeval with Manwë, but covetous and desiring kingship and dominion over Manwë. He is described as a "liar without shame," and moves from the desire of light to "darkness and fire." His greatest servant was Sauron, who served as maiar of Aüle, concerning the substance of the earth.

63. Tolkien, *Silmarillion*, 18.

64. Tolkien, *Book of Lost Tales 1*, 62. Christopher Tolkien points out that the introduction of this separate moment of physical creation is one of few developments between the early and late versions of *The Ainulindalë*.

If we are to seek a direct creative account in the Scriptures, of angelic beings helping fashion the world via celestial music, then we will not find it in the book of Genesis. This may be another deliberate attempt by a deft writer to avoid obvious biblical allusions, but also because we can read it out of a less obvious source: the book of Job, which describes the heavenly host accompanying the creation of the world with their singing, "On what were its bases sunk, or who laid its cornerstone, when the morning stars sang together, and all the sons of God shouted for joy."[65] Furthermore, King David enjoins the whole of creation to lift up its praise to God, and in similar fashion the angelic host sing their timeless praise to God in the company of the martyred saints.[66] David Bentley Hart summarizes his own scriptural analysis:

> there are abundant biblical reasons, quite apart from the influence of pagan philosophy, for Christians to speak of the *harmonia mundi* [. . .] the pleasing conceits of pagan cosmology aside, theology has all the warrant it needs for speaking of divine composition, a magnificent music, whose measures and refrains rise up to the pleasure and the glory of God.[67]

In that same sense of harmony and order, we read in the *First Letter of Clement to the Corinthians*:

> The heavens move at his direction and obey him in peace. Day and night complete their course assigned by him, neither hindering the other. The sun and the moon and the choirs of stars circle in harmony within the courses assigned to them, according to his direction, without any deviation at all.[68]

This text has a generally accepted dating of 95–96 AD, and we find therefore in the very early apostolic period the influence of Greek ideas of number, harmony, and hierarchy of being. Hart is correct, in that biblical and early Christian texts can open up to us creation as having integrity in terms of its origin in a divine Creator. However, we see already in a text thought to be consonant with the dating of John's Gospel—which itself incorporated Greek philosophical concepts in its own *Prologue*—language which stands outside of the Christian revelation in Scripture. This is certainly suggested in Tolkien's own account, whereby it is already anticipated that "a greater [music] still shall be made before Ilúvatar by the choirs of the Ainur and the

---

65. Job 38:6–7.
66. 1 Chr 17:23, 31–33; Rev 5:8–12; see also Ps 96:11–12.
67. Hart, *Beauty of the Infinite*, 275.
68. *1 Clem.* 20:1–3.

children of Ilúvatar after the end of days."[69] For Tolkien, the music originates in the One, but is mediated by free intellectual creatures.

The philosophical background to this organization of music and number may be seen to rest in the pre-Socratic Pythagorean school, and that Aristotle writes of them that

> since they [the Pythagoreans] saw further that the properties and ratios of the musical scales are based on numbers, and since it seemed clear that all other things have their whole nature modelled upon numbers, and that numbers are the ultimate things in the whole physical universe, they assumed the elements of numbers to be the elements of everything, and the whole universe to be a proportion [or harmony] or number.[70]

Given the classical premise that 'like effects resemble like causes,' it may be asserted that the Pythagorean concept of world or cosmic harmony is more than simple metaphor and/or allegory, but in related concepts such as Aquinas' analogy of attribution, the heavenly ordering becomes the means whereby the reality of human music was ultimately derived. In Plato's *Timaeus*, it has been shown that ratios are the basic principle by which the World Soul is immanent in the cosmos, and gives its order and structure.[71] There is a continuous flow of metaphors from the human (and divine) sphere to nature and back again to human activities, which are considered as imitating the artistic orderliness and harmony of nature.[72] The Pythagoreans held that bodies of such vast a size as the planets must emit a considerable volume, and that their relative speed and distance ratios are in the same ratios as musical chords.[73] According to the Myth of Er at the end of the *Republic*, each of the planets gives out a sound together with the fixed stars beyond them, so that their total harmony of eight notes constitutes a vast concord.[74] Aristotle decried these Pythagorean claims as absurd, since a principle feature of the heavenly bodies is their very silence.[75]

---

69. Tolkien, *Silmarillion*, 15.

70. *Metaphysics I-XI*, 1.5.986a2; *De Caelo I and II*, 2.9.290b12.

71. *Timaeus*, 35b–36a. In the *Republic* (546b-c), skill in understanding ratios can disclose the perfect 'nuptial number,' determining the times when good or bad offspring are conceived.

72. Spitzer, *World Harmony*, 8–9.

73. Chadwick, *Consolations of Music*, 79.

74. *Republic*, 617a–b.

75. *De Caelo*, 2.9.290b15.

It is by means of a similar kind of Pythagorean family resemblance that Tolkien undertakes by means of fictional deities when he writes of them in *The Ainulindalë* how,

> the voices of the Ainur, like unto harps and lutes, and pipes and trumpets, and viols and organs, and like unto countless choirs singing with words, began to fashion the theme of Ilúvatar to a great music.[76]

Given my assertion that Tolkien was influenced by a range of Christian (and pre-Christian) Neoplatonist concepts and *modus operandi* in creation, he shared none of the skepticism of Aristotle's views on the *Timaeus*, but rather embraced them via the works of Augustine, Pseudo-Dionysius, and Boethius. Indeed, in the *Timaeus*, we may see the influence of Plato on Tolkien in a passage which alludes to the music of the spheres, when he suggests that an analogous structure was placed by the Demiurge in the World Soul:

> The body of the heaven is visible, but the soul is invisible and endowed with reason and harmony, being the best creation of the best of intelligible and eternal things.[77]

The manner in which the Ainur's music antedates and pre-contains the entire history of the world resembles Plato's realm of Forms/Ideals, in which the physical world of sensible things participate. This being so, we may see here the foundation for a later Neoplatonic philosophy of 'being and gift' by virtue of its participation in the highest being, but in this case via the mediation of intermediary and free agents, the Ainur. In the *Timaeus*, Plato brings about his creation myth via these eternal Forms, to which the Demiurge/Craftsman has fashioned the material world. In the case of Tolkien, we see creation as a process arising out of the mind of Ilúvatar, and shared with his quasi-divine beings, the Ainur, who have the freedom to modify, and even challenge, the divine theme. Plotinus, writing some six hundred years after Plato, applied this musical analogy, in that, "certainly all music since the ideas which it has are concerned with rhythm and melody, would be of the same kind, just like the art which is concerned with intelligible number," and thus like the other arts would have "its principles from the intelligible world."[78]

---

76. Tolkien, *Silmarillion*, 15.
77. *Timaeus*, 36e–37a.
78. *Enneads*, 5.9.11.

2.2.2 Augustine's Ordering of Creation in His *De Musica* and the *Confessiones*

It was principally through the works of Plotinus that the works of Plato were mediated to Augustine, whose treatise *De Musica* was the first Christian work to shape significantly the way music was studied in the Latin West, and paved the way for Boethius' own exposition of the subject. In his *Homily on Psalm 42*, a work written some nine years after his *De Musica*, he continues his Platonic trajectory, declaring that when a man is close to death, the mind becomes detached from this world and hears an 'intellectual music':

> a certain sweet and melodious strain strikes on the ears of the heart, provided only the world do not drown the sounds. [. . .] As he walks in this tabernacle, and contemplates God's wonderful works for the redemption of the faithful, the sound of that festivity charms his ears, and bears the "hart" away to "the water-brooks."[79]

Furthermore, his tract *On Christian Instruction* postulates that music and number are keys to unlock the exegesis of Scripture. As numbers are governed by immutable ratios, so they become signposts to an immutable Creator. The science of numbers was not ordained by men, but rather investigated and learned by them.'[80] In this way, we see how Augustine placed firmly at the heart of his 'poetic cosmology' the earlier Platonic language about numbers, order, and harmony as pathways to the truth of who and what God is.

Whilst the majority of Augustine's *De Musica* is devoted to matters of musical theory, the sixth and final book addresses some of the cosmic implications of music, the ascent from rhythm in sense to the immortal rhythm which is in truth. In the course of his discussion, Augustine enumerates five different kinds of rhythm, the highest and most 'immortal' of which he calls *iudiciales numeri* (judicial rhythm), a form of rhythm that "it appears those judicial numbers are not confined to a span of time," is nevertheless in some sense eternal and resides in the soul, enabling it to "pass judgment on things given even if varied within certain lengths, by approving harmonies in them and rejecting discords."[81] The judicial rhythm within the soul, enabling it to judge the presence or absence of rhythm outside the soul, however, is also a property of the cosmos as a whole:

---

79. *EnPs*, 42.8.
80. *De Doctrina Christiana*, 2.16.26; 2.38.56,
81. *De Musica*, 6.7.18.

to each living thing in its proper kind and in its proportion with the universe is given a sense of places and times, so that even as its body is so much in proportion to the body of the universe whose part it is, and its age so much in proportion to the age of the universe whose part it is, so its sensing complies with the action it pursues in proportion to the movement of the universe whose part it is?[82]

In Book 11 of the *Confessions*, Augustine's idea of this judicial rhythm in the cosmos, similar to the Ainur's music, is represented as the agent through which the Creator's own act of creation is somehow mediated. As Augustine enquires of God:

But how did you speak [in creation]? [. . .] The utterance came through the movement of some created thing, serving your eternal will but itself temporal. And these your words, made for temporal succession, were reported by the external ear to the judicious mind whose internal ear is disposed to hear your eternal word. But that mind would compare these words, sounding in time, with your eternal word in silence.[83]

Quoting Psalm 33:6 and 33:9, Augustine here changes the medium of creation from music to word, and these divine words correspond to the one Word, which is the Son. Augustine is keen to stress Christian orthodoxy via the Trinity, but does so using language which is steeped in both Plotinian ideas and biblical texts. Thus, "In this beginning, God, you made heaven and earth, in your Word, in your Son, in your power, in your wisdom, in your truth speaking in a wonderful way and making in a wonderful way," may be read as a lexical equivalent to his analysis in *De Musica*.[84] There is still a divine mediator, but here He is the second person of the Trinity, corresponding to Plato's Demiurge, and I would therefore postulate, Tolkien's Ainur. Leo Spitzer points to an important shift from the pagan to Christian mediation of creation, which is clearly derived from Augustine's understanding of world harmony:

According to the Pythagoreans, it was cosmic order which was identifiable with music; according to the Christian philosophers, it was love. And in the *ordo amoris* of Augustine we have evidently a blend of the Pagan and the Christian themes: henceforth, 'order' is love.[85]

82. Ibid., 6.7.19.
83. *Conf*, 11.6.
84. Ibid., 11.9.
85. Spitzer, *World Harmony*, 19–20. See also Hart, *Beauty of the Infinite*, 276.

CREATION AND THE METAPHYSICS OF MUSIC

Brian Brennan makes an important point in addition to Spitzer, in that the personal element that links Augustine's philosophical speculations on the nature of music is his own experience of the Ambrosian music of the Milanese church at the time of his conversion and baptism in 387 AD. Brennan cites *Confessions* 9.6, in that Augustine,

> wept during your hymns and songs! I was deeply moved by the music of the sweet chants of your Church. The sounds flowed into my ears and the truth was distilled into my heart. This caused the feelings of devotion to overflow. Tears ran, and it was good for me to have that experience.[86]

It was through the music of the Milanese church that Augustine attained a oneness with God, and yet it is by rising above the pleasures of the senses that the soul may find supreme enjoyment in contemplation of the One.[87] Like Plato before, and Boethius later, Augustine recognizes an ethical as well as aesthetic sense in music, and that music is the science of measuring well.[88] The Perfect numbers in the soul are those termed by Augustine judicial, and within the soul these *iudiciales numeri*, unlike other transient numbers, are alone immortal.[89] Number is perfect and has its origin in the One.[90] It is also reflected in that which he has created—*carmen universitatis*, the poem of the universe.[91] It is particularly apposite therefore, that Augustine should choose to illustrate his number theory by reference to the Ambrosian hymn *Deus Creator Omnium*, since his work describes God in terms reminiscent of the Platonic One:

> Creator of all things.
>
> You rule the heavens.
>
> You clothe the day with light
>
> And night with the grace of sleep.[92]

Music contains number, but is never abstract: good music is the perfect *numerositas*. The soul, therefore, illuminated and aided by God's gift of the judicial numbers, goes forward to confront such music and judge it as being good.

---

86. Brennan, "Augustine's *De Musica*," 267.
87. *Conf*, 4.10.
88. *Republic*, 398c–399e; *De Musica*, 1.2.
89. *De Musica*, 6.7.17
90. Ibid., 6.17.67.
91. Ibid., 6.11.29.
92. *Conf*, 9.12; *De Musica*, 6.17.57.

That Tolkien was aware of, and followed Augustine's *De Musica* as a primary source of influence, is demonstrated in his own creation myth. The Music of the Ainur can therefore be judged according to the relation of Number to the One, and its variance from the One may be evaluated as a divine gift. That Melkor sowed discord and mischief via dissonance in music is not simply an aesthetic observation, but one which corresponds to Augustine's 'science of music' in his early writings. For Augustine, the correct ethical disposition is found only in one who allows God to operate on the rational soul and guide its judicial sense to appraise music by the standard of divine truth. Man's—or in the case of Tolkien's music, Melkor's pride—may disrupt God's plan and disrupt the soul from what is good in music by diverting attention to that which is below the soul—sensible pleasure.[93] Indeed, Augustine's discussion makes use of the Plotinian imagery of the fall of the soul, in that it is itself nothing: if it were something, then "it would be subject to change and suffer a fading away from being." Whatever the soul is, comes from God, but when the soul turns its back on God, "it puffs up with pride" and becomes "less and less."[94] At this lower level, the soul focuses its attention on bodily pleasure, and has already fallen from the contemplation of the divine numbers of wisdom received from God, and strays/lapses farther from the One, becoming "less and less" as it falls down the scale of lower numbers.

What may at first appear to be a bland and impersonal work may be seen in a highly personal and liturgical light, given that the hymn *Deus Creator Omnium* brought Augustine great solace following the death of his mother, Monica. Furthermore, but more generally, later comments on music in the *Confessions* reveal that he was extremely conscious of the powerful influence that music exerted over him. His later works made him suspicious of music altogether, since it is perceived through one of the bodily senses. Indeed, it was this fear of sensual pleasure that led Augustine to consider banning music altogether from church services.[95]

Spitzer's focus on *ordo amoris* may go some way to answer the accusation of deism in Tolkien's cosmo-genesis, where Ilúvatar is almost entirely disinterested with the evolution and activities within Middle-earth, once it becomes reality.[96] For Augustine, number, music, and order are never entirely distinct from the source—the One—and it might be said that even the

---

93. *De Musica*, 6.13.

94. Ibid., 6.13.

95. *Conf*, 10.33; Brennan, *Augustine's De Musica*, 276, 277.

96. Spitzer clarifies the particular focus of *caritas* in the Christian harmonizing of ancient thought into the *ordo amoris* of Augustine, in particular the use of feeling in 1 Corinthians 13:1. Only through charity can man reach true music. *World Harmony*, 19.

most degrading or discordant music may still have some faint suggestion of the divinely ordered pattern, yet dimly perceived. Tolkien lifts this concept to a new height by his assertion that Eru—the One—makes good out of such discord and dissonance: it is not simply ignored or left to languish in a moral void. I shall demonstrate in Chapter 3 that this blending of pagan and Christian themes in Tolkien's professional studies of *Beowulf,* alongside other Anglo-Saxon literature, highlights the distinction from a largely deterministic pagan worldview, and a freedom within the providence of God, arising out of the Christian understanding of free will that Augustine is so keen to stress in his readings of Genesis chapters 1–3. The development of this freedom in Tolkien owes as much to Boethius as it does to Augustine, and it is to his own treatise on music that I now turn.

2.2.3 Boethius' Threefold Division of Musical and Cosmic *Ordo*

This work was intended to be read alongside his *De Institutione Mathematica*, and may have been one of four works setting out the foundations of Platonic scientific education: arithmetic, music, geometry, and astronomy.[97] Boethius' early works record in Latin what he was reading in Greek. In his *De Institutione Musica* Boethius intended to treat only peripherally the actual theory of music: his focus was knowing. For Boethius,

> it appears beyond doubt that music is so naturally united with us that we cannot be free from it even if we so desired, and for this reason the power of the intellect ought to be summoned, so that this art, innate through nature, might also be mastered, comprehended through knowledge.[98]

The means of coming to know music is uncompromisingly Pythagorean: number. In Boethius' exposition, music has both religious and moral overtones: music began in a state of grace, as it were. This tradition dates back to Pythagoras' observations of sounds in a smithy, resembling four strings sounding intervals of the octave divided by a fourth and fifth, intervals embodying the tetractys 12:9:8:6. In this age of gods and demigods nothing discordant was found in music, and this historical allegory reaches back to the most ancient of Greek prehistory, naming inventors of strings who had been associated with the inventions of modes. The tonal genesis brings the development of musical system to its completion in fifteen notes, but a

---

97. Bower and Palisca, *Fundamentals of Music,* xix.
98. Ibid., 1.1.187.

value judgment is clear throughout: namely that, as music moved away from the state of simplicity and purity expressed in the Pythagorean tetractys, its integrity was compromised.[99] We see here hints of a *lapsus* or declination from an ideal, so universal in Greek and early Christian Neoplatonism, that it would not be difficult to harmonize Tolkien's use of Boethius, and a pessimistic reading of discordance and disharmony as a tragic decay in harmony. Boethius' musical treatise is a dialectical balance between mythic and mathematical poles, and represents an exercise in faith and reason. It should come as no surprise, therefore, that it was through the *De Institutione Musica* that classical musical theory was primarily transmitted to the Middle-Ages and the Renaissance.[100]

Towards the beginning of his thesis, Boethius distinguishes three specific kinds of music, in order of priority and importance: the music of the universe (*musica mundana*), human music (*musica humana*, the music of body and soul), and instrumental music (*musica instrumentalis*).[101] The first kind is embodied (and further sub-divided) into the movement of celestial bodies, the harmony of the four elements, and the four seasons. These movements denote a tension between both their movements and the 'sounds' which they emanate, so that

> all revolve with such equal energy that a fixed order of their courses is reckoned through their diverse inequalities. For that reason, a fixed sequence of modulation cannot be separated from this celestial revolution.[102]

Boethius thinks it impossible that "so swift a heavenly machine moves on a mute and silent course," and that "such extremely fast motion of such large bodies should produce absolutely no sound."[103] In a later chapter Boethius even correlates each of the planetary spheres with the various musical strings, and rank within Roman society:

> a seventh string was added by Terpender of Lesbia, obviously in likeness to the seven planets. The lowest one called 'hypate' [. . .] for this reason they call Jove 'Hypatus.' They also call a consul by the same name because of the loftiness of his rank.

---

99. Ibid., xxii.
100. Ibid., xxiv.
101. Ibid., 1.2.187.
102. Ibid., 1.2.188.
103. Ibid., 1.2.187.

This string was attributed to Saturn because of its slow motion and low sound.[104]

For Boethius, the differences (or potential discord) among the four elements are harmonised by a chain of being that helps to balance and co-ordinate them in order to produce the plenitude of creation. This harmony is reflected in the music of the universe:

> so that we perceive that in the music of the universe nothing can be excessive to destroy some other part by its own excess, but each part brings its own contribution or aids others to bring theirs.[105]

Although it is with this classical idea of the music of the spheres that commentators have most often compared the Music of the Ainur, it is worth noting that nowhere in *The Ainulindalë* does it ever refer to celestial bodies, nor anywhere else in the Tolkien *corpus*. Of greater relevance, therefore, are Boethius' second and third sub-divisions of the *musica mundana*, namely the harmony of the elements and the seasons. Of the former, for example, Boethius asks, "If a certain harmony did not join the diversities and opposing forces of the four elements, how would it be possible that they could unite in one mass and contrivance?"[106] Similarly, in *The Ainulindalë* it is in a state of Boethian harmony that the four elements first appear to the Ainur in the vision:

> And they observed the wind and the air, and the matters of which Arda was made, of iron and stone and silver and gold and many substances: but of all these water they most greatly praised. And it is said by the Eldar that in water there lives yet the echo of the Music of the Ainur more than in any substance else that is in this Earth; and many of the Children of Ilúvatar hearken still to the voices of the Sea, and yet know not for what they listen.[107]

As for the third category of the *musica mundana*—the harmony of the four seasons—Boethius compares the consonance of the four seasons with the attunement of lower and higher strings of an instrument, such that

> the whole corpus of pitches is coherent and harmonious with itself [. . .] for what winter confines, spring releases, summer

---

104. Ibid., 1.20.206.
105. Ibid., 1.2.188.
106. Ibid., 1.2.188.
107. Tolkien, *Silmarillion*, 20.

heats, and autumn ripens, and the seasons in their turn either bring forth their own fruit or give aid to others in bringing forth their own.[108]

This consonance of the seasons has an earlier source in *1 Clement*, in that "The earth, bearing fruit in the proper seasons in fulfilment of his will, brings forth food in full abundance for both men and beasts and all living things which are upon it, without dissension or altering anything he has decreed."[109] These are interpretations of Scripture rooted in the Catholic tradition, and yet framed in the more ancient usage of classical Greek philosophy: all life is divinely ordered, and yet is in an interconnected state of harmony and peace. This short passage on creation is appended by the statement, "All these things the great Creator and Master of the universe ordered to exist in peace and harmony, thus doing good to all things, but especially abundantly to us who have taken refuge in his compassionate mercies through our Lord Jesus Christ, to whom be the glory and the majesty for ever and ever. Amen."[110]

In a comparable text in *The Ainulindalë*, recalling the accord between seasons and weather patterns, upset only by the dissonance of Melkor, Ilúvatar informs the Vala, Ulmo:

> Behold the snow, the cunning work of frost! Melkor hath devised heats and fire without restraint, and hath not dried up thy desire nor utterly quelled the music of the sea. Behold rather the height and glory of the clouds, and the ever-changing mists; and listen to the fall of rain upon earth! And in these clouds thou art drawn nearer to Manwë, thy friend whom thou lovest.[111]

Ilúvatar did not plan for Melkor's rebellion, nor his temporal effect in Middle-earth via his discordant music becoming reality. However, Melkor's freedom is but an opportunity for the greater diversity, plenitude, and experience of grace in creation as gift, such that Ulmo could respond:

> Truly water is become now fairer than my heart imagined, neither had my secret thought conceived the snowflake, nor in all my music was contained the falling of the rain. I will seek Manwë, that he and I may make melodies for ever to thy delight![112]

---

108. Bower and Palisca, *Fundamentals of Music*, 1.2.188.
109. *1 Clement*, 20.4.
110. Ibid., 20.11–12.
111. Tolkien, *Silmarillion*, 20.
112. Ibid.

Herein is found an expression of Tolkien's *felix culpa,* that even through the interference of Melkor, the Ainur become more co-operative in their sustaining and developing of Arda: not simply as shepherds of what already is, but co-workers within the providence of a God who is able to bring delight out of mischief. The participatory ontology of the Music of the Ainur is but one expression of the giftedness of being within Tolkien's cosmo-genesis, and I shall demonstrate below how this is expressed more universally in how Tolkien can be read in a more Thomistic light, via the work of Jacques Maritain.

2.2.4 Recapitulation: The Musical Interface of Metaphysics and Reality

In *The Ainulindalë,* the focus is on music as the creative and visual agency, whereby the mind of God, mediated via his demigods, creates reality. The reader is an observer of events that are transpiring prior to the beginning of space/time. The medieval depiction of the various hierarchies of angels singing continuously around the throne of God (cf Isaiah 6; Revelation 4) is recalled in this account of creation, and is a powerful exemplar of medieval cosmological theory in action. That music is the creational and binding agency that sets in motion the whole drama of Middle-earth, as *Eä,* the world that is, not only emphasizes the first category of music that Boethius describes—the music of the universe—but also binds Tolkien in the rest of his mythological work to construct and illustrate music's power through the other two types of music as well (human and instrumental).[113] For if Eru Ilúvatar and the Ainur from the beginning are both bound and set free by the power of cosmological music, then even more so are the creations and creatures contained in Middle-earth. This is not lost on Boethius' analysis either, as any discourse about music highlights a bridge between what is physical and what is metaphysical, such that, "the order of our souls and bodies seems to be related somehow through those same ratios of melodious notes, joined together and united."[114] Here 'ratio' is a translation of *proportio,* itself being a rendering of *logos*—a concept in Christian theology rich in incarnational meaning, but here appears to be limited to the technical ordering of mathematical ratio. Chadwick postulates that in this immediate context Boethius is speaking in analogical terms, there being a direct link between the body/soul (and hence physical/metaphysical) interface

---

113. Eden, "Music of the Spheres," 185, and Tolkien, *Silmarillion,* 15–20.
114. *Fundamentals,* 1.1.186.

on the one hand, and that of music and the World Soul on the other.[115] The *musica humana* exemplifies this soul/body unity, for what unites the incorporeal nature of reason and corporeal nature of the body is a certain harmony, "a careful tuning of low and high pitches as though producing one consonance."[116] It would appear that here Boethius is modifying the Aristotelian principle of harmony being the principle whereby the two parts of the soul—rational and irrational—are harmonised together with the body, and not simply constituting the two parts of the soul.[117]

For those Ainur who choose to enter Middle-earth as Valar (immanent 'demigods'), and assist in its progress (or evolution), then music comes to be the creational energy whereby they, in imitation of Eru, are able to bring forth the results of the Great Music (above) by means of the Valar's respective powers in singing. In the *Quenta Silmarillion* (*Of the Beginning of Days*), Yavana, who controls the production of fruits,

> sang a song of power, in which was set all her thought of things that grow in earth [. . .] and as they watched, upon the mound there came forth two slender shoots [. . .] under her song the saplings grew and became fair and tall, and thus there awoke in the world the Two Trees of Valinor.[118]

In contrast Ulmo, the Vala of water, gives rise to different kinds of music, "in the deep places he gives thought to music great and terrible; and the echo of that music runs through the veins of the world in sorrow and in joy."[119] Later in the tale, as the Valar depart Valinor for ever, and return to *Eä*, then all music ends: "for it is said that after the departure of the Valar there was silence, and for an age Ilúvatar sat alone in thought."[120] In this juncture, Ilúvatar designs the fate of both elves (Quendi) and men (Atani). Therefore, it may be seen that not only does music appear to bring about great creational activity on a cosmological scale, but the silence or absence of music also appears to bring about cosmological implications as well.[121]

---

115. Chadwick, *Consolations of Music*, 7, note 30.

116. *Fundamentals*, 1.2.188.

117. Chadwick, *Consolations of Music*, 10, n41. The relevant text here would be the *Nichomachean Ethics*, 1.13.1102–3. He notes also that it is significant that Boethius does not quote *De Anima* 432A–B, where Aristotle finds the division 'rational-irrational' less than satisfactory.

118. Tolkien, *Silmarillion*, 43.

119. Ibid., 45–46.

120. Ibid., 47.

121. Eden, "Music of the Spheres," 187.

If it is through the agency of music and song that construct the philosophical background to the 'efficient cause' whereby things come into being, then by that same principle in human music do we see the generational force out of which the drama of Middle-earth and its inhabitants unfolds itself. For instance, not only is the entire Beren and Lúthien story framed in the context of song, the man Beren first discovers Lúthien dancing under the rise of the moon. The motif of 'creation by music' therefore represents an original and significant aspect of Tolkien's project, and forms "the relation of the One, the transcendental Creator, to the Valar, the 'Powers,' the angelic First-created, and their part in ordering and carrying out the Primeval Design."[122] It is her singing like a nightingale that draws him.[123] However, Eden finds in this stylistic verse another exemplar of Tolkien's philosophical motif, demonstrating this time the ethereal and persuasive nature of music in one so gifted.[124]

The medieval philosophy of the music of the spheres can be seen, therefore, to pervade throughout Tolkien's early Middle-earth writings. At first reading, there appears to be an unconscious decay of cosmological theory written into *The Silmarillion* that can only be detected by one who is intimately knowledgeable about the entire mythological reality that is Middle-earth. Each theoretical step taken away from the 'Great Music,' which sets everything in motion, is a slow descent away from the divine. This is a strong thread throughout the writings of Plato and Aristotle, that each gradation and division of music away from the 'pure' or 'universal' results in a type of gradual descent downward in spirit and soul. Rowan Williams exemplifies this aspect of privation theory by referring to discord on a musical instrument being not the result of the instrument being interfered with by an external agency *called* discord, but a functioning of the workings of what is already there, of what constitutes the instrument itself.[125] The discord of Melkor, therefore, was a free act of rebellion of a created 'being' who being

---

122. Carpenter, *Letters*, 345. Tolkien gives a summary of the tale by Strider (Aragorn at) Weathertop, *LOTR*, 208–9. The full tale is found in *The Silmarillion*, 194–225, and represents some of the earliest aspects of Tolkien's project. A letter, dated 16th July 1964, testifies to this tale being one of his earliest whilst on sick leave from the Army in 1917, and predates his cosmogonical myth. Appendix B gives a full synopsis of the *Tale*.

123. Tolkien, *Silmarillion*, 198: 'Keen, heart-piercing was her song [. . .] and the song of Luthien released the bonds of winter, and the frozen waters spoke, and flowers sprang from the cold earth where her feet had passed.'

124. Two examples cited are when Luthien offers to sing before Melkor, and the beauty of her song temporarily blinds him (*Silmarillion*, 209–10); and where she seeks the spirit of Beren in the halls of Mandos (the place of the dead). Again, her song overpowers the Valar, but this time by its melancholy sorrow (*Silmarillion*, 224–25).

125. Williams, "Insubstantial Evil," 112.

"offspring of his [God's] own thought," sought to compete with and dominate the "great theme."[126] This strand of 'descent' and 'falling away' is acknowledged in Tolkien's own *Letters*, and is highly suggestive of an Augustinian approach to the problem of evil, linking his (Tolkien's) own concepts with the tendency of created being towards mutability and corruption. Tolkien distinguishes between his own myth and the Christian 'mythology':

> In the latter the Fall of Man is subsequent to and a consequence (though not a necessary consequence) of the 'Fall of the Angels'—a rebellion of created free will at a higher level than Man.[127]

In Tolkien's myth, death is not a punishment for sin, but part of the nature of 'un-fallen' man,

> the Fall or corruption, therefore, of all things in it and all inhabitants of it, was a possibility if not inevitable [. . .] there cannot be any story without a fall—all stories are ultimately about the fall—at least not for human minds as we know them and have them.[128]

2.3 Creation and Fall in *The Ainulindalë*

Tolkien was, first and foremost, a philologist and not a philosopher-theologian. We do well to constantly revisit this reality, as this investigation delves into both his extant self-published works, and those published posthumously. In his study of Tolkien's co-creation, Shippey introduces the term "asterisk-reality" to denote the philological quest to reconstruct not only the forms of lost words, but also the worldviews that those words and languages describe. The difficulty of this task could be seen in the production of asterisk-realities simply reduced to pure imagination.[129] However, Tolkien's works were too well-rooted in the mythology and lore of ancient European cultures and languages—constructs that have their origins in some discernible reality—and he was far too adept a storyteller to allow his co-creation to be the subjective imagination of the reader. This would be the stuff of constructed allegory, something which he persistently denied in his own works.

In the opening section of *The Silmarillion*, Tolkien gives what he calls the elves' "cosmogonical drama": *The Ainulindalë*.[130] Houghton ascribes

---

126. Eden, "Music of the Spheres," 191.
127. Carpenter, *Letters*, 286.
128. Ibid., 286–87; 147.
129. Shippey, *Road to Middle Earth*, 22–26.
130. Carpenter, *Letters*, 146.

the term "asterisk-cosmogony" to this tale, "an imagined account of the creation of an 'asterisk-reality' and, as the hobbits fit neatly into the historical world (including an Old English etymology), then *The Ainulindalë* fits neatly among the real cosmogonies known to early Western medieval Europe."[131] Whilst early medieval thinkers had access to various Christian writers of late-antiquity, and pagan commentaries on Plato's *Timaeus* (all of them more or less reflecting the doctrine of the Neoplatonist philosopher Plotinus), and to various patristic writings on the *Hexameron*, their primary resource for cosmological reflection lay in the writings of Saint Augustine. Deely makes an important distinction in that the 'occasion of Neoplatonism' reveals a bias that Plotinus held towards the absolutism of Plato, especially in his theory of ideas about the Good. It was not, however, a question of examining the two thinkers (Plato and Aristotle), then rejecting the work of the latter in favour of the former. Neoplatonism attempted to reconcile the agreements in their respective doctrines, over and above where they essentially disagree. Far from being a hostile critic of Aristotle, Plotinus can be presented as a philosopher sympathetic to Aristotle, but who concluded that Plato "in the end had got things just about right."[132]

Had medieval theologians encountered the early versions of *The Ainulindalë*, they would have found its picture of double-creation—creation as music in the Song of the Ainur, and then as fact in the word of Eru—The One—as reassuringly easy to fit into the schema of Augustine's Christian-Neoplatonist synthesis, and the writings of others such as Pseudo-Dionysius and Dante. In Tolkien's own analysis, however, he testifies to himself having devised a "world of 'natural theology', with an absence of churches, temples, or religious rites or ceremonies, simply because the Third Age was not a Christian world."[133] Given the account of creation, as we have it in Augustine's dogmatic refutation of Manichaeism, it is not difficult to reconcile this account with *The Ainulindalë* of Tolkien's *The Silmarillion*, though we have no direct reference or clear indication that the one influenced the other. Houghton shares this view, but as these Augustinian writings were not obscure, Tolkien may have made some recourse to them in his development. Furthermore, whilst I have suggested that he was influenced by Neoplatonic commentaries, his own reading of creation lends itself much more to the *De*

---

131. Houghton, *Augustine*, 171, reminds us that Latin Christian thinkers in the early medieval period inherited two cosmogonies representing the disparate beginnings of their tradition in Jerusalem and Athens: the Hexameron—the Genesis creation myth of *creatio ex nihilo*, and the *Timaeus* of Plato, translated into Latin.

132. Deely, *Medieval Philosophy*, 57–58. Flieger, "Naming the Unnameable," 127, describes Plotinus as an "Aristotelian systematizer of Platonic thought."

133. Carpenter, *Letters*, 220.

Genesi than the writings of Plotinus. Nowhere in Tolkien do we read anything approximating to Plotinus' three successively emanating hypostases (such as The One, Intellect, and Soul).[134] The opening pages of *The Silmarillion* reveal a cosmogony that is rich in imagery, and forms the basis of an account of creation and fall: what it is to be created being, under grace, and what it is to fall from that grace. This theme requires some detailed analysis, if the whole is to be understood in context (as also in the case of Augustine).

Ainulindalë means the 'Music of the Ainur,'[135] and music is the overriding symbol of the whole cosmogony, and provides the means by which all things come into being. In the beginning there was Eru (the One, or 'he who is alone'), who is called Ilúvatar ('Father of all'). The literary use of the title, 'One,' in Tolkien's cosmo-genesis is suggestive of Plotinus, and makes no specific reference to the Judaeo-Christian deity. It is strongly reminiscent of Plotinus' theology in the *Enneads*, but I have already ruled out an emanationist theory of existence in matter. Plotinus' doctrine of deity as 'The One' is the absolutely simple first principle of all. It is both 'self-caused' and the cause of being for everything else in the universe. There are, according to Plotinus, various ways of showing the necessity of positing such a principle. Plotinus found it in Plato's *Republic* where it is named 'the Idea/Form of the Good' and in his *Parmenides* where it is the subject of a series of deductions.[136] For Plotinus, The One or the Good, owing to its simplicity, is indescribable directly. We can only grasp it indirectly by deducing what it is not.[137] Even the names 'One' and 'Good' could be described as the 'least worse' manner of description. Therefore, it is wrong to see The One as a principle of oneness or goodness, in the sense in which these are intelligible attributes. The name 'One' is least inappropriate because it best suggests absolute simplicity. Ilúvatar made first the Ainur, the Holy Ones, offspring of his thought.[138] But Tolkien's use of the verb 'made' in the text parallels his reference to the Ainur as 'created' and 'angelical first-created' in letters from 1958 to 1964. In

---

134. Houghton, *Augustine*, 180.

135. They were the greatest of the Ainur who witnessed the vision of Ilúvatar and so came to create Arda. Each was granted insight into a specific part of Ilúvatar's thought, and was therefore more aligned in spirit with that part. The Ainur also witnessed the unfolding of the history of Arda in the vision, but not all of it. Parts of it, and certain parts of Ilúvatar's thought, such as the true nature and destiny of the Children of Ilúvatar, remained hidden from them. Thus they were not gods or masters unto the Children, but rather their elders and guides, and were therefore unable to force the minds of Eldar and Edain, although they had power over their bodies.

136. *Republic*, 508e, 510d; *Parmenides*, 137c.

137. *Enneads*, 5.3.14; 6.8.8; 6.9.3

138. Tolkien, *Silmarillion*, 15; Flieger, *Splintered Light*, 50, considering this latter phrase in light of the Neoplatonic traditional concept of 'emanations,' says of the Ainur: "They are powers or principalities emanating directly from the godhead, and are developed in the text as aspects of his nature."

addition, Ilúvatar declared in *The Silmarillion* itself that the Ainur have 'being as a gift.'[139] This reading of Tolkien's cosmo-genesis would argue (at this point) against an emanationist view of the Ainur (and creation), or of their actually sharing the divine nature, though as creatures they may reflect parts of it: Creator and created 'angelic-being' are distinct.

Flieger correctly observes that, "quite literally setting the tone for the whole of creation in this sub-created world is the music, the initiating force and the design in which all is contained."[140] The origin of this mode of creation is, as I have demonstrated above, traceable to the Pythagerean philosophy that the heavens, and especially the solar system, form a musical scale whose ratios create heavenly harmony. A viable concept well into the Middle Ages, the concept of the music of the spheres proposes that each planet was supposed to ride on its own crystalline sphere, sounding a harmonic vibration with the others.[141] This medieval cosmological phenomenon survived into the early modern period, and is evidenced by Nicholas Brady's *Hail! Bright Cecilia* (1687), set to music by Henry Purcell in 1692. The fifth and sixth stanzas read,

> Soul of the World! inspir'd by thee /
>
> The jarring Seeds of Matter did agree /
>
> Thou didst the scatter'd Atoms bind /
>
> Which, by thy Laws of true proportion join'd /
>
> Made up various Parts, one perfect Harmony /
>
> Thou tun'dst this World below, the Spheres above /
>
> Who in the Heavenly Round to their own Music move.[142]

Flieger observes also that Tolkien took the twin ideas of celestial harmony and Melkor's dissonant theme, and melded them together, making each concept dependent on, as well as the source of the other. Rebellion is conflict, and conflict is disharmony, and for Tolkien what must now be metaphoric in our primary world, is literal in his created secondary one.[143] In an attempt to exclude overt Christian references from this cosmo-genesis, Tolkien asserts clearly that the rebellion of created free-will precedes the creation of the world:

> In this Myth the rebellion of created free-will precedes the Creation of the World (Eä); and Eä has in it, subcreatively

---

139. Carpenter, *Letters*, 284, 345; Tolkien, *Silmarillion*, 15.
140. Flieger, *Splintered Light*, 57.
141. Ibid., 58.
142. Dennison, "Ode on St Cecilia's Day 1692," 31–45.
143. Flieger, *Splintered Light*, 58.

introduced, evil rebellions, discordant elements of its own nature already when the *Let it Be* was spoken.[144]

Therefore, as Melkor's discord becomes an active part of the music, so his rebellion and disharmony effects the shape and being of the world that is to be: music is not the physical act of creation, but only its blueprint.[145] It is the pattern of the world *in potentia*, and as the music is transfigured into vision then reality, the Valar descend into Middle-earth, and make real the musical pattern and vision.

Many of the Ainur then entered into creation (as Valar), only to find that it was not yet developed according to the shape of the Great Music. Time had begun with their entry into the world: the music, vision, and creation had taken place in the timelessness of the presence of Ilúvatar.[146] The resonances here with Augustine's account of creation, suggests a high degree of dependency, and Houghton is correct in making obvious the links. He notes, however, two differences between the two schemata: first, the predominant musical images function in *The Ainulindalë* in the way that speech and light, taken together as intellectual illumination, do in Augustine's reading of Genesis. Furthermore, in the way the Ainur act as sub-creators, developing the themes proposed by Eru Iluvatar, whereas Augustine focuses upon God as sole Creator, via the agency of the *logos*.[147]

For Augustine, the angels are free, rational, and powerfully spiritual beings, and in this sense play a part in the unfolding of creation (viz the gardening analogy and seminal reasons, above).[148] The music of the Ainur develops the themes of Iluvatar, but it is not the full tale of creation. They are sub-creators, and they also have a part to play in the enfolding of things later in the tale. If Tolkien had knowledge and understanding of Augustine's philosophy at this point, then he crafted it into his cosmogony very astutely. This stylized departure from Augustine is in the mode of agency, and not necessarily departing from his philosophical model. Thus, in showing Melkor the results of his rebellion, Ilúvatar states his own omnipotence:

> Thou shalt see that no theme may be played that hath not its uttermost source in me, nor can any alter the music in my despite. For he that attempteth this shall prove but mine instrument in

---

144. Carpenter, *Letters*, 286–87.
145. Flieger, *Splintered Light*, 58.
146. Tolkien, *Silmarillion*, 20.
147. Ibid., 18–19.
148. Houghton, *Augustine*, 173–75.

the devising of things more wonderful, which he himself hath not imagined.[149]

The idea expressed here would harmonize with *De Genesi*, though Augustine does not here use musical imagery. Augustine does specifically state that, whilst discussing the temptation of Adam and Eve, God will bring good from Satan's actions, despite what the Devil intends.[150] Given that Melkor has exercised free will, and that Ilúvatar has allowed Melkor's dissonance to mix in the divine theme, it can be rightly said that freedom originates in Ilúvatar himself.

Keith Jensen discusses this significant and often overlooked aspect of the divine music, that Ilúvatar does not punish Melkor, but patiently suffers through the two themes in the divine music, "changing them to counterbalance Melkor's dissonance."[151] *The New Grove Dictionary of Music* defines dissonance as "an antonym to consonance, hence a discordant sounding together of two notes perceived as having 'roughness' or 'tonal tension.'"[152] The third musical theme in fact makes use of the dissonance that interweaves the 'triumphal notes' into its own 'solemn pattern.'[153] Melkor's dissonance is not only allowed to merge with that of the Ainur, but that it is also a part of Ilúvatar's divine plan from the outset. One may ask, if such suffering as we read comes about by Melkor's free acts, whether or not Tolkien's deity is of himself malicious, and why such a (good) deity may embrace evil so readily. It shall be seen below in Chapter 5 in the discussion of mutability and evil that for Augustine, wrongdoing arises out of free choice, and that the agent is entirely culpable. In his rejection of Manichaeism, that evil was some substantial and malignant mind creeping over the earth, ready to corrupt and mar that which is essentially good, Jensen reads Augustine's free-will defence in terms of God's immutability and omnipotence: that evil is 'simply' a lapse from that initial state of good in creation. Before the fall, the choice was simple—doing good or evil. After the fall, the choice was between one sin and another.[154] Tolkien was a storyteller at heart, and stories need conflict in order to create a backdrop for the journey, struggle and hero. In musical terms, "the build-up and release of tension (dissonance and resolution) [. . .] is to a great degree responsible for what many listeners

---

149. Tolkien, *Silmarillion*, 17–18.

150. *De Gen ad Lit*, 11.22.29. Here we perceive overtones of Augustine's 'aesthetic theodicy,' discussed in chapter 5.

151. Jensen, "Dissonance in the Divine Theme," 105.

152. Sadie, *New Grove Dictionary of Music*, 380.

153. Tolkien, *Silmarillion*, 17.

154. Jensen, "Dissonance in the Divine Theme," 103.

perceive as beauty, emotion, and expressiveness in music."[155] Essentially, dissonant chords or notes are necessary to fill out and complete a musical selection, and such dissonance can only be created through individuality. David Matthews observes that dissonance in music can both challenge the listener, and be a demonstration of a composer's maturation in both style, and in developing the ideas of others. Commenting on Britten's works from the April of 1930 onwards, he notes that they "employ both a high level of dissonance and a blurring of tonality."[156] This is highly significant, as in the case of the maturing Benjamin Britten it acknowledges a young man who is branching out on his own, recognizing the originality of his contemporaries, whilst expressing in his own music his struggles with the past:

> Schoenbergian modernism, the language of an isolated and anguished prophet, was for a while an appealing path for the ultra-sensitive, lonely schoolboy, conscious of the superiority of his taste and abilities to those of his so-called elders and betters.[157]

Nowhere is this seen to better effect than in his 1945 opera, *Peter Grimes*. After the exclamation, "And God have mercy on me," at the end of Act II, Grimes finds himself standing defiantly alone against the village. His frustration, along with the suffering of his apprentice, is led and repeated by a solo viola (Britten's own instrument), increasing in momentum and ferocity. In the background, and in parallel, we hear the more peaceful and tuneful strains of the village church service. As the passage reaches a climax, Grimes submits himself to the Borough, and his fate is sealed.[158] We see this tragicomic aspect in Tolkien's own use of music, understandably arising out of his own traumatic past and recent combat experience, as he begins to draft his cosmo-genesis as early as 1917. It is because Ilúvatar chooses to work with Melkor's dissonance that elves and men, dwarves and hobbits, will have to live with sorrow, tragedy, and other difficulties: they are not the cause of it; they are the inevitable victims of a quasi-divine free act. As Flieger aptly points out, "Elves and Men [...] come after the fall but do not cause it and are not part of it."[159] This is a notable and important departure of Tolkien's *mythos* from the Christian one, with which it is so often compared and associated.

155. Sadie, *New Grove Dictionary of Music*, 380.
156. Matthews, *Britten*, 13.
157. Ibid.
158. Ibid., 75–76.
159. Flieger, *Splintered Light*, 128.

In allowing Melkor the sin of pride and dominance, Ilúvatar incorporates free will as an essential part of the world. In the fact that Melkor sins in actuality, and that Arda is changed as a result, the world of Middle-earth is becoming, and finds a purpose. Due to suffering and vulnerability, the kindreds of Middle-earth have the capacity to grow or regress, and it is through both consonance/order and dissonance/struggle that these peoples can choose these options.[160] Flieger is correct to point out that the elves are bound to the patterns of the music, but men are not.[161] The Children of Ilúvatar in the third musical theme were, "conceived by him alone; and they came with the third theme."[162] The preposition 'with' and not 'in' is significant for Flieger, as this makes them independent of Melkor's rebellion and fall, as Ilúvatar works with the discordant theme, and uses it to his own ends. For all their deliberate and cryptic origin, "Elves and Men will find their lives complicated and profoundly affected by the music, which accomplished their placement in the world."[163] This is critical, in that the entry into the space/time of Middle-earth of these two kindreds is also a procession into mutability, psychological sorrow and grief from the outset.[164] There was no Edenic earthly paradise to which they may hark back, and we see this reflected in the Boethian/Anglo-Saxon elegiac *ubi nunc* tradition in section 3.3.3. Flieger is correct to note that,

> After Melkor—and to some degree because of him—Elves and Men will live in a world of immeasurable sorrow as part of a pattern that can take the most triumphant of the discordant notes and weave them into the whole.[165]

In the Music of the Ainur, each of the deities is given both the Flame Imperishable and the freedom to adorn the Great Music with "his [Eru's] own thought and devices."[166] In weaving this Great Music towards a thing of beauty, Melkor seeks to "bring into it things of his own," and thus opposing Ilúvatar's plan (or so he thinks) by musical dissonance.[167] Whilst Melkor has been allowed to create his own dissonance, then it was because he had been granted the freedom to do so, and that same freedom comes from Ilúvatar

---

160. Jensen, "Dissonance in the Divine Theme," 106.
161. Flieger, *Splintered Light*, 128.
162. Tolkien, *Silmarillion*, 128.
163. Flieger, *Splintered Light*, 128.
164. Jensen, "Dissonance in the Divine Theme," 105.
165. Flieger, *Splintered Light*, 128.
166. Tolkien, *Silmarillion*, 15.
167. Ibid., 16.

himself. Musical dissonance and consonance, therefore, can be woven into a greater theme, and used to much greater effect, and I shall demonstrate that Tolkien's 'aesthetic' approach to the problem of evil has a strong resonance with Augustine's 'aesthetic' theodicy.

It is equally significant that the kindreds of Middle-earth are not the cause of their suffering (in the Augustinian sense): the absence of a (Middle) earthly fall/lapse, such as we read in Genesis 3 (and expounded by St Paul), absolves these creatures from guilt. These kindreds are left to make the best of their situation, as history unfolds and Ilúvatar fades into a deistic background, apparently unconcerned and unaffected by the affairs of and within Arda. It is noteworthy that Ilúvatar permits selfish and rebellious evil to exist, so as to serve his own divine providence, and whilst he has allowed discord in the creative Music of the Ainur as a corporate body of deity, he will not give it limitless licence. The third theme ends in wrath, and Melkor's crimes are eventually punished, and he is incarcerated in prison (in chains), for a time. In the case of men we later read that they have,

> a virtue to shape their life, amid the powers and chances of the world, beyond the Music of the Ainur, which is as fate to all things else; and of their operation everything should be, in form and deed, completed, and the world fulfilled unto the last and smallest.[168]

Arda would not be what it is/was without the musical dissonance and attendant struggle; there would be no place for virtues such as courage and justice, and no opportunity for personal growth. Such is the case for the inhabitants of Middle-earth, except in the case of men: men can change the music, and they are free in a way in which the elves are not.[169] It is through the actions of men that the world shall be fulfilled or brought into actuality: Ilúvatar willed that "the hearts of Men should seek beyond the world and should find no rest therein."[170] The purposes of Ilúvatar and Melkor appear never to be fixed in time, but constantly in a state of flux. Jensen makes an apposite point in that Luthien Tinúviel's decision to become mortal, whilst it brought grief to her father and the elves, gave her a second chance of life with the man she loved (Beren). From this union sprang Aragorn and Arwen (the latter making the same choice as Luthien). They became King and Queen of a new era—a Golden Age of Men at the end of the Third

---

168. Tolkien, *Silmarillion*, 47.

169. The themes of fate, free will, and order are key themes in the third section of this thesis, and the word 'fate' here is to be understood in the Boethian sense which is discussed in section 3.3.

170. Tolkien, *Silmarillion*, 47.

Age of Middle-earth—and this 'doom' arose out of the free choices of Beren and Luthien in a previous age. These two protagonists are the central focus of Chapter 3, as we establish what 'being and gift' mean for free creatures within the providence of God.

Given that Tolkien was passionate in establishing—or more appropriately—restoring the power of myth, and of language itself, then it is unsurprising that he stands alongside Augustine in re-ordering a creation myth, using almost precisely those concepts which were used to engage with the contemporary worldview of early Christianity in North Africa.[171] If myths contain powerful truths, then Augustine's analysis serves to assert that truth, and Tolkien's *mythopoesis* transposes the power of the story of creation. Augustine implies that, if Christians wish to have their neighbors believe in the miracles of the Gospels, then it is necessary to avoid interpretations of Scripture that conflict with what pagans know to be true from reason and experience.[172] The theologian faces the task of recovery, of restoring the power of images and stories that have grown weak from cultural change or from mere familiarity. In this sense the theologian's task is not to demythologize, but to 're-mythologize'; either searching for new models of religious language, or to recast old truths into new moulds. Tolkien's fantasy writings were not primarily religious works, but grew in the making. In a letter to his friend Fr Robert Murray SJ, on the 2nd December 1953, Tolkien acknowledges that,

> The Lord of the Rings is of course a fundamentally religious and Catholic work; unconsciously so at first, but consciously in the revision. [. . .] I have cut out practically all references to anything like 'religion,' to cults and practices, in the imaginary world. For the religious element is absorbed into the story and the symbolism.[173]

The same can at least be said of *The Silmarillion*. Given that Tolkien's writings have gained a new audience in a post-modern context, his recast myth may prove to be a 'meta-narrative' in its own right, conveying ancient truths for a generation who are retreating from the self-confident and

---

171. Burrell notes that Augustine's rejection of Platonism, in favour of following Jesus in the context of the Church, was a local phenomenon. He further notes that Clement of Alexandria, Gregory of Nyssa (amongst others) had already demonstrated how to read Plato as breaking ground for God's revelation in Christ, precisely by displaying how these writings could usefully be employed in showing that revelation to be the highest wisdom—or 'true philosophy.' *Faith and Freedom*, 23.

172. *De Gen ad Lit*, 1.19.39.

173. Carpenter, *Letters*, 172.

religiously-critical claims of modernity. Houghton is forceful in his summing of his interpretation of Tolkien's cosmogony:

> Neither Augustine nor Tolkien would countenance for a moment the proposition that his own work could supplant the foundational story of Genesis. Ultimately, power lies not in translation but in the language of the myth.[174]

Tolkien's 1958 letter to Rhona Beare explicitly denies any primary world religious status to his myths, but rather asserts that they are built upon certain religious ideas, as opposed to being allegories of them.[175]

2.4 Music, Vision, and Reality in Creation

2.4.1 Neoplatonism's Tragic Decline towards Reality

I have demonstrated that Tolkien's music-metaphor is rooted in both the classical and medieval philosophical heritage of Neoplatonism, in that it consists in the gradual unfolding of a primeval, cosmic symphony, containing both consonance and dissonance, acquiescence with the will of the One, and opposition from it. Either way, the omniscience of God is prior to all other hierarchies, and his creative thought transcends the independent free will of even the greatest of his demi-gods, the Ainur.[176]

It would be wrong at the outset of this section to suppose that the cosmic music is the causal power of materiality in Middle-earth, and a succession of scholars have (in my view) misread Tolkien here. Eden's Boethian interpretation of *The Ainulindalë* overestimates the contribution of the Ainur's music in creation.[177] Similarly, Flieger and Bradley Birzar overreach themselves in this regard; the former suggesting that music is the 'initiating force' and 'ordering force of the universe,' and the latter suggesting that the Ainur's inherited "wisdom and power [...] sang the universe into existence."[178] Whilst the music of the Ainur is the means by which the world comes into being, its true importance lies in its correspondence to the ensuing vision, prior to reality. If the music is said to be a truly creative

---

174. Houghton, *Augustine*, 85.

175. Carpenter, *Letters*, 283.

176. Jonathan McIntosh's 2009 PhD thesis, "The Flame Imperishable: Tolkien, St Thomas and the Metaphysics of Faërie," and his 2010 article, "*Ainulindalë*: Tolkien, St Thomas, and the Metaphysics of Music," covers similar ground to my investigation here, though less developed in its sense of life as 'being and gift.'

177. Eden, "Music of the Spheres," 185–58.

178. Flieger, *Splintered Light*, 57–9; Birzar, *Tolkien's Sanctifying Myth*, 53.

source, then we would have to concede in the Platonic fashion that every other motion away from this primeval music as metaphysically enfeebling, or in the analysis of Augustine (above), things become 'less and less.' This 'tragic metaphysics' of Neoplatonism, informed as it is by Plotinus' reading of Plato, ascribes to 'everything that derives from the One or the forms is necessarily decadent,' and of Classical Greek thought generally, "insofar as it [treats] finitude, temporality, bodiliness, and limitation as philosophical and practical 'problems' that must be either transcended or grudgingly accepted."[179] Whilst the carefully crafted delineated and successive stages of Tolkien's sub-creation may indeed *suggest* a likeness to the successively emanating hypostasis of Plotinian cosmogonic theory, I propose that it would be a misreading of Tolkien as presenting a sub-creation involving a gradual diminution of being as the Ainur's music passes into vision and subsequent reality. The Ainur do not mediate between The One and the physical world in the manner of the World Soul in the *Timaeus*, since in Plato's *Republic* the world is not reality, but famously a world of shadow and opinions.

This is the interpretation of Eden. He views Boethius' three-fold classification of music as Neoplatonic progression, or *digression*, from highest to lowest, and the pattern around which the subsequent history of Middle-earth is allegedly structured: the gradations of music's power in Middle-earth from its first appearance in *The Silmarillion*, all the way down to the Fourth Age in *LOTR*, reflects a Neoplatonic heirarchy of being, from the highest form of music down to the lowest—from the *musica mundana* to the *musica instrumentalis*.[180] According to Eden, elves and men are farther away in both time and space from the music of the spheres, and closer to the third and lower type of music in the Third Age.[181] On this Platonic reading of Tolkien, each stage of his creation myth and subsequent mythical history involves this necessary decay—a *lapsus*—from the pure and divine origins of the 'music of the Ainur,' so that physical reality itself finally emerges, as it does in Plotinus, as a veritable metaphysical catastrophe or accident, necessary yet tragic. In the posthumously published *Morgoth's Ring*, there is an interesting description of the Valar's role in the development of the Blessed Realm—Aman—which is reminiscent of Plato's description of the Demiurge in *The Timaeus*: "The Valar were like architects working with a plan 'passed' by the Government. They became less and less important as the plan was more and more nearly achieved. [. . .] (The wiser they became

---

179. Leithart, *Deep Comedy*, 46, 38; cf. *Enneads* 5.1.3.
180. Eden, "Music of the Spheres," 192.
181. Ibid., 190–91.

the less power they had to *do* anything—save by counsel)."[182] This might suggest what we rejected above: that Tolkien's material world is indeed a diminution from perfection, and things within it fade, but only after they have finished their function. In this discussion the same is said of elves and men. However, this 'fading' is said to be bound up with the end of history, and has a more apocalyptic than lapsarian sense.

This *lapsus* or 'splintering' from perfection is present in *The Silmarillion*, but its medium is light in addition to music. In Verlyn Flieger's influential study—*Splintered Light*—she stresses this sense of tragic loss accompanying the loss of the two lamps set up in Middle-earth by the Vala, Aulë, in response to the prayer of Yavanna.[183] The light of these lamps pervades throughout Middle-earth, and yet was subsequently destroyed by Melkor. This desecration had cosmic consequences, as not only were the lights destroyed beyond repair, but their lamps "spilled destroying flame [. . .] out over the earth. And the shape of Arda and the symmetry of the waters and its lands was marred in that time, so that the first designs of the Valar were never restored."[184] The two lamps were replaced by two trees, but these lights were inconstant, following the cyclic forms of the tree's blossoming—though accelerated: "Thus in Valinor twice every day there came a gentle hour of softer light when both trees were faint and their gold and silver beams were mingled."[185] Flieger observes rightly that, though new light is brought into being, it is qualitatively different from the former light, and that this difference "conform[s] to the pattern of fragmentation and diminution that underlies the whole mythology [. . .] the trees give light in waxing and waning cycles of flower and fruit."[186] As Flieger interprets Tolkien's imagery of light,

> from ancient unity to the fragmentation and splintering of light, of perception, of society, and of self, Tolkien's sub-created world mirrors our own. And through its people, their wars and turmoils, their triumphs and disasters, we come gradually to recognize our world, to see and hear it as Tolkien saw and heard it.[187]

It is worth noting firstly that Rowan Williams' comments above are equally apposite here: the main cause behind the succession of lights in

---

182. Tolkien, *Morgoth's Ring*, 405.
183. Tolkien, *Silmarillion*, 39.
184. Ibid., 41.
185. Ibid., 43.
186. Flieger, *Splintered Light*, 63.
187. Ibid., 65.

Middle-earth is not due to any tragic flaw within the light itself, but the malicious destruction caused by the rebellion of Melkor. Secondly, each time the previous source of light is replaced, then this has less to do with a Neoplatonist 'entropy' with which we are now familiar, but with the nature of Tolkien's crafted metaphysics. The nature of light in *The Silmarillion* is that which is both gratuitous and sacrificial. When the Vala Yavanna laments her inability to remake the Two Trees after Melkor and Ungoliant's attacks on them, she exclaims that "even for those who are mightiest under Ilúvatar there is some work that they may accomplish once, and once only. The Light of the Trees I brought into being, and within Eä I can never do so again."[188] If there is a diminution of light in Middle-earth, then it is not caused by a tragic loss of being, but the sheer 'giftedness' of being for which there is no absolute assurance—and indeed a degree of fragility, at least in the present age from the perspective of finitude—of it ever being received back in full.

I have already alluded to a *felix culpa* dimension in Tolkien's loss of perfection, and it would seem that without this loss of light, or splintering, there can be no 'eucatastrophic' return and restoration that Tolkien celebrates in his poem *Mythopoeia*:

> man, sub-creator, the refracted light
>
> through whom is splintered from a single White
>
> to many hues, and endlessly combined
>
> in living shapes that move from mind to mind.[189]

Without the splintering of light, there can be no subsequent refraction of light, and hence raising his sub-creation to new heights of being. He hints at this in a draft intended to follow a lengthy letter to Rhona Beare, but which was never sent. On the subject of death and immortality, he expounds this Catholic principle:

> A divine 'punishment' is also a divine 'gift,' if accepted, since its object is ultimate blessing, and the supreme inventiveness of the Creator will make 'punishments' (that is changes of design) produce a good not otherwise to be attained: a 'mortal' Man has probably a higher if unrevealed destiny than a longeval one.[190]

---

188. Tolkien, *Silmarillion*, 91.
189. Tolkien, *Tree and Leaf*, 87.
190. Carpenter, *Letters*, 286.

2.4.2 Aquinas' Mathematical Music and Beauty

It is my intention to substitute those (understandable) misreadings of Tolkien above with a more positive metaphysics of 'being as gift,' and one that is influenced more by his reading of St Thomas Aquinas than earlier Christian Neoplatonist scholars, at least in respect of this ordering of the cosmos. I am indebted here to the work of Jonathan McIntosh, who extrapolates this reading of Aquinas in his recent book, 'The Flame Imperishable: Tolkien, St Thomas, and the Metaphysics of Faerie'. The whole *musica universalis* tradition appears to have made very little impression on Aquinas. Spitzer comments that he does not appear to have had "the Augustinian ear for world harmony, ascribing to music a holy character only insofar as it was an element of the liturgy. As an Aristotelian he reflects the world as it is, rather than attempting to recreate it by forging it together into a unit."[191] Aquinas' personal interest in music, such as it was, was informed by direct experience with sacred music as part of the religious duties as a priest.[192] His education would have required of him a particular familiarity with the musical analysis of both Augustine and Boethius, and his command of some of the more technical and mathematical details of the latter work may be seen in his commentary on Aristotle's *De Anima*.[193] Aquinas' experience of the technical order and rhythm of polyphonic music, only recently introduced into the liturgical life of thirteenth-century Paris, would have influenced his treatise on music, alongside his particular Platonic interpretation of divine *ordo*: "for if any one thing were bettered, the proportion of order would be destroyed, just as if one string were stretched more than it ought to be, the melody of the harp would be destroyed."[194]

McIntosh observes that, in his commentary on Boethius' *De Trinitate*, Aquinas closely associates music with mathematics on account of the way music derives its first principles from arithmetic, and subsequently applies these principles to natural things:

> In another way, one science is contained under another as subalternated to it. This occurs when in a higher science there is given the reason for what a lower science only knows as a fact. This is how music is contained under arithmetic.[195]

---

191. Spitzer, *World Harmony*, 74.

192. *ST*, 2–2.91.2, *Of Taking the Divine Name for the Purpose of Invoking by Means of Praise*.

193. Eco, *Aesthetics*, 131–32.

194. *ST*, 1.25.6 ad 3.

195. *SBT*, 5.1 ad 5; McIntosh, *Flame Imperishable*, 130.

For Aquinas, music represents an 'intermediate' stage between mathematics and natural science, yet it bears a closer affinity to mathematics since music is more formal, and thus more separated from matter and motion than is the case in natural science: music considers sounds, not inasmuch as they are sounds, but inasmuch as they are proportionable according to numbers.[196] Behind Aquinas' argument is his understanding that, although both mathematical and natural objects involve an act of mental abstraction, separating their intelligible principles from the physical, it is via self-same sensible substances in which these principles are mediated and experienced. Mathematics and natural science nevertheless differ in their respective degrees of abstraction.[197] Music is therefore a highly abstract reality that is ultimately concerned with sound, not *qua* sound as experienced audibly, but as a peculiarly mathematical and proportionate kind of sound. It appears then that his approach to sound is more scholastic and theoretical in respect of music, than the participatory ontologies of Augustine and Boethius. Between mathematical theory and the quantity, number, etc., contained in matter/form there is a distinctive abstract separation in the two concepts. Eco observes how the intellectualism and purely contemplative attitude found in Aquinas' account of music "gives a justification to the disinterested contemplation of music independent of music's effects or its function."[198]

In this abstract formalism of Aquinas' theory of music we may read a metaphysical 'disinterest,' which is also characteristic of his aesthetics generally. This is not congruous with the later aesthetics of Kant, but an account of beauty and form that can exist *in intellectu*, but need not take material existence. What is essential here to beauty and form (for example) is that form determines the organic structure of things—in the Aristotelian sense—and that "form in its simplest and, it would seem, most worthy aspects is pure organic structure."[199] This 'formalism,' however, represents only one half of an *aporia* that Eco locates at the heart of Aquinas' aesthetics, for if the bare essence of beauty can indeed be reduced to its mere form, in the way that music can be expressed in pure mathematical abstraction, independent of its utility, then everything other than this essential beauty is an extra richness—something superadded, and:

> in the last analysis these extra items increase the beauty and even determine how suitable it is for human experience. [. . .]

---

196. Ibid., 5.3.
197. Ibid., 5.1–2; McIntosh, *Flame Imperishable*, 130.
198. Eco, *Aesthetics*, 134.
199. Ibid., 87.

This distinction between beauty as a principle and beauty as a fact is found in Aquinas and is never completely resolved.[200]

For Aquinas, the more beauty a thing has the more existence or being will be implicated in that beauty, given his definition of beauty as "that which pleases when seen."[201] The pleasure or delight the object of beauty is able to bestow on those who perceive through their senses, implies the existence of some independent subject-object rationale, capable of acting on the senses in aesthetically pleasing ways. Human sense faculties have as their proper activity and end the perception of sensible objects—especially beautiful sensible objects—and aesthetic pleasure or delight consists in this activity being brought to completion. In the sensible properties of the object of beauty, first stimulating and gratifying the senses, in turn effects a corresponding intellectual apprehension of, and a satisfaction in, the form or internal structure of the physical object. In this manner a harmonious, pleasing, and nature-fulfilling correspondence is established between the object and the perceiving subject, and between the subject's own perceptual and intellective faculties.

This is developed below in relation to Maritain's renewal of Thomist aesthetics, and its influence upon Tolkien and his contemporaries. However, the basic principles are spelled out as follows. Tolkien's philosophy of 'being and gift' lies not so much in the tragic metaphysics of early Christian Neoplatonism, but in the more positive metaphysics of Aquinas. Therefore, before I can assert the influence in Aquinas' distinct philosophy of being, arising out of his sense of musical 'disinterest' and subject-object *apprehensio*, I shall establish what it is in the (beautiful) object that is responsible for eliciting the affective response in the individual. Aquinas lists three objective properties of beauty: integrity, proportion, and clarity.[202] By integrity (or perfection), Aquinas means what Tolkien understands as his own sub-creation's inner constancy of reality: it refers to a thing's completeness, wholeness, and formal structure which is proper to its essence or nature. Secondly, proportion (harmony or consonance), is of Pythagorean extraction, and designates in his usage a sense of qualitative proportion or *convenientia*. It is the harmony of beauty, the pleasing correspondence between the parts and metaphysical

---

200. Ibid., 88.

201. *ST*, 1.5.4 ad1 (*pulchrum dicuntur quae visa placent*). Although Thomas' definition emphasizes visual beauty 'as seen,' there is also a contemplative *apprehensio* aspect to the definition. Elsewhere he proposes that, 'let that be called beauty the very perception of what pleases' (*pulchrum autem dicitur id cuius ipsa apprehensio placet*), *ST*, 1–2.27.1. Resp3.

202. Ibid., 1.39.8.resp. For a complete analysis of these properties in light of their development in Western thought prior to Aquinas, see Eco, *Aesthetics*, 64–121.

principles both within the object and between the object and the sensory faculties of the perceiver. Finally, the clarity (brightness or splendor) is a 'shining forth of form,' or the radiating of intelligible light radiating from the beautiful object, and a word which Robert Wood suggests is linked with the Greek word *doxa* (glory), and which Tolkien images in *The Ainulindalë* when the Ainur first glimpse the world, for "they had become enamoured of the beauty of the vision and engrossed in the unfolding of the World which came there to being, and their minds were filled with it."[203] These three aesthetic properties of beauty are expounded in much greater detail in section 2.5.4, as they are key in distinguishing Tolkien's turn, from a purely Platonic lapsarian declension of being. It is sufficient for the present to acknowledge this underlying 'existential realism' in Aquinas' philosophy of being, in which he references the act of existence—*esse*—as the "actuality of all acts and the perfection of all perfections."[204] In identifying a thing's essence in this superlative way, his epistemology and metaphysics locate the primary order of being as something actual, real, and concrete, over and above its intelligible, contemplatable essence or form. In emphasizing this existential hyper-dimension in its actualized sense, Aquinas offers a radically new interpretation of being, transforming previous Greek and Latin concepts of being, which gave primary place to form. On the one hand, it is true that, for Aquinas, "natural things [. . .] have being absolutely in the divine mind more truly than in themselves, because in that mind they have uncreated being, but in themselves a created being."[205] In other words, things are more real in the divine mind than they are in their own created being. However, rather than implying a Neoplatonic diminution of being as they become created, it is precisely the inferiority of created being in comparison to their divine origin that renders the act of creation for Aquinas not metaphysically tragic, but comic. He continues by further asserting that

> to be this particular being, a man, or a horse for example, is realized more truly in its own nature than in the divine mind, because it belongs to the truth of man to be material, which as existing in the divine mind he is not.

In a phrase which has direct relevance to our reading of the 'music of the Ainur,' Aquinas states that

> even so a house has nobler being in the architect's mind than in matter; yet a material house is called a house more truly than the

---

203. Wood, *Placing Aesthetics*, 109; Tolkien, *Silmarillion*, 21.
204. Armand Maurer, in Aquinas,' *On Being and Essence*, 10.
205. *ST*, 1.18.4 ad 3.

one which exists in the mind, since the former is a house in act, the latter only in potency.[206]

McIntosh summarises this independence in created being, such that things have more truth, more being, more perfection and goodness, more actuality in God than they do in themselves. However, in the divine mind 'things' enjoy this super-eminent truth, being, perfection, etc., not 'as themselves' as created beings, but as certain aspects of God's own uncreated being. To have any kind of reality as themselves, things must be given their own being *qua* individual things, namely that kind of being which they do not possess in the divine mind. Therefore, returning to his musical 'indifference', the purely logical existence that mathematical entities possess in the mind—and upon which music is based—"do not subsist as realities [...] otherwise they would be in some sort good if they subsisted."[207] Similarly, therefore, an individual man, because he has individual matter, has "something in him" which the intelligible essence of a man alone does not.[208]

2.4.3 The Divine Extravagance in Aquinas' Philosophy of Being and Gift

Aquinas' positive analysis of matter as a created, intelligible, and objectifying force, combined with the role he reserves for the body in the sensual perception of beauty, means that instead of rendering created being as a tragic lapse from an ideal in the mind of God, the corporeality of human life makes philosophy comic because matter is no longer an irrational given contrary to intelligibility, but the created principle to which all human thought must return. The gratuitous character of creation as a principle is stated in *ST,* 1.19.2, in that it belongs especially to God to will the existence of "things apart from himself" *(alia a se),* which serve no other purpose than to give Him something to which He might communicate his inherent goodness. It is not for His own sake, since God is already perfect and replete: God creates to benefit that which would otherwise not even exist, unless he first created it, or more succinctly, "He alone is the most perfectly liberal giver, because He does not act for His own profit, but only for His own goodness."[209] For Aquinas, creation is not a metaphysical decadence: it is a divine extravagance.

---

206. Ibid., 1.18.4 ad 3.
207. Ibid., 1.5.3 ad 4.
208. Ibid., 1.3.3. Resp; McIntosh, *Flame Imperishable*, 135.
209. Ibid., 1.44.4. resp 1; McIntosh, *Flame Imperishable*, 136.

If God's gratuitous nature leads Him to effect the existence of things other to Himself, then this principle is true also of rational beings made after His own image and likeness: angels and men. For Aquinas, a thing approaches God's likeness the more perfectly it resembles Him in more things.[210] The creature approaches more perfectly to God's likeness if it is not only good, but can also act for the good of other things, than if it were good only in itself. Consequently, no creature could act for the benefit of another creature unless plurality and inequality existed in created things, for the agent is distinct from the patient and superior to it. Therefore, in order that there might be in created things a perfect representation of God, the existence of diverse grades among them is therefore necessary. God creates other things in order to communicate his own goodness, but a corollary of this divine action is that part of the 'character' of this goodness which He gives to other things is precisely his own propensity for bestowing goodness on others.

> Thus, in order for creatures to receive God's goodness, they themselves must have things other than themselves unto whom they in turn—yet in imitation of God—might pass on this goodness. Hence, the fulfilment of the nature of created things necessitates the existence of things other than themselves towards whom they might manifest their (and their Creator's) benevolence.[211]

And so I return to Tolkien's metaphysics of music, and apply Aquinas' more positive metaphysics of being in how that music transposed itself into vision and reality.

2.4.4 The Music of the Ainur Becomes Revelation and Theodicy

In the earliest editions of *The Ainulindalë*, Ilúvatar had created the world and hidden from the Ainur, simultaneously with their playing and singing of their music, with the vision of the world's history being given only after the act of creation. The final edition in *The Silmarillion* demonstrates Tolkien's heightened sense of drama, of placing the vision chronologically between the music and creation. At its simplest level, the vision is a counterpart to the music, in that they perceived "sight where before was only hearing." More profoundly, however, Ilúvatar proclaims to the Ainur, "Behold your Music!

---

210. SCG, 2.45.4.
211. McIntosh, *Flame Imperishable*, 137.

[...] each of you shall find contained herein, amid the design that I set before you, all those things which it may seem that he himself devised or added."[212] The vision contained those things that the Ainur had devised or added to the themes of Ilúvatar—even those rebellious inventions of Melkor—and "things that they had not thought" in the music, chief amongst them were the Children of Ilúvatar (the elves and men), and the habitation prepared for them. They had sung the themes without knowing that they had contributed to their conception in the vision.

An obvious aspect of difference between the music and the vision, is that the latter is revelatory of both the music of the Ainur, alongside the secret creative devices of Ilúvatar. The music gave an opportunity for participation and mediation; the vision revealed the mind of Ilúvatar anew, and they "learned yet a little more of his wisdom, which otherwise had been hidden even from the Ainur."[213] Here we see revealed that Thomist existential desire to recognize in other created beings the work of God, in which they had —without direct cognition—been participating via the music: "Therefore, when they beheld them, the more did they love them, being things other than themselves, strange and free."[214] There was no jealousy, nor resentment in the revealing of the vision, save in the mind of Melkor, and the Ainur delighted and wondered at what the vision contained, and how the world *in potentia* may yet be in actuality. This reading of Tolkien's co-creative vision makes no sense when viewed from the standpoint of the Neoplatonist principle of diminution and decline, and even the rebellious and discordant music of Melkor is an opportunity on the part of the Ainur for 'theodicy,' in that whilst his strident effort to subvert the music is not suppressed, it is made use of and contributes to the whole. It is in the vision that the Ainur perceive this aspect of Ilúvatar's wisdom. The vision manifests what the music in its own forms and rhythms contained prior to the vision, and not *vice versa*. The vision reveals the 'divine extravagance,' such that the Ainur—as created being—may delight in the offspring of their thought. This is coherent with Aquinas' own 'metaphysics of music,' in that music represents that intermediate stage between pure mathematics and natural science: mind-reality and created-reality, and in Tolkien, the crafted vision becomes the crossover point of contact between the two. In Alison Milbank's words, in showing the actualization of the divine music, "he shows them themselves."[215]

---

212. Tolkien, *Silmarillion*, 18.
213. Ibid., 19.
214. Ibid., See also Carpenter, *Letters*, 147 and 285.
215. Milbank, *Chesterton and Tolkien*, 19.

The principle that goodness is imputed from the Creator to intelligent created beings, in order that they also impute creatively goodness in beings which are distinct from themselves, is fully worked out in this vision. This reading of Tolkien is therefore radically affirmative of created being as a gift, and that given freely. It has no sense of the tragedy of the readings of Eden and Flieger, influenced as they are by both Augustine and Boethius.

2.5 The Thomist Revision under the Influence of Jacques Maritain

2.5.1 The Intellectual Foundations of Tolkien's Philosophy of Being

I shall demonstrate in my exposition of Eriugena's philosophy of (unfallen) human nature (chapter 4), that all of God's attributes can be found in human nature, the distinction being that God is Himself *per essentiam*, whereas man is God *per participationem*. For Eriugena, the Creator-creation distinction is at times very blurred, and God is variously both everything and nothing. Aquinas, however, clarifies that distinction to great effect, upholding both the unique and transcendent nature of God, juxtaposed with the realized and immanent nature of humanity.

Tolkien would have known Aquinas' theological and philosophical framework of faith through many years of attending Mass, "and thus sat through sermons by those trained in Aquinas, [but] owned a copy of the *Summa* which has some marginal notes."[216] Tolkien's intellectual formation in Thomistic ideas spans from the early 1920s, and Milbank links the burgeoning Catholic intellectual community with the recently translated works of Jacques Maritain into English. The influence of Maritain had a significant influence on G. K. Chesterton, Tolkien, and their contemporaries, and "Maritain's *Art and Scholasticism* served as a sort of text book during the periods of the early twenties that Jones spent with Gill at Ditchling and Capel-y-ffin."[217] In addition to the renewed focus on Aquinas in English seminaries, Maritain and Etienne Gilson were enormously influential on the theological formation of lay Catholics such as Chesterton and Eric Gill, "formulating a unified theory of civil and cultural life."[218]

---

216. Ibid., 15. Note 38 lays claim to the veracity of this important piece of evidence, and the notes contained in the text may date back to his early courtship with Edith. I understand that this source now belongs in a private collection, and resides in Italy.

217. Miles, *Backgrounds to David Jones*, 6.

218. Milbank, *Chesterton and Tolkien*, 16.

That Tolkien would have been steeped in a Neoplatonic outlook, in its Thomist revision, is due partly also to a historical turn in the nineteenth century. Pope Leo XIII expounded the role that the early apologists and fathers held, in using philosophy coupled with faith, but the greatest accolade rested upon Thomas Aquinas—the Angelic Doctor—who "single-handed, victoriously combated the errors of former times, and supplied invincible arms to put those to rout which might in after-times spring up."[219] His future legacy within Catholic moral theology is secured at this point, and his pre-eminence is further championed by being appointed by Pope Leo XIII as universal patron of Catholic schools (1880). *Aeterni Patris* issued a reminder that it was the *Summa Theologiae* which was placed upon the altar, along with the Bible, at the Council of Trent, and that his philosophy and wisdom be a safeguard against errors. Paragraph 31 reads,

> We exhort you, venerable brethren, in all earnestness to restore the golden wisdom of St. Thomas, and to spread it far and wide for the defence and beauty of the Catholic faith, for the good of society, and for the advantage of all the sciences.

Aquinas represents, therefore, the summation of a tradition that stretches back into the patristic period, and he stands at the summit of the scholastic project of assimilation, seeking to reconcile reason and revelation, and to construct a theology that relates all things to God.[220] His breadth of reference—biblical and patristic (Latin *and* Greek), Platonic and Aristotelian, Christian, Jewish, and Islamic—has not been surpassed.

The Neo-Thomism to which Tolkien and others became attached was not merely a retro-Scholasticism or attempted recovery of some halcyon intellectual past, but desired that Thomist philosophy should be extended to comprehend events and developments (in society) since the thirteenth century: "the old must be nourished by the new."[221] These principles of neo-Thomism, originating in *Aeterni Patris* gave an 'impetus' to what Frederick Copleston suggests was "an already existing movement."[222] Christopher Dawson, in his Introduction to Maritain's *Religion and Culture*, drew attention to "the remarkable revival of Catholic intellectual life" that had "taken place during the last twenty five years." It was this revival, Copleston adds, that "coincided with the revival of Thomism."[223] The *Syllabus errorum* of 1864—a

---

219. *Aeterni Patris*, para 18.
220. *ST*, 1.1.7. resp.
221. Copleston, *Aquinas*, 258–59.
222. Ibid., 264, note 1.
223. Dawson, "Introduction" to Jacques Maritain, xx; Copleston, *Aquinas*, 247.

list of eighty propositions, displaying a rejection of modern thought—provided "a counterweight: an anti-modern intellectual framework."[224] *Aeterni Patris* was not so much a beginning of Neo-Scholasticism, but a high tidemark of ultramontanism which also included the promulgation of dogmas such as the immaculate conception (1854) and papal infallibility (1870). In the period between *Aeterni Patris* and the 1920s, a Neo-Thomism gradually established itself as exclusive and all-pervading: "The vicious circle created by the Magisterium on the one hand, which granted Scholasticism the highest authority, and Neo-Scholasticism on the other, which constituted the Church's only intellectual conceptual framework, was reinforced by an ambitious handbook tradition and the republication of prominent scholastic thinkers."[225] This intellectual milieu provided little room for creativity and renewal within Catholic theology, and against such a backdrop, little if any innovation and spirit can be detected.

Leo XIII's response to the call for a philosophical foundation for theology, as a means to allow the Church to enter dialogue *with* modernity on a philosophical-theological basis, evolved into a philosophical superstructure, with modernity as *the* enemy. Furthermore, it "evolved into a rod for punishing those who (in the Church's mind) presented themselves as Modernist, as well as those who did not demonstrate enough anti-Modernism."[226] This was the immediate context and background prior to Maritain's more aesthetic approach, reflecting that human intuition pointed to an integration of contemporary (artistic) culture with this emergent Neo-Thomism. The development and popularity of Maritain's works grew alongside the spirit of *ressourcement* in the 1930s to 1940s. Amongst further development of this *retour à la scolastique*, Vatican II was to recognize this plurality of tendencies, and it was perhaps that the Council Fathers "did not yield to the partially curial pressure to declare Thomas' sanctity yet again by canonising his philosophy as the pinnacle of Roman Catholic wisdom,"[227] that Tolkien was piqued enough to declare his hand in objection. Tolkien was enough of a conservative to have approved of the restatement of traditionally expressed certainties (viz Thomism), amidst the challenge to faith of modernism and the growing independence of science. It will be evident from my analysis of Maritain's aesthetics, inspired as they are by a more theological reading of Neo-Thomism, that Tolkien's own aesthetics of beauty and goodness is rooted in this Catholic understanding of how being has a radical giftedness in creation. This in turn is a personal *ressourcement* of that tradition which

224. Mettepenningen, *Nouvelle Théologie*, 18.
225. Ibid., 20.
226. Ibid., 24.
227. Laarhoven, "Thomas op Vaticanum II," 113–27.

had emerged out of the development of Neo-Thomism since Leo XIII, and was the founding basis for art, poetry, and intellectual expression from the 1920s onwards. And yet in the 1960s he was not hopeful of further innovations with which he was faced.

Tolkien further demonstrated in his *Letters* a degree of support for the reforms of Pope (St) Pius X, and a certain ambivalence toward those of the Second Vatican Council. Writing to his son Michael, on the 1st November 1963, he asserted his concern about what may yet befall the Church: "I suppose the greatest reform of our time was that carried out by St Pius X: surpassing anything, however needed, that the Council will achieve."[228] One year into the Council, Tolkien's concern for the new 'trends in the Church' reveal the great changes he is forced to endure:

> But imagine the experience of those born (as I) between the Golden and the Diamond Jubilee of Victoria. Both senses or imaginations of security have been progressively stripped away from us. Now we find ourselves nakedly confronting the will of God, as concerns ourselves and our position in time.[229]

Tolkien was an English Catholic of the Old School, and he took his faith very seriously. It is claimed by his biographer that he viewed his mother's death as little short of a martyrdom, due to the rejection she faced when she and the boys were received into the Catholic Church in 1900. Even at the time of Edith's reception into the Church on the 8th January 1914, and the months after, she still missed the worship and community at her Anglican parish in Cheltenham. Despite many short lapses, Tolkien was for the greater part of his life a convinced, committed, and devout Catholic.[230]

The link between Tolkien and Chesterton's works rests firmly on both personal and documentary evidence. Firstly, Milbank recalls a private conversation with Tolkien's daughter—Priscilla—"who kindly confirmed both her father's liking for Chesterton and his possession of *The Coloured Lands*, which was published the year before he gave the St Andrews Lecture that

---

228. Carpenter, *Letters*, 339. The reference here has a footnote, hinting that the context is in reference to children's reception of Holy Communion, and Pius X's recommendation of daily communion. This is in contradistinction to the Reformers' allegation of the 'blasphemous fable of the Mass.'

229. Ibid., 393–95. This letter was variously dated between 25th August 1967 and 11th October 1968, by which time Pope Paul VI's Apostolic Constitution, *Missale Romanum*, 3rd April 1969, and the attendant changes to the liturgy, had been anticipated by Tolkien. Much had been stripped away of what was previously familiar; and much was added to what had previously been omitted.

230. Ibid., 31–33; 39–40; 73–77.

became *On Fairy-Stories*."²³¹ Secondly, we find in his own *Letters* that he read Chesterton's *The Ballad of the White Horse* to his daughter, Priscilla, and that he considered the work as being overrated, "G.K.C. knew nothing whatever about the 'North,' heathen or Christian."²³² After his own conversion to Catholicism in 1922, Chesterton became the leading public intellectual of pre-war Britain. His popular fictional character Father Brown—based on his friend Monsignor John O'Connor—helped promote the English Catholic identity, despite the deep resentment faced by the likes of the Tolkien family.²³³ Tolkien's quotation of Chesterton's intellectual journey to faith—*Orthodoxy*—is proof that he read at least chapter 5, and that Chesterton's book—*Saint Thomas Aquinas: The Dumb Ox*—could hardly have escaped his notice, given his owning a copy of the *Summa*.²³⁴ Tolkien's famous essay, based on his lecture "On Fairy-Stories," quotes from Chesterton's *The Coloured Lands*, though his own method of sub-creation is said to display more freedom and originality in its reality. Milbank postulates that it is a phrase from Maisie Ward's 1938 *Introduction* to *The Coloured Lands* that Tolkien derives his sub-creative ideals:

> Cheerful fantasy is the creation of a new form wherein man, becomes creator, co-operator with God.²³⁵

Tolkien's comparison between his own sub-creation and Chesterton's own fantasy lies in that

> it [Chesterton's] has, I think, only a limited power; for the reason that recovery of freshness of vision is its only virtue.²³⁶

In discussing a reference to Dickens' discovery of a new word—*Mooreeffoc*, whilst it sounds fantastical, it is merely a disorientated 'coffeeroom' sign, viewed from a new angle (i.e., through a mirror). This kind of Chestertonian fantasy may at first sight appear to belong to an altogether different time, understandably given that H. G. Wells' *The Time Machine* had been published only eleven years prior to Chesterton's *Charles Dickens: A Critical Study*. Tolkien cedes that it can do only that—give an impression of timelessness—when, in point of fact, "it act[s] as a time-telescope

---

231. Milbank, *Chesterton and Tolkien*, xiii.

232. Carpenter, *Letters*, 92. (References to Chesterton's ideas are discussed in pp. 246 and 402. Carpenter alludes to regular trips out in the car with the family to White Horse Hill and Waylands Smithy, Oxfordshire (*Biography*, 163).

233. Milbank, *Chesterton and Tolkien*, x.

234. Carpenter, *Letters*, 402.

235. Chesterton, *The Coloured Lands*, 195.

236. Tolkien, *Tree and Leaf*, 58–59.

focused on one spot," like Wells' *Time Machine*, which moves through time only, but not spatially.[237] However, Tolkien admits of his own interpretation of fantasy, as being "made out of the primary World, but a good craftsman loves his material, and has a knowledge and feeling for clay, stone and wood which only the art of making can give."[238] In creating fantasy Tolkien cannot escape from the real world: instead Tolkien, like Chesterton, seeks to inject into the experience of the mundane, "the wonder of the things, such as stone, and wood, and iron; tree and grass; house and fire; bread and wine."[239] It is this "freshness of vision," which is a common denominator between their respective approaches to fantasy, that links them at this juncture. Tolkien's artistry as a writer paints (literally) new world opportunities, in reference to what we experience in our own. Instead of Chesterton's "queerness of things that have become trite," viz Mooreefoc, Tolkien's interpretation are all the more potent—containing things supraabundant—because "they deal largely, or (the better ones) mainly with simple or fundamental things, untouched by fantasy, but these simplicities are made all the more luminous by their setting."[240]

Milbank highlights a commonality between these two fantasy authors, both in their "relation of paganism and Christianity, and to English history. Common also is a religious tradition and its expression in fiction."[241] What is central to both writers is a view of art as revealing the createdness of the world, and the creation of the artist in remaking it:

> Each writer sees art itself as mediatory: a theological tool for opening human eyes to see the reality of God and the reality, albeit contingent, of the world beyond the self.[242]

2.5.2 Otherness and Independence in the Reality of Being.

Having placed Tolkien firmly amongst his contemporaries within a conservative post-Edwardian Catholic context, we can now trace how Tolkien's own mythology arises out of the intellectual basin and thought of his own

---

237. Ibid., 59. Tolkien makes several references to Wells' Morlocks throughout this essay.

238. Ibid.

239. Ibid., 60.

240. Ibid., 58–59.

241. Milbank, *Chesterton and Tolkien*, xiv.

242. Ibid.

day. Returning, therefore, to his metaphysics of music, we observe a significant movement in Tolkien's use of the music of the Ainur, in that he describes their music as mere "abstract form," a quality which calls to mind Aquinas' analysis of music as an incidentally physical embodiment of otherwise ideal, mathematical harmonies or proportions.[243] As with Aquinas' apparent musical 'disinterest,' the Ainur for their part enjoy the music simply for what it is—music. There is a kind of stoic oblivion to the possibility of their subordinating the music to some ulterior and/or utilitarian purpose beyond itself. This is in contradistinction to Melkor's more 'interested' stance who, failing to enjoy the music for what it is, sought rather to bend his own will, and to bring into being the thoughts of his imagination so that he might exercise dominion over them.

There is something therefore significant in both Aquinas' and Tolkien's disinterest in, and indifference to music: an 'other-ness' which is both within the music, but also radically transcendent when it appears in the vision. Tolkien's use of this characterisation is very profound, such that when confronted with this vision, there is amongst the Ainur a sense of wonder in the possibility of things "other than themselves, strange and free."[244] Here we see a distinct similarity of intention between Aquinas and Tolkien: as God creates things 'other than' Himself, then this is precisely because the Creator in a very real sense is already an 'other to Himself' (viz the Trinity).[245] This is brought into dramatic effect in Tolkien's cosmogony when one of the Valar—Aulë—creates the dwarves in the darkness of Middle-earth, though Ilúvatar knew of the act. When the Vala was chastised for overreaching his 'power and authority,' his defence was that,

> I did not desire such Lordship. I desired things other than I am, to love and to teach them, so that they too might perceive the beauty of Eä, which thou hast caused to be.[246]

The likeness to the divine goodness is displayed in the desire to create a plurality and inequality of creatures in which higher beings (Vala)—in

---

243. Carpenter, *Letters*, 284.
244. Tolkien, *Silmarillion*, 18.
245. *ST*, 1.27.1.resp: "Procession, therefore, is not to be understood from what it is in bodies, either according to local movement or by way of a cause proceeding forth to its exterior effect, as, for instance, like heat from the agent to the thing made hot. Rather it is to be understood by way of an intelligible emanation, for example, of the intelligible word which proceeds from the speaker, yet remains in him. In that sense the Catholic Faith understands procession as existing in God."
246. Tolkien, *Silmarillion*, 49.

imitation of God—might communicate to others the goodness they have received in their own origin. In continuing his defence Aulë exclaims,

> It seemed to me that there is great room in Arda for many things to rejoice in it, yet it is for the most part empty still, and dumb. [...] Yet the making of things is in my heart from my own making by thee; and the child of little understanding that makes a play of the deeds of his father may do so without thought of mockery, but because he is the son of his father.[247]

We have in this early mythology of Tolkien a paradigm of his Thomist understanding of 'being as gift,' in relation to the Creator. If there is unlimited freedom in God's own being to create, then by participation in nature that self-same freedom and desire extends to the Ainur and Valar. Created being—or being coming into reality—is not a lapse from an ideal, but an extension of the creative affections of the One. Milbank draws this important aspect of Tolkien's philosophy of being, in contrast to Eastern philosophical ideas of reality:

> In Thomas this leads to a rejection of nominalism, and promotion of a moderate and participatory realism. For Tolkien the element I would stress is the objectivity of things. Only through the reality of the world can the mind, according to Thomas, reach out to otherness and become the object.[248]

This sense of 'making the other,' derives from Aquinas' discussion in the *Summa* on the nature of the good, who cedes that, whilst God is *the* Good, both supremely and in essence, "all things are good, inasmuch as they have being. But they are not called beings through the divine being, but through their own being; therefore all things are not good by the divine goodness, but by their own goodness."[249] Milbank draws our attention to Maritain's exposition of this idea, that it is in "its totality reaching out towards the object, towards the other *as* other; it needs the dominating contact of the object, but only that it may be enriched by it [...] fertilised by being, rightly subjected to the real."[250]

Tolkien's world, though fictional, is full of real-world possibilities, and "to invent a world at all, as fantasy writers continue to do, is to commit to metaphysics."[251] The fantasy writer does not only mimic a divine act of cre-

---

247. Ibid., 49–50.
248. Milbank, *Chesterton and Tolkien*, 17.
249. *ST*, 1.6.4. resp.
250. Maritain, *Theonas*, 9.
251. Milbank, *Chesterton and Tolkien*, 18.

ation, "but he or she, by creating a self-consistent, independent world also witnesses to the existence of an Is: to *Ens*."²⁵² Hart captures this sense of the 'desire for other,' as we see demonstrated by the Ainur's love of creation and the Children of Ilúvatar, in that,

> Beauty invokes desire [. . .] precedes and elicits desire, supplicates and commands it (often in vain), and gives shape to the will that receives it. Second, it is genuinely desire, and not some ideally disinterested and dispirited state of contemplation, that beauty both calls for and answers to: though not a coarse, impoverished desire to consume and dispose, but a desire made full at a distance, alongside what is loved and possessed in the intimacy of dispossession.²⁵³

This desiring things for their sheer and radical 'otherness' is based on a Thomist and not a Kantian metaphysics, though Tolkien does allude to his knowledge of the latter in a passage immediately preceding the comparison of his own work and that of Chesterton's:

> Recovery (which includes return and renewal of health) is a re-gaining—regaining a clear view. I do not say 'seeing things as they are' and involve myself with the philosophers, though I might venture to say 'seeing things as we are (or were) meant to see them.'²⁵⁴

The 'things in themselves' are *das Ding an sich*—the *noumenon*—of Kant's first *Critique*, and are epistemologically unknown and inaccessible to us. Here Tolkien rejects the disinterested metaphysics of Kant's idealism, and Milbank asserts the originality of Tolkien's approach:

> Despite his apologetic tone, Tolkien is actually saying something quite radical: that fiction in the form of fantastic recreation of the world can give us access to the real by freeing the world of objects from our appropriation of them.²⁵⁵

She draws our attention to Maritain's criticisms of Kant in this respect, and that Kant's mistake was in believing "that the act of knowing consists in *creating* the other, not in *becoming* the other, he foolishly reversed the order of dependence between the object of knowledge and the human intellect and

---

252. Ibid.
253. Hart, *Beauty of the Infinite*, 19.
254. Tolkien, *Tree and Leaf*, 57–58.
255. Milbank, *Chesterton and Tolkien*, 19.

made the human intellect the measure and law of the object."²⁵⁶ Tolkien's understanding of the Thomistic participatory relationship between Creator/created avoids the confusion that things are limited to the subjective perception of the senses, but can in fact be real in and of themselves. In the music-vision-reality procession of Middle-earth we do not see the Ainur as those who wonder before great works of art, but as those who repeatedly set free those things and peoples to be themselves.²⁵⁷

2.5.3 Tolkien's Art Viewed through a Scholastic Looking Glass

Given that we can now locate Tolkien's true art, as both original and dependent upon Aquinas' philosophy of 'being and gift,' then we do so through the 'looking glass' of Maritain's influential essay published in 1920: *Art and Scholasticism*, and David Jones' 1959 response—*Art and Sacrament*. It has been stated already that directly or indirectly Tolkien was informed by the writings of Maritain, and perhaps nowhere is this seen more than in the creative and gratuitous sense that life and being display that radical giftedness which is occasioned by its participation in the divine. In Tolkien's world, there is no need for an immanent deity, it "does not need gods or a Christian subtext to be a religious work: because there is a mediatory radiance in every detail of its world."²⁵⁸ In this section, I shall demonstrate how Maritain's Neo-Thomist outlook can be identified within Tolkien's artistic and mythological project, and that his project as a whole—and not just things in it—is both a product of 'undeviating reason,' and has a sacramental aspect also.²⁵⁹

The influence of Aquinas crept upon Maritain almost without knowing, and this sense of surprise is relayed in his earliest (1914) work:

> In thus completely accepting, without quibble or reserve, the authentic reality and value of our human instruments of cognition I was already a Thomist without being aware of it. When [. . .] I came upon the *Summa Theologica* its luminous flood was to find no opposing obstacles in me.²⁶⁰

Central to Maritain's aesthetics and theory of creative activity is the role played by the intellect and human intelligence. The opening paragraph of

---

256. Maritain, *Theonas*, 9.
257. Milbank, *Chesterton and Tolkien*, 20.
258. Ibid., 25.
259. Jacques Maritain, *Art and Scholasticism*, 9.
260. Maritain, *Bergsonian Philosophy*, 16–17.

Art and Scholasticism situates the term 'art' as an intellectual virtue distinguished not only from the other intellectual virtues, but from the moral virtues as well. John Trapani argues that for Maritain, following Aquinas,

> the intellect is not an inferior and limiting knowing power (Bergson), nor is it an active knowing power, where anything that is suprasensible in the knowing mind is exclusively its own structure (Kant), nor is it an isolated knowing power turned in solely upon the contents (ideas) of its own mind (Descartes).[261]

According to Maritain, "the intellect is a superior, immaterial knowing power that operates together with the instrumentality of the senses in a diversity of ways, and, having being itself as its proper object, it puts us in direct and immediate contact with reality itself."[262] Because we can see, we can delight in beauty (unlike Kant). In Thomas Aquinas, "Maritain found not only this defence of an integral, spiritual intellect, but one who knew how to put things in their proper place."[263]

For Maritain, art (poetry) has a high transcendent quality reaching beyond itself: "Poetic intuition is directed towards concrete existence as connatural to the soul pierced by a given emotion."[264] He speaks of this moment of Idea as being the "transient motion of a beloved hand," existing in an instant only, disappearing from the human sphere, but being preserved out of time only in the memory of angels. Maritain continues, by stressing the dynamic nature of art, in that 'poetic intuition catches it in passing, in a faint attempt to immortalize it in time. But poetic intuition does not stop at this given existent: it goes beyond and infinitely beyond." It is precisely because poetic intuition has no conceptualized object that it tends and extends to the infinite. It tends towards all reality, universally, and also to "the infinite reality which is engaged in any singular existing thing, either the secret properties of being involved in its identity and in its existential relation with other things."[265] Art is therefore not just a demonstrative knowledge of reality, but extends both within and beyond that reality in a hyperontic way: in like manner to which God extends creation within and yet beyond its own boundaries. There is an inherent reality about creation, and yet there is also its transcendental form which is eternal in the mind

---

261. Trapani, *Poetry, Beauty and Contemplation*, 34.
262. Maritain, *Bergsonian Philosophy*, 145.
263. Trapani, *Poetry, Beauty and Contemplation*, 21.
264. Maritain, *Creative Intuition*, 126.
265. Ibid., 126.

of God.[266] It is highly unlikely that Tolkien would have known Maritain's late and American work, *Creative Intuition*. However, Maritain is drawing on strands of his Neo-Thomist theories on art and poetry which had influenced Tolkien almost two decades earlier, in both the content of his ideas, and the method of inception.

The context of Maritain's exposition centres on the distinction between speculative and practical order. The speculative virtues are said to perfect the intellect, "the intellect itself as such aims to know. The intellect acts, indeed its act is, absolutely speaking, life 'par excellence.'"[267] Its act is an immanent one which remains wholly within the intellect to perfect it, and through which the intellect "draws it into itself—it eats being and drinks being—so as itself to become, in a certain fashion, all things."[268] The practical order, on the other hand, is opposed to the speculative order, and in this sphere man tends to something other than knowledge only: if he knows, it is no longer to rest in the truth, and to enjoy it (*frui*). It is to use it (*uti*), knowledge with a view to some work or action.[269] Art, arising out of the intellect, therefore belongs to this practical order, turning towards action and not merely pure interiority of knowledge. We can then begin to see how this sense of creating things 'other than itself' has its origin in the Thomist metaphysics of both *agibile* (*praktikon*, or doing) and *factibile* (*poiēton*, or making).[270]

Here *praxis* consists in the free use—as freedom—of our faculties, in the exercise of free will not in regard to the things that we do, but with regard to the use which we make of that freedom. The sphere of *praxis* is one of morality, and in this Maritain champions the virtue of prudence—practical wisdom—in that "prudence [. . .] measures our acts with regard to an ultimate end which is God himself Sovereignly loved."[271] In contrast, *poiesis* is chiefly concerned with 'productive action,' the sphere of art in the most universal sense. *Poiesis* is not so much concerned with the use of our freedom, as in the case of *praxis*, but with the thing produced or to the

---

266. We see this hyperontic reality when describing God in relation to materiality and cognitive sense in Pseudo-Dionysius' *Mystical Theology*, chapter 5. God is said to be "beyond assertion and denial [. . .] being the perfect and unique cause of all things [. . .] free of every limitation, beyond every limitation; it is also beyond every denial" (*Complete Works*, 141).

267. Maritain, *Art and Scholasticism*, 5.

268. Ibid.

269. Ibid., 6. Here Maritain is referring to Aquinas' *In II metaphysics*, lecture 2 of Aristotle, 995b.

270. Ibid., 7.

271. Ibid.

work done in and of itself. The action is good in itself, and not to any common end of human life.[272] For Maritain, therefore, art stands outside the human sphere, "as it has an end, rules and values, which are not those of man, but those of the work to be produced." There is for art but one law, "the exigencies and the good of the work."[273] If art is not human in the end that it pursues, it is human—essentially human—in its mode of operating. It must have upon it the mark of man—*animale rationale*—and this is chiefly why in Tolkien's world of Middle-earth, artefacts have a moral value: the art of making imbibes a virtue or malice of the artisan (*artifex*). In a letter to Rhona Beare (14th October 1958) he highlights that "The Ring of Sauron is only one of the various mythical treatments of the placing of one's life, or power, in some external object, which is thus exposed to capture or destruction with disastrous results to oneself."[274] In 'philosophizing' this myth, Tolkien asserts that "*potency* (or perhaps rather *potentiality*) if it is to be exercised, and produce results, has to be externalized and so as it were passes, to a greater or lesser degree, out of one's direct control." The same could be said by extension, of the whole of Tolkien's co-creation in relation to Ilúvatar's great theme, shared with the Ainur. In creating free creatures, there is a liberation from control and determinism, whose "making and nature [. . .] were the two chief secrets." Tolkien continues to explain his ontology of being such that,

> The Children of God are thus primevally related and akin, and primevally different. Since also they are something wholly 'other' to the gods, in the making of which the gods played no part, they are the object of the special desire and love of the gods.[275]

David Jones' response to Maritain—*Art and Sacrament*—is an essay which adopts a more earthy approach that would have appealed to Tolkien. In the sense of the practical order of which Maritain writes in a theoretical sense, Jones responds such that "there is no surrogate for being 'on the job'";[276] "Art is an infantryman's job";[277] and that "for the artist the question is 'Does it?' rather than 'Ought it?'"[278] Jones does not distinguish between a painted or written work of art, as "the problems and dilemmas at least

---

272. Ibid.
273. Ibid, 9.
274. Carpenter, *Letters*, 279.
275. Ibid., 147.
276. Jones, *Epoch and Artist*, 12.
277. Ibid., 183.
278. Ibid., 18.

'feel' all one to me. Over the whole of these matters I feel the same despairs and the same occasional hopes."[279] The respective realms of *praxis* and *poiesis*—doing and making—are those of *prudentia* and *ars*. What *prudentia* attempts to achieve in the ordering of life, *ars* attempts to achieve in the ordering of a thing to be made.[280] The difference between *ars* and *prudentia* is in respect of ends rather than operations. Jones wrote his *Art and Sacrament* essay partly to indicate that

> there seems little or no purpose imposing the kind of questions which so often are posed touching *Prudentia* and *Ars*, as though these were two comparable qualities in opposition to each other or two jurisdictions or figures in a hierarchy having claims against each other.[281]

This debate originates in Maritain's use of Aristotle's *Ethics* (6.4.114a), whereby he contrasts the intellectual virtues of 'doing and making,' in that Maritain pointed out that the ancients did not differentiate between fine arts (e.g., poetry) and the useful arts (e.g., boat-building): the division between them "derives from the end pursued."[282] Jones refuses to take for granted the distinction between art and prudence: the former is an activity, whereas the latter is a quality of an activity. Rowan Williams' exposition of this debate exposes Jones' true intention: "Prudence is about how we make lives significant, not about how we meet our needs. Therefore, art is a necessary accompaniment to prudence."[283] Jones notes, that *prudentia* is a contraction of *providentia*, and that in English 'providence' is still related to the "Divine Providence."[284] For Jones, in contrast to Maritain, art moves beyond itself: 'man is a maker [. . .] a maker of things,'[285] and yet "man is unavoidably a sacramentalist and that his works are sacramental in character [. . .] this creature has, for about fifty millenniums [. . .] made works, handled material, in a fashion that can only be described as having the nature of a sign."[286] There is something intrinsically religious, and not merely abstract or disinterested, in the manner of the making of art. Speaking of *Homo Neanderthalis*, and of all primitive and "merest rough, bungled incision, or the daubed on red ochre," Jones testifies to what "would appear already to be in the domain of sign

279. Ibid., 17.
280. Miles, *Backgrounds to David Jones*, 8.
281. Jones, *Epoch and Artist*, 147.
282. Maritain, *Art and Scholasticism*, 119–20, note 39.
283. Williams, *Grace and Necessity*, 85.
284. Jones, *Epoch and Artist*, 145.
285. Ibid., 158.
286. Ibid., 155.

(sacrament), of anamnesis, of anathemata."[287] *Anamnesis* here is a Platonic idea, but Jones utilizes that sense of which Dom Gregory Dix writes in his *Shape of the Liturgy*: "a sign then must be a significant of something, hence of some 'reality,' so of something 'good,' so of something sacred. That is why I think that the notion of sign implies the sacred."[288]

Just like Maritain's recognizing his non-cognitive but intrinsic Thomism, Jones asserts that it was "with relative suddenness, the analogy between what we call 'the arts' and the things that Christians call Eucharistic signs became (if still but vaguely) apparent."[289] For Jones, it became increasingly evident that this analogy applied to the whole gamut of 'making.' In a manner similar to Tolkien, the freedom to co-create things other than itself, which are both good and beautiful after the maker, then freedom is a necessary attribute of art. Jones links this to the etymology of the words *religio* and *obligation*, the latter implying

> a binding of some sort is indicated. The same root is in ligament, a binding which supports an organ and assumes its freedom of use as part of a body. Man's making—the juxtaposing concepts of *prudential* and *ars*—implies that binding, in order that freedom to make becomes possible.[290]

For Jones, the binding makes possible the freedom: "cut the ligament and there is atrophy—corpse rather than *corpus*."[291] There is a common cause preventing (non-rational) animals from being prudential beings or artists. The beauty of animals creating (e.g., Ant, spider, nuthatch) is 'transitive': "human activity aims at the embodying of meaning by deliberate choices, and this gratuitous element in what is human makes the difference between us and other creatures." For Christian theology, God's act of creation is utterly gratuitous, describable as "a kind of play."[292]

We can stand back at this juncture, and assess Tolkien's project through the dual lens of *praxis* and *poiesis* as art—being more akin to that of Jones than Maritain—in that his freedom to create a mythology is one which creates the 'otherness' of his imaginary world, which is at the same time our world. As Tolkien asserted that, whilst Middle-earth is a non-religious sphere in its outward vesture, the whole is imbued with a Catholic understanding of what

287. Ibid., 156.
288. Ibid., 157.
289. Ibid., 171.
290. Ibid., 158.
291. Ibid.
292. Ibid., 85.

life and being are, in relation to The One. Its *exitus* and *reditus*, discussed in section 3.4, are expressed as they are here, as participatory ontologies having a superabundant value in respect of their proximity as 'things other than God,' and not merely subsumed into or by God (as might be said in the case of Eriugena). In Maritain's terms, Tolkien's art is imbued with ideas from which he cannot release himself. As a committed and practising Catholic of his generation then it would have been a work of pure fiction had he created a world entirely independent of his own religious worldview. What we read throughout Tolkien's *legendarium* is an arrangement of ideas which are made real by the fact of his understanding a reality beyond himself to which he is ontologically related, and in Jones' reading of the process of art—sacramentally related. If the whole *corpus* of his *legendarium* demonstrates the duality of *praxis* and *poiesis*—*prudentia* and *ars*—then it is unsurprising that the peoples and things within it display the dual characteristics of both a freedom of the will and the use of that freedom to co-create, such that Middle-earth becomes a 'good in itself,' principally because practical order arises out of an analogical relationship of *prudentia*—whose chief aim is to reflect this cardinal virtue as it is approximated in God's 'beyond being,' but in the reality of an immanent created world. I have already demonstrated that, for Aquinas, in the divine mind 'things' enjoy this super-eminent truth, being, perfection, etc., not 'as themselves' as created beings, but as certain aspects of God's own uncreated being. To have any kind of reality as themselves, things must be given their own being *as* individual things, namely that kind of being which they do not possess in the divine mind. And so, in Tolkien's mythology, both the world and those things contained within it have a formal cause which is brought into actuality, and therefore have an integrity of being as gift.

Maritain extends this notion of subjectivity to the process of creating art itself, as things in and of themselves. The subjectivity of the poet is essential to the work of art. Here subjectivity does not limit itself to "the inexhaustible flux of superficial feelings," but is,

> subjectivity in its deepest ontological sense, that is, the substantial totality of the human person, a universe unto itself, which the spirituality of the soul makes capable of containing itself through its own immanent acts, and which, at the centre of all the subjects that it knows as objects, grasps only itself as subject.[293]

This he links to the divine creative intellection, arising out of perfect and complete self-knowledge in God, whereas the poet acts analogously—"a

---

293. Maritain, *Creative Intuition*, 113.

grasping by the poet—of his own subjectivity in order to create." God's intellect is determined or specified by nothing else that his own essence: "It is by knowing Himself, [...] that he knows his works, which exist in time and have begun in time, but which He eternally is in the free act of creating."[294] Maritain links this analogously to the free creativity of the human spirit in the creation of poetry and art, and yet in an inferior sense:

> Well, it is too clear that the poet is a poor god. He does not know himself. And his creative insight miserably depends on the external world, and on the infinite heap of forms and beauties already made by men.[295]

The poet/artist cannot free himself from his immediate context, and this is evidently true of Tolkien who, in writing his own mythology, weaves into it Neoplatonic religious themes simply because this is the manner in which he has received his own faith in his own day, alongside his own personal experiences of family, education, war, and trauma.

Maritain discusses art in terms of a formal cause as "its thought before being made" in a mind, prior to passing into matter: "its formal element, what constitutes it in its species and makes it what it is, is its being ruled by the intellect."[296] He signifies human works in contradistinction to that of a beast or machine, in that,

> when work becomes inhuman or sub-human, because its artistic character is effaced and matter gains the upper hand over man, it is natural that civilization tends to Communism and to a productivism forgetful of the true ends of the human being.[297]

For Maritain, following Aquinas (above), art resides primarily in the intelligence of the *artifex*; art is the undeviating determination of works to be made (*recta ratio factibilium*), and whilst the work to be made is only the matter (or material and efficient cause) of art, its form is undeviating reason.[298] Jeanette Winterson described this process in contrast to contemporary fashions of spontaneity in art, such that,

> Art always dresses for dinner. Does this seem stuffy in the jeans and T-shirt days of popular culture? Perhaps, but without a

---

294. Ibid., 133.
295. Ibid., 113.
296. Maritain, *Art and Scholasticism*, 9.
297. Ibid., 9, note 4. This is discussed at some length by Milbank, *Chesterton and Tolkien*, 81–83.
298. Ibid., 10.

formal space art cannot do its work. To be exact is to clear away the clutter from what is essential. [. . .] Contrary to the bohemian stereotype, the true artist is highly organised and must constantly select and order her material, choosing only that which can be shaped to an ultimate purpose.[299]

Maritain reminds us that the doctors of the Middle Ages were interested in the whole mass of mankind, but even so they still studied their Master: they knew that the virtue of art is predicated pre-eminently of God, as are goodness and justice.[300]

Aquinas lists three objective properties of beauty: integrity, proportion, and clarity (*cf.*, 2.3.2 above) arising out of a discussion in the *Summa* on the essential attributes of God within the Holy Trinity, and not on the abstract nature of art *per se*.[301] This is significant in putting Maritain—and by association Tolkien—into perspective: our intellect, which is led to the knowledge of God from creatures, must consider God according to the mode derived from creatures, and this mode is by analogy from the perspective of humanity.[302] From the Trinitarian perspective, integrity, proportion, and clarity correspond to the Son's like-nature, image, and art of the omnipotent God, respectively. The consummation of these ideas of Maritain, as they impact on Tolkien's own philosophy of 'being as gift,' require an exposition of these three properties of beauty—integrity, proportion, and clarity—as they are key to how Tolkien fashioned his co-creative ideas of Middle-earth out of the Thomistic worldview of his own day.

2.5.4 Beauty as an Approach to God

Maritain's definition of beauty resides in the phrase *id quod visum placet* (what gives pleasure on sight), and is a derivative of Aquinas' own definition of *pulchra enim dicuntur quae visu placet* (beautiful things are those which please when they are seen).[303] Umberto Eco claims that there are consider-

---

299. Winterson, *Art Objects*, 98.

300. Maritain, *Art and Scholasticism*, 21.

301. *ST*, 1.39.8. resp.

302. Ibid., 1.5.2. resp 1: "Dionysius discusses the Divine Names (*Div Nom*, 1.3) as implying some causal relation in God; for we name God, as he says, from creatures, as a cause from its effects."

303. Maritain, *Art and Scholasticism*, 23; cf *ST*, 1.5.4.ad1 : "Beauty and goodness in a thing are identical fundamentally; for they are based upon the same thing, namely, the form; and consequently goodness is praised as beauty. [. . .] Hence beauty consists in due proportion; for the senses delight in things duly proportioned, as in what is after their own kind, because even sense is a sort of reason, just as is every cognitive faculty."

able differences in these two definitions, the former being a "sociological fact," and the latter amounts to a "metaphysical definition."[304] Kevin O'Reilly defends Maritain's development of Aquinas' definition of beauty, as being a true development of "a body of thought already imbued with metaphysical worth," and not a corruption. Whilst at first reading he appears to misquote, the conflation itself is quite legitimate: "Maritain neither adds nor detracts from Aquinas' own essential understanding of beauty."[305] Maritain argues that the intellect comes into contact with beauty only through the senses, because only these faculties posses the capacity for intuition which is required for perceiving beauty. Beauty is apprehended "in the sensible and by the sensible, and not separately from it."[306] O'Reilly describes this reaction to beauty, and this is analogous to what we see in the wonder of the Ainur at the sight and revelation of Arda, in that:

> the intellect does not exercise powers of abstraction, since it does not have to extricate anything from the matter in which it is buried and then examine step by step the various attributes of what it has extricated.[307]

It rejoices, rather, "without work and without discourse" as it "drinks the clarity of being."[308] This aesthetic moment can thus be interpreted as "contemplative, uncritical, blessed."[309] In terms of the Ainur's *visio*, the three formal elements of beauty—integrity, proportion and clarity—are three ways in which form can be considered as a whole, beauty being rooted in form, "and their hearts rejoiced in light, and their eyes beholding many colours were filled with gladness."[310] These three elements are "mutually implicative notions," and according to Eco:

> Form is proportion with integrity which manifests itself as such; form is the totality of a relation as it manifests itself; form is the self-signifying proportion of some whole. The three criteria are reciprocally implicative, each continually referring to the other, and no description of any one of them can be allowed to obscure

---

Now since knowledge is by assimilation, and similarity relates to form, beauty properly belongs to the nature of a formal cause."

304. Eco, *Aesthetics*, 240 note 22.
305. O'Reilly, *Aesthetic Perception*, 30.
306. Maritain, *Art and Scholasticism*, 25.
307. O'Reilly, *Aesthetic Perception*, 14.
308. Maritain, *Art and Scholasticism*, 26.
309. Eco, *Aesthetics*, 60.
310. Tolkien, *Silmarillion*, 19.

the reality of the other two. The reality of form is the permanent substratum of this interplay of references.[311]

In this interplay of references, clarity signifies the capacity of form to communicate itself, which requires the cognitive faculty of sight. Given both Maritain's and Aquinas' definitions, then what *claritas* communicates when actualized is the object's true beauty. O'Reilly observes that as *ST* 1.5.4 is concerned with "goodness having the aspect of a final cause," then *Objectio* 1 and its corresponding *Responsorio* has the word *pulchrum* occurring seven times. This contrasts with the single use of the word, *pulchra*.[312] This suggests that in terms of aesthetics, Aquinas' attention is focused on beauty per se, rather than on beautiful things: *pulchrum* rather than *pulchra*. The aim of the response is to distinguish between goodness and beauty—*bonum et pulchrum*—and according to Aquinas they are based on the same thing: form. That is why goodness is praised as beauty. They differ in that "goodness properly relates to the appetite (goodness being what all things desire); and therefore it has the aspect of an end (the appetite being a kind of movement towards a thing). On the other hand, beauty relates to the cognitive faculty," as it has a reference to the ocular senses—it delights when seen.

We have seen how Aquinas ascribes three objective properties to beauty: integrity, because the intellect is pleased in fullness of being; proportion, because the intellect is pleased in order and unity; radiance (or clarity), because the intellect is pleased in light and intelligibility.[313] Maritain invests the greater part of his treatise of these properties upon radiance/clarity, or splendor, which is the essential characteristic of beauty—*clarita est de ratione pulchritudinis*.[314] But radiance is a splendor of intelligibility—a *splendor formae*, for the form is "the ontological secret that they bear within them, their spiritual being, their operating mystery."[315]

Armand Maurer locates Aquinas' aesthetics of beauty in our knowledge of the real world via our senses. His analysis focuses upon a thing's existence, form, and action as its ground of being, and the mystery of its beauty is tied up with these symbolic components.[316] If there were a *thing* or *being* that was pure and unqualified existence, presenting no form or action, then its existence, its beauty, would reside in the actuality of its

---

311. Eco, *Aesthetics*, 121.

312. O'Reilly, *Aesthetic Perception*, 28.

313. *ST*, 1.39.8.

314. Maritain, *Art and Scholasticism*, 24. Here he is quoting from Aquinas' *Commentary on the Book of Divine Names*, Lecture 6.

315. Ibid., 24.

316. Maurer, *About Beauty*, 8.

pure and (unknowable) infinite existence. For Aquinas, such a being could only be God, and therefore beauty seems inseparably connected with actuality. Aquinas uses the phrase *formositas actualitas* (the beauty of actual existence).[317] For Aquinas, the first and most profound sense of actuality is *existence*. To be (*esse*) is "the actuality of all acts and consequently the perfection of all perfections."[318] Whatever actuality a being has over and above its existence, it owes it to its existence: without existence there is no being, nothing. So the actuality of existence is the source and origin of the whole being, including its beauty. In terms of actuality, Maurer cites the illustration of completed and unfinished works of art: "the half-finished sculptures of Michelangelo in the Accademia of Florence are hauntingly beautiful, but they cannot compare with his actually completed 'David.'"[319] These can be observed in Appendix A. There is no doubt that the unfinished works in potentiality have a beauty of their own, but they lack the *integritas* of the finished work. The primary meaning for Aquinas here is existential: it expresses the primal perfection of a thing, which is found in its essence. It lacks nothing, taking into account the sort of thing that it is. In a second sense, a thing is integral when it is perfect in operation: "wholeness demands perfection in its being and action."[320] Lacking any of the parts, or failing in its operation, it falls short of the wholeness due to it, and to this extent it is ugly. Hence, Figures 1–3 in Appendix A may be considered ugly, after this second sense, merely because they are incomplete and lack any discernible function, compared to the completed David. As studies, they are good in themselves, and have the potentiality to be great, but nobody pays their money to see the incomplete works, and they are not what catches the eye when walking into the gallery.[321] Interestingly, the mature Maritain speaks of "finite beauty or finishedness" in the work being always incomplete at some level, "limping like the biblical Jacob, from the encounter with what cannot be named."[322] Achieved art always has the kind of imperfection through which infinity wounds the finite.[323]

The second aspect of actuality is a thing's *form*. This concept is hinted at in the Latin language itself:

317. *QDP,* 4.2.ad 31.
318. *ST,* 1.4.1.ad 3.
319. Maurer, *About Beauty,* 7.
320. Ibid., 11.
321. That is not to diminish the importance of the *Non Finito* movement in art, inspired by Plato's views that no work of art can fully resemble its ideal form in the World of the Forms.
322. Maritain, *Creative Intuition,* 166–67.
323. Williams, *Grace and Necessity,* 21.

One of the words for beauty is *formositas*, from the adjective *formosus*, which means-well formed. This suggests that the beautiful is well formed, well shaped ; and because *forma* means not only figure and shape, but also appearance and 'look,' the beautiful is also the well appearing and the good looking.[324]

The third meaning of actuality in Aquinas is *act* or *action*. In a discussion concerning whether or not there is power in God, Aquinas describes actuality in the sense that:

> Now act is twofold; the first act which is a form, and the second act which is operation. Seemingly the word 'act' was first universally employed in the sense of operation, and then, secondly, transferred to indicate the form, inasmuch as the form is the principle and end of operation. [325]

Action completes the actuality of existence and form. Maurer uses another example from the arts to express this idea—that of a dancer: "a dancer asleep is still a dancer, but he is most completely a dancer when he actually dances."[326] Therefore if, as Aquinas teaches, beauty is located in actuality, then the fullness of beauty will be found in action. I shall demonstrate below that Tolkien's ideas of beauty are not located in abstract concepts, but in real things, and that is why, therefore, Maurer's examples of statuary and movement are apposite in understanding the dynamic procession of Tolkien's co-creative narrative in *The Ainulindalë*. As things come into existence, and take form, they cannot have the kind of being which *is* God: their *formositas actualitas* draws its existence from the source, and is sensually bound to the material world in both form and action. *Eä* as speech and reality is *the* actuality of beauty, insofar as it is apprehended by the senses. In being apprehended, it brings delight in those things which are good and beautiful, after God's own transcendent attributes of the Beautiful and the Good.

Developing these Thomist ideas of beauty in actuality, Maritain expounds these ideas in that form is above all the proper principle of intelligibility, the proper clarity of every thing. Every form is a vestige or a ray of the Creative Intelligence imprinted at the heart of created being. Conversely, every order and every proportion is the work of intelligence. Maritain, developing the aesthetics of Plotinus, states that "beauty is the splendour of the form on the proportioned parts of matter [. . .] a flashing of intelligence

---

324. Maurer, *About Beauty*, 8.
325. *QDP,* 1.1.Resp.
326. Maurer, *About Beauty*, 8.

on a matter intelligibly arranged."[327] Here he is developing Plotinus' *Ennead* 1.6.1, and a kind of democratic aesthetic principle, such that:

> Almost everyone declares that the symmetry of parts towards each other and towards a whole, with, besides, a certain charm of colour, constitutes the beauty recognized by the eye, that in visible things, as indeed in all else, universally, the beautiful thing is essentially symmetrical, patterned.[328]

This Platonic outlook is reinforced by Plotinus' maxim that "all the loveliness of this world comes by communion in Ideal-Form." It is clear that Maritain (and Tolkien) interpret Aquinas and his own sources in that the Platonic principle of participation in the divine, and its attendant idealism is never far from the forefront of dialogue with these classical ideas of beauty. These notions of participation are at the heart of all being, and located not so much in the abstract but in the particular.

Following Aquinas, Maritain identifies the beautiful as essentially delightful: it stirs desire and produces love, whereas truth as such only illuminates.[329] It is for her beauty that Wisdom is loved (Wis 8:2), and love in its turn produces ecstasy—a standing outside of oneself, of which the soul experiences a diminished form when it is seized by the beauty of the work of art, "and the fullness when it is absorbed, like the dew, by the beauty of God."[330] Aquinas, following Dionysius, constantly affirms that the beautiful and the good are the same thing in reality, and differ only in notion or idea.[331] It is so with the transcendentals—they are identified in the thing, and they differ in idea.[332] Strictly speaking, beauty is the radiance of all the transcendentals united: wherever there is anything existing there is being, form, and proportion; and wherever there is being there is beauty. Pseudo-Dionysius stretches this sense of participation in delight by suggesting that God's love causes the beauty of what he loves; whereas our love is caused by the beauty of what we love. In contemplating the abundance of God's goodness, the subject suffers this ecstasy of love in some way: God's love diffuses into all things a participation of His splendor. Just as within the hierarchy of being, "all comes from the universal Cause and Source of goodness. From this Source it was given to them to

---

327. Maritain, *Art and Scholasticism*, 25.
328. *Enneads*, 1.6.2.
329. Maritain, *Art and Scholasticism*, 26.
330. Ibid., 26.
331. *ST*, 1.5.4.ad1 (cf *Div Nom*, 4.704B).
332. *De Veritate*, 22.1.ad 12; *ST*, 1–2.27.1.ad 3.

exemplify the Good, to manifest that hidden goodness in themselves, so to speak."[333] For Pseudo-Dionysius, nothing—not even non-being—can exist without its prior causation in the absolute being of God:

> This—the One, the Good, the Beautiful—is in its uniqueness the cause of the multitudes of the good and beautiful. From it derives the existence of everything as beings, what they have in common and what differentiates them.[334]

Whilst stressing that there are higher and lower ranks of beings, and that there are similarities and dissimilarities, there is an essential interrelationship between them also, which transcends the "providence of the higher ranks": there is "an innate togetherness of everything." Pseudo-Dionysius continues by postulating a universal desire for the Beautiful and the Good: "Because of it and for its own sake, subordinate is returned to superior, equal keeps company with equal, superior turns providentially to subordinate."[335] It is here that we find Maritain's emphasis on desire, his participatory *id quod visum placet*, wherein "the Cause of all things loves all things in the superabundance of his goodness [. . .] the divine longing is Good seeking good for the sake of the good."[336] If there is here implied a necessary emanation in the creation of beings capable of knowing and reflecting that same beauty and goodness, then it is because the nature of these two concordant properties desire issue, such that they may have being themselves. As this superabundant life exists within the created order, then it is so because there is an analogous relationship here between lover and beloved, such that:

> This divine yearning brings ecstasy so that the lover belongs not to self but to the beloved. This is shown in the providence lavished by the superior on the subordinate. It is shown in the regard for one another demonstrated by those of equal status. And it is shown by the subordinates in their divine return towards what is higher.[337]

Things in creation are free in themselves to be what they are, but they are never free from the providential care, and yearning for its source in the Creator. In quoting St Paul, the writer strikingly admits to the intimacy of that Creator/creature co-existence:

---

333. *Div Nom*, 4.696B.
334. Ibid., 4.704B.
335. Ibid., 4.708A.
336. Ibid., 4.708A-B
337. Ibid., 4.712A.

This is why the great Paul, swept along by his yearning for God and seized of its ecstatic power, had this inspired word to say: "It is no longer I who live, but Christ who lives in me." Paul was truly a lover and, as he says, he was beside himself for God.[338]

It is important to stress, therefore, that for Maritain the beautiful is 'connatural' to man, and that which is proper to human art is seized in the sensible and through the sensible, and not separately from it.[339] The intuition of artistic beauty thus stands at the opposite extreme from the abstraction of scientific truth: it is through the very apprehension of the sense that the light of being penetrates the intelligence. Stressing the reality of being implied by a metaphysics of participation, Maritain describes the delight, "like a stag at the gushing spring, intelligence has nothing to do but drink; it drinks the clarity of being."[340] For Maritain, following Aquinas, beauty is not conformed to a certain ideal and immutable type—there are no Platonic forms beckoning the artist to construct and create in a predetermined form. Aquinas denotes beauty from the moment the shining of any form on a suitably proportioned matter succeeds in pleasing the intellect. That beauty is in some sense relative—not in any post-modern subjective sense—but relative to the proper nature and end of a thing, and to the formal conditions under which it is taken. However beautiful a thing may be, it can appear so to some and not to others because it is beautiful under certain aspects, which some discern and others do not. If this is so, it is so precisely because the Beautiful belongs to the order of the transcendentals—objects of thought which transcend every limit of genus or category; they do not allow of themselves to be enclosed within any class because they imbue everything and are to be found everywhere. Like the transcendental properties of the one, the true, and the good, so the beautiful is being itself considered from a certain aspect: it is a property of being. It is not an accident superadded to being: it adds to being only a relation of reason. Beauty is being considered as delighting, by the mere intuition of it, an intellectual nature. Thus everything is beautiful, just as everything is good, or at least in a certain relation.[341] Because created being has an ontological participation in God's super-essential being, then it is able to demonstrate those

---

338. Ibid. quoting Galatians 2:20. One can see in readings such as this how Eriugena later developed, in his own mystical way, a blurred distinction between the Creator/creature, in his own attempt to expound a mystical philosophy of being based upon a participatory ontology.

339. Maritain, *Art and Scholasticism*, 25.

340. Ibid.

341. Ibid., 30.

transcendental aspects, but only in an analogous manner.[342] Beauty, like being and other transcendentals, is essentially analogous: it is predicated for diverse reasons (*sub diversa ratione*) of the diverse subjects of which it is predicated. Each kind of being *is* in its own way, is *good* in its own way, is *beautiful* in its own way. Analogous concepts are predicated of God pre-eminently; in Him the perfection they designate exists in a 'formal eminent' manner, in the pure and infinite state. We meet them as a "dispersed and prismatized reflection of the countenance of God": thus beauty is one of the divine names.[343] God is beautiful through Himself and in Himself, beautiful absolutely, and in the extreme (*superpulcher*), "because in the perfectly simple unity of His nature there pre-exists in a super-excellent manner the fountain of all beauty."[344] It is from this absolute beauty (and goodness) that Maritain is able to own for himself that sense of participation that we see in both Pseudo-Dionysius and Aquinas: being beauty itself, God gives beauty to all created beings, according to their particular nature and rank, "and because He is the cause of all consonance and all brightness every form indeed [. . .] every light, is a certain irradiation proceeding from the first brightness [. . .] a participation in the divine brightness."[345]

2.5.5 Beauty as an Approach to Actualized Humanity

It is noteworthy that, as Maritain draws his analysis of beauty and participation to its climax, he introduces the musical term 'consonance.' In speaking of art generally, Robert Fallon notes that Maritain acknowledges the influence of the greater world on a poet's subjectivity. In focusing on the genesis of the artwork, the subject frequently adapts metaphors of music to describe poetic knowledge. For Maritain, music is the first step of artistic creation, "the very first effect, the sign, of poetic knowledge and poetic intuition, as soon as they exist in the soul—and even before the start of any operative exercise—is a kind of musical stir produced in the depths of the living springs

---

342. *ST*, 1.13.2. resp.1: "when we say, 'God is good,' the meaning is not, 'God is the cause of goodness,' or 'God is not evil'; but the meaning is, 'Whatever good we attribute to creatures, pre-exists in God,' and in a more excellent and higher way. Hence it does not follow that God is good, because He causes goodness; but rather, on the contrary, He causes goodness in things because He is good; according to what Augustine says (*De Doctr. Christ*. i, 32), 'Because He is good, we are.'"

343. Maritain, *Art and Scholasticism*, 30. *Div Nom*, 4.701C.

344. Ibid., 31.

345. Ibid., Here he quotes from Aquinas' *Commentary on the Divine Names, Lessons 5 and 6*: '*ex divina pulchritudine esse omnium*.'

in which they are borne."³⁴⁶ Here Fallon is quoting from Maritain's *Creative Intuition*,³⁴⁷ and highlights the fact that Maritain's influence in this respect spread far beyond the literary ambitions of the English Catholic *intelligentsia*. It is said that in France, his Neo-Thomism exerted "a strong but understated influence on Igor Stravinsky," though he had no ear for Stravinsky's 'impure' music which "like Wagner," tends to "dull or debauch the eye, the ear, or the mind."³⁴⁸ Here we may find parallels to Tolkien's own approach to musical consonance and dissonance. A footnote to this later edition of *Art and Scholasticism* alludes to the fact that Maritain had heard only the *Le Sacre du Printemps*—a work seething with dissonance and riotous disorder.³⁴⁹ As Stravinsky's work became more "disciplined," and as he was "renewing it in light," so Maritain became to recognize his later genius. If, in fact, Tolkien was aware of Maritain's variant views on the work of Stravinsky, then he may have been opportunistic in borrowing from this tension between writer and composer, and it would make some sense of the procession and evolution of the three musical themes in *The Ainulindalë*. After the initial order descends into chaos, struggle and discordance, the third theme brings with it things unseen—elves and men, to the delight of the Ainur. Fallon further notes that it was because of Stravinsky's turn to a more neoclassical style between 1920 and 1923, that Maritain was able to acknowledge Stravinsky's more mature craft, and this would have appealed to Maritain's "anti-art-for-art's-sake aesthetics."³⁵⁰ Despite the relationship becoming sour, Stravinsky's famous Norton Lectures delivered at Harvard University in 1941 refer several times to Maritain, and borrowed his neo-Thomist definition of a composer as a medieval artisan who orders and disciplines his craft.³⁵¹

In Tolkien's own metaphysics of music, we have observed a teleological aesthetic in its various forms. As the One (Eru) exerts his dominance on the themes, the development is towards a consonant beauty, which demonstrates the Thomistic integrity, proportion, and clarity in form. This in turn brings forth the 'issue' in creation, of which Pseudo-Dionysius speaks: the beloved of the absolute lover, and their appearing brings both delight and wonder amongst the Ainur. If all this discussion of artistic and musical abstraction appears to deflect from Tolkien's co-creative project, then

---

346. Fallon, "Maritain's Poetic Knowledge," 286–87.

347. Maritain, *Creative Intuition*, 300.

348. Fallon, "Maritain's Poetic Knowledge," 288; Maritain, *Art and Scholasticism*, 60.

349. Fallon, "Maritain's Poetic Knowledge," 288.

350. Ibid., 289.

351. Ibid., 290.

we find that personal sense of wonder in his own devotion to the Blessed Virgin Mary. For Tolkien, his admission that the *LOTR* is "a fundamentally religious and Catholic work" is preceded by a curious statement on his approach to aesthetics: "your references to Our Lady, upon which all my own small perception of beauty both in majesty and simplicity is founded."[352] This letter of the 2nd December 1953 is addressed to his good friend Fr Robert Murray SJ, who read and commented on many typescripts of *LOTR*, and there is a note appended to the letter that Fr Murray was impressed with a "strong sense of a positive compatibility with the order of grace, and compared the image of Galadriel to that of the Virgin Mary." Tolkien was by 1958 aware of, and had a profound appreciation for, the newly stated dogma on Mary's *Assumptio*, and the *Munificentissimus Deus* of Pope Pius XII (1950). In a note added to an unsent letter to Rhona Beare, dated 14th October 1958 (above), Tolkien demonstrates his keen understanding of the dogmatic statement when discussing the incorruption of the elves:

> The Assumption of Mary, the only *unfallen* person, may be regarded as in some ways a simple regaining of unfallen grace and liberty; she asked to be received, and was, having no further function on Earth. Though, of course, even if *unfallen* she was not 'pre-Fall.' Her destiny (in which she had cooperated) was far higher than that of any 'Man' would have been, had the fall not occurred.[353]

Tolkien's own reflection on the assumption relates to original and restored states of grace, and Mary's role in the redemption of fallen humanity. Her unique vocation required that state of grace as if the fall had not happened—in her singular particularity. This may be said to be a logical outworking of the dogma relating to her immaculate conception, and that despite the fall of the mass of humanity, she was spared both physical and moral corruption. Tolkien continues:

> It was also unthinkable that her body, the immediate source of Our Lord's (without other physical intermediary) should have been disintegrated, or 'corrupted,' nor could it surely be long separated from him after the Ascension.

The incarnation event required a free agent in terms of her decisive *fiat*, and that her body be free of the corrupting elements associated with the fall. Small wonder that in the Easter Vigil's joyfully sung *Exsultet* we encounter the phrase, "Our birth would have been no gain, had we not been

---

352. Carpenter, *Letters*, 172.
353. Ibid., 286.

redeemed," immediately juxtaposed with the *O felix culpa*—"O happy fault that earned so great, so glorious a redeemer!"[354] If all created being displays analogously the beauty and goodness of its primary cause, then how so much more is the human race engraced with these redeemed qualities, because the Beautiful and the Good has touched the earth in his own particularity via the incarnation event.

If Tolkien's aesthetics of beauty are focused upon a created being, then the Aristotelian principle of 'like effects resembling like causes' brings into light the true teleological and analogical human nature without any imperfection. In his discussion on whether or not we should ascribe goodness to God, Aquinas expounds the Dionysian text (above), such that:

> Now everything seeks after its own perfection; and the perfection and form of an effect consist in a certain likeness to the agent, since every agent makes its like; and hence the agent itself is desirable and has the nature of good. For the very thing which is desirable in it is the participation of its likeness. Therefore, since God is the first effective cause of all things, it is manifest that the aspect of good and of desirableness belong to Him; and hence Dionysius (Div. Nom. iv) attributes good to God as to the first efficient cause, saying that, God is called good "as by Whom all things subsist."[355]

The key to understanding Aquinas here is not to equate 'efficient cause' with the likeness of the effect in the sense that a builder is the same essence and form as the building he makes. What Aquinas is saying about causation is that a like effect has a familial resemblance to its efficient cause, in so far as the cause acts upon and within the effect: God is an agent expressing himself in something other that himself, causing things to become other than he is. In this sense, "we are his workmanship, created in Christ Jesus for good works,"[356] and it is worth repeating here the point I made at the beginning of this section, that for Maritain, art stands outside the human sphere "as it has an end, rules and values, which are not those of man, but those of the work to be produced." There is for art but one law, "the exigencies and the good of the work."[357] In this Pauline sense, we are created in Christ as intrinsically

---

354. *Roman Missal*, 389.

355. *ST*, 1.6.1 resp.

356. Ephesians 2:10. The *Jerusalem Bible* renders the phrase beginning *autou gar esmen poiēma* as, "we are God's work of art, created in Christ Jesus to live the good life as from the beginning we were meant to live it."

357. Maritain, *Art and Scholasticism*, 9.

good free and rational creatures, independent of, but participating in God's superessential goodness.

Brian Davies explains this succinctly:

> Insofar as creatures aim and attain to what is desirable for them, they reflect what God is as bringing it about that they do so, since he is the source of all that they are and all that they succeed in being. The idea here is that the good at which creatures aim and sometime obtain is in God as their maker before it is in them.[358]

As the Creator of all creatures, God accounts for all the perfections that they have and aim for, and that these reflect him as their maker. When Tolkien, therefore, sees beauty in the Blessed Virgin Mary he does so in the Neo-Thomist sense that she is also good (after God), and in being Beauty she reflects that integrity, proportion, and clarity which is analogous to God whom Dionysius names the Beautiful. At her life's completion, she is also in that state of actuality which is the realization of her full potentiality as a human being. In her assumption she is now completely human in her unique existence, and also in her unique proximity to the Trinity.

We cannot call God Beautiful because we see beauty in a thing, but we can name God as such precisely because God has those transcendent qualities as part of his superessential being, and that which is desirable in humans is but a participation in those self-same superabundant attributes as they exist in God. This same sense of wonder can be read out of the Ainur's response to their first experience of the children of Ilúvatar, and Aulë's co-creative work in bringing forth the dwarves. Where there was participation in the music, there is revealed beauty in both the vision and reality of Middle-earth. In their wonder, the Ainur do not burst forth into psalmodic praise of God, but in recognizing the super-essential beauty in created being 'other' than God, they wonder in its being precisely because it is an issue of the beauty which God is and has, in and of himself. The mind has truly become reality: it is actualized in real things, issued from the hidden mind and desires of God. They exist, have form, and are a result of some action.

---

358. Davies, *Aquinas on God and Evil*, 59–60.

I am an old man who has experienced much.
I have been a man of action and have fought for my King
and country at sea.
I have also read books and studied and
pondered and tried to fathom eternal truth.
Much good has been shown me and much evil,
and the good has never been perfect. There is
always some flaw in it, some
defect, some imperfection in the divine
image, some fault in the angelic song,
some stammer in the divine speech. So that the
Devil still has something to do with
every human consignment to this planet of earth.[1]

---

1. Herbert, *Operas of Benjamin Britten*, 183.

3

The Concept of Life as 'Being and Gift' in Tolkien's Literary Corpus

3.1 Towards a Mythology for England

The words above are taken from the *Prologue* of E. M. Forster's libretto for Benjamin Britten's opera *Billy Budd*: a sea tale of adventure, betrayal, and redemption. Stories of literary heroism and adversity, like Herman Melville's own *Billy Budd*, pervade through the canon of boys' own novels, and create within the English psyche a worldview which is accessible both to the immediate physical senses, and yet suggests an altogether transcendent quality also. What at first glance appears to be rooted in the experience of flawed humans on a quest is, at the less ephemeral level, a searching for, and aiming toward, the heart of philosophy's greatest questions. Like the subject of Forster's libretto, Tolkien was an old man by the time he had published his most famous works—*The Lord of the Rings* Trilogy, but had begun his literary career, and his Middle-earth writings, as a young man recovering from his experiences of the First World War. These early manuscripts, now published posthumously, illuminate with skilful precision the development of his earliest works, and arguably the project that he most desired to publish in his own lifetime—*The Silmarillion*. In this developed and evolved 'cosmo-genesis' we read the origins of Tolkien's sub-creation, with features strikingly similar with those mature reflections above. However, the literary origins of this (posthumous) work do not begin chronologically with a creation myth, but with two tales: *The Fall of Gondolin* and *The Tale of Tinúviel*.[1] It is in the latter that I propose to focus on a key philosophical theme, that of 'being and gift' within the context of Tolkien's broader literary and aesthetic oeuvre. Tolkien, whilst he focuses on general conditions of mortality/immortality, is also aware of the particularity of individual freedom when its

---

1. Carpenter, *Biography*, 100, 105; Shippey, *Road to Middle Earth*, 284.

'virtue' is enfolded within a *telos* which is incorporeally boundless, and has unlimited potential in its return.

3.1.1 *The Tale of Tinúviel*: A Real 'Life Drama'

The focal point of this investigation is *The Tale of Tinúviel*, a story which is integral to *The Silmarillion*, and one which evolved up to and beyond Tolkien's death.[2] The gravestone of Tolkien, alongside that of his wife Edith, bear the names of the two lovers—Beren and Lúthien—and have given rise to much speculation as to the origins of the tale.[3] A synopsis of the *Tale* as it appears in *The Silmarillion* may be read in Appendix B. The theme of dangerous love and the inter-marriage of elf and human is a thread woven at significant points in his works, and therefore needs special attention if we are to fully understand what is meant by life as 'being and gift' within Tolkien's wider project.

One place where Tolkien makes explicit the metaphysical foundation of myth and faërie is in his unfinished and little-known time travel fantasy, *The Notion Club Papers*. Here we find an allusion to a broadly Aristotelian and hierarchical understanding of reality, and hence of the different sciences responsible for studying that reality. When one interlocutor asks what is the source or soil of "ancient accounts, legends, myths, about the far past, about the origins of kings, laws, and the fundamental crafts" if these accounts are to be something more that "wholly inventions" or "mere fiction," the response is a sober reply:

> In Being, I think I should say [. . .] and in human Being; and coming down the scale, in the springs of History and in the designs of Geography—I mean, well, in the pattern of our world as it uniquely is, and the events in it as seen from a distance.[4]

---

2. This is the title of the first edition of the narrative, and has existed in many forms until the final (posthumously) published draft in *The Silmarillion* (1977): simply, *Of Beren and Luthien*. I use this deliberately, as it marks the origin of the tale's long history, and represents also its origin in Tolkien's immediate context: that of recovering from injuries and sickness arising out of his participation in the Battle of the Somme. The themes of evil, darkness, recovery, change and death are consonant with his life in this period.

3. Stevens, "Catastrophe to Euchatastrophe," 119–32.

4. Tolkien, *Sauron Defeated*, 227. This idea of a great chain of being can be traced to Plato's division of the world into the Forms, which are full beings, and sensible things, which are imitations of the Forms and are both being and not being. Aristotle's teleology recognized a perfect being, and he also arranges all animals by a single natural scale according to their physical properties and the degree of perfection of their souls.

It is inconceivable that Tolkien would have been unaware of the idea of the *scala naturae*—the great chain of being—a concept derived from Plato and Aristotle, and developed fully in Neoplatonism. It details a strict, religious hierarchical structure of all matter and life, believed to have been decreed by God. The chain starts from God and progresses downward to angels, demons (fallen/renegade angels), stars, moons, kings, princes, nobles, men, wild animals, domesticated animals, trees, other plants, precious stones, precious metals, and other minerals. Mythology then, has its roots in the fertile soil of metaphysics, in a certain intuition of the being of things, and the same certainly holds true of Tolkien's own mythology. Tolkien alludes to this same hierarchy, or 'scale of being,' and its 'patterns of being' in a letter to Camilla Unwin—the daughter of his publisher. Answering her question as to the purpose of life, he replies:

> As for 'other things' their value resides in themselves: they ARE, they would even exist if we did not. [. . .] If we go up the scale of beings to 'other living things,' such as, say, some small plant, it presents shape and organization: a 'pattern' recognizable (with variation) in its kin and offspring [. . .] and since recognizable 'pattern' suggests design, [human curiosity] may proceed to WHY? But WHY in this sense, implying reasons and motives, can only refer to a MIND.[5]

Tolkien's line of reasoning here is explicitly teleological, as he is directly pointing to an intelligent designer—a Creator—who imputes both organization and purpose into created being. He makes explicit reference to an analogical function, similar to Aquinas' analogy of attribution that,

> Only a MIND can have purposes in any way or degree akin to human purposes. [. . .] Is there a God, a Creator-Designer, a Mind to which our minds are akin (being derived from it) so that It is intelligible to us in part.[6]

Things exist for Tolkien only because of their gratuity—or giftedness—from that Mind to which he corresponds to God who is ultimately ineffable. To the larger questions of philosophy he could only answer in the negative, "because that requires a complete knowledge of God, which is unattainable. If we ask why God included us in his Design, we can really say no more than because He Did."[7] Flieger observed that from one vantage point the

---

5. Carpenter, *Letters*, 399. This is dated the 20th May 1969.

6. Ibid. See also *ST* 1.13.5 and 1.13.10 on the univocal and equivocal use of language, as they refer to the attributes of God and humanity.

7. Carpenter, *Letters*, 400.

whole of Tolkien's *Silmarillion* represents an "exploration of the implications and ramifications of the one word *Eä*," the Elvish word meaning either the indicative 'it is,' or the imperative 'let it be'—the word Ilúvatar speaks when he at last brings the physical world into being.[8] I shall demonstrate in section 3.4.1 that this Aristotelian-Thomist exposition of *being* is linked to this sense of hierarchy and, more significantly, participation in the Platonic sense of the 'ground of being,' which is God's own nature.

3.1.2 Tolkien's Emerging Myth in a Multi-Layered World

Verlyn Flieger's description of Tolkien's *mythos* as "its very own complex manuscript tradition of multiple and overlapping story variants" is reflected in the repeated themes and character portrayals across the broad canvas of his entire corpus.[9] She poses the question, whether or not *The Tale of Tinúviel* is to be compared or linked to tales of a similar genre, such as that of Guinevere and Lancelot, Tristan and Isolde.[10] *The Tale of Tinúviel* has no social restriction or illicit nature. Stevens speculates that it is Ovid's *Metamorphoses*, and the lovers Pyramus and Thisbe that are the origin of the 'doomed' lovers. Whilst this hypothesis has some merit, there is no documentary evidence to verify the case. Their fate was to be in the wrong place at the wrong time, whereas Beren and Lúthien appear to be ensnared in a fate that was woven by many. Beren himself is enmeshed in a series of oaths and loyalties. He is given aid by King Finrod Felagund because of an oath that Finrod made with Beren's father, Barahir. This aid in turn forces Finrod to leave his kingdom because of the wrath of the sons of Fëanor, who are bound up with their own father's oaths to regain the Silmarils that results in bringing the 'Doom of Mandos' upon them. This doom also ensnares Thingol when he gives Beren the quest of bringing back a Silmaril from the crown of Morgoth. Thus, although Beren and Lúthien are, to some extent, trapped by events beyond their control, these circumstances were conceived by the (free) choices made by the inhabitants of Middle-earth, "rather than some 'doom' apparently randomly or otherwise distantly handed down by omniscient gods."[11] These fates are as yet uncertain, as Huan the dog advises Beren.[12] Unlike the relentless chain of events in Pyramus and Thisbe, there are moments in the lives of

---

8. Flieger, *Splintered Light*, 59.
9. Flieger, "Matter of Britain," 55.
10. Ibid., 53.
11. Stevens, "Catastrophe to Euchatastrophe," 127.
12. Tolkien, *Silmarillion*, 215.

Beren and Luthien in which more than one outcome may be achieved. The 'doom' is thus not a form of predestination or hard-deterministic fate, but in part subject to the choices and decisions of others.

The most likely origin of this tale lies in Tolkien's own life, and love of Edith, who eventually became his wife.[13] As a young officer serving on the home-front during the First World War, when he could get leave Edith would engage a babysitter, and they would take long walks in the woods; a favorite spot being a glade near Roos (Yorkshire), with an undergrowth of hemlock: "Her hair was raven, her skin clear, her eyes bright, and she could sing—and dance."[14] And, like the description of Beren's first 'chance' meeting with Lúthien Tinúviel, she danced also.[15] Carpenter notes that of all his 'tales' Tolkien loved this one especially, not least because of the association with his own wife. There is a sense of despair in a letter to his son, Michael, dated 1972: "I met the Tinúviel of my own personal 'romance' with her long dark hair, her face and starry eyes, and beautiful voice. [. . .] But now she has gone before Beren, leaving him indeed one-handed, but he has no power to move the inexorable Mandos, and there [. . .] is no Land of the Dead that Live."[16] In a letter later that year to his other son, Christopher, he declares that "I never called Edith 'Lúthien'—but she was the source of the story that in time became the chief part of The Silmarillion."[17] In this, he reveals that he expresses himself best "about things deepest felt in tales and myths," rather than in other forms of discourse.

The Tale of Tinúviel is preceded by the saga of Túrin and the Fall of Gondolin, but occupies a central place in his *legendarium*, as it speaks not only of the victory of the elves over Morgoth from within his own stronghold, and the recovery of a single Silmaril, but also it hints at, and develops his own philosophical ideas of an emergent anthropology of Middle-earth: *that* things are, and *what* things are. Tolkien himself attests to the central place of this tale amongst his wider and later works, in that *The Lord of the Rings* is but a sequel to the *Tale of Tinúviel*.[18] The tale has a complex

13. In this I concur entirely with Richard West, in his "Real World Myth," 259–67.
14. Carpenter, *Biography*, 104–5.
15. Tolkien, *Silmarillion*, 198.
16. Carpenter, *Letters*, 417.

17. Ibid., 420. It was in this letter that Tolkien made clear how he wished the name 'Lúthien' to appear on her grave stone. This is adduced elsewhere in a letter (No.165) to the Houghton Mifflin Company in 1955 (exact date unclear), 221: "she was (and knew she was) my Lúthien."

18. Carpenter, *Letters*, 180: "The tale of Beren and Lúthien [. . .] is constantly referred to, since as Sam [Gamgee] points out this history [LOTR] is only a further continuation of it."

history, and has been both expanded and contracted in form.[19] It features in all volumes of the posthumously published *The History of Middle-earth*. In describing its literary genre, Tolkien defines it, "as such the story is [...] heroic-fairy-romance, receivable in itself with only a general vague knowledge of the background."[20] It stands alone, and as such provides a crucial backdrop to all that follows.

The intermarriage of elves and men is a recurring theme in Tolkien's works, though Beren is originally an elf (gnome). Yet after a number of incarnations in the succeeding editions, he reappears as a mortal (man). Lúthien is always an (immortal) elf, and their dangerous liaison is echoed in other characters: Thingol, Lord amongst the Eldar, is a lesser being than Melian, who is a Maia: a quasi-angelic being (like Gandalf and Sauron); Aragorn, a human, and Arwen, an elf. What is interesting in the latter pair is that they are both descended from Beren and Lúthien. Arwen was, in point of fact, a late addition to the cast of characters in *The Lord of the Rings*, and all references to her are what Tolkien called "constant rewriting backwards."[21] Within this tale are interwoven features of other myths and stories, which Tolkien would have known. For example, both Lúthien and *Rapunzel* escaped captivity by their use of unnaturally long hair; like the *Sleeping Beauty*, Lúthien charged the drinks of her captors with a sleeping draught; as in the case of *The Twelve Dancing Princesses*, Lúthien escapes by way of an invisibility cloak, reminiscent in principle to the Tarnhelm in Wagner's Ring Cycle, and a feature also of the Harry Potter novels. The biting off of Beren's hand by the wolf Carcharoth, is a clear reference to the *Prose Edda*.[22] Tolkien here is freely borrowing from a variety of traditions, and "these tastes and whiffs and echoes resonating from other mythologies only add to the appropriateness of their setting in Tolkien's own mosaic. His myth seems like the real thing."[23] The melding of fictional and inter-textual sources gives the whole a feeling of reality: Tolkien's commentary on the *Old English Exodus* demonstrates that this literary 'borrowing' was epidemic.

---

19. Shippey, *Road to Middle Earth*, 292–96; 357–58, gives a complete and detailed analysis of the composition of the tale, and its evolution from 1917 up to the end of Tolkien's life.

20. Carpenter, *Letters*, 149.

21. Ibid., 258.

22. 'Gylfaginning' chapter 25, in Sturluson, *Prose Edda*, 35–36. Shippey, *Road to Middle Earth*, 193–94, claims that the hunting of the great wolf recalls the chase of the boar Twrch Trwyth in the Welsh *Mabinogion*.

23. West, "Real World Myth," 265.

3.1.3 Life and Being in the Tale of Beren and Lúthien

Given the long and complex history of the tale, I have utilized the final text in *The Silmarillion*, but where it departs significantly from previous versions—so far as it pertains to this investigation—then my theme will develop accordingly.

Andrew Louth explains how, before the developments of late medieval views on the physical body, the human body is a microcosm reflecting in itself a cosmic story, whereas it later became seen as an interpreter of human inwardness.[24] In this analysis, Louth cites the use of Plato's *Timaeus* in that the cosmos is understood as an analogy in the human person: the human person is a copy, reflection, image of the cosmos, which is a living creature endowed with soul and reason.[25] The cosmos is seen as a great body: the human being as a little body, and both owe their life and form to the indwelling soul and reason. Similarly different views were attached to how creation or physical nature was viewed, as medieval cosmology formed: the later period, instead of *integrating* the Other, was objectified *in relation* to the Other, and is linked to the development of Eucharistic theology and doctrine in the late medieval period. The linguistic changes objectified the *Corpus Christi* or *corpus verum*, whereby the Body of Christ is no longer the Church realized as a worshipping community. The consecrated host instead becomes an object of devotion and adoration in itself. Louth sees in this subtle but significant dislocation of focus, a shrinking or collapse from the notion of sacred space. The body on a cosmic scale becomes 'The Body' (of Christ) in a reduced scale (or volume).[26] This cosmic understanding of human anthropology in Tolkien's *legendarium* has its origins in a possible use of the works of John Scotus Eriugena, and that human nature in its participation in the divine becomes some thing, and yet still retains an almost divine aspect when viewed from eternity. Eriugena, perhaps more than any other Christian Neoplatonist scholar, integrates the objectified body with the nature of God's own being, via what are the divine energies or theophanies.

Tolkien's creation myth in *The Silmarillion* shows how layers of both history and spiritual presence intermingle with the physical scenery and subject in Tolkien's textual "spots of time."[27] The Earth as a whole is imbibed with that same numinosity as might be envisaged by man-made burial mounds being portals for the Otherworld in pre-Christian narrative. We

---

24. Louth, "The Body," 129.
25. Ibid., 112 and *Timaeus* 30B.
26. Ibid., 124. See also Siewers, *Strange Beauty*, 16–19.
27. Ibid., 146.

now know, for example, that Tolkien regularly visited ancient sites in the wider Oxfordshire countryside, such as Wayland's Smithy.[28] Here it is said that the Neolithic long-barrow was named after the smith-spirit *Weland*, who inspired the work of smiths, whose own craft was imbued with magic. King Alfred refers to it, and when Beowulf boasts of the fine mail coat he is wearing, he remarks at Line 453–55 that "if the battle takes me, send back this breast-webbing that Weland fashioned and Hrethgel gave me, to Lord Hygelac. Fate goes ever as fate must."[29] There is a numinous and transcendent nature about the objects in this world, but even with the magical charm of this mail coat, it could not hold back the fate of Beowulf.[30] Earth becomes more powerfully alive than metaphor for the multidimensional life of an integrated spirit and body. Chapter 4 provides an exposition of these themes of fluid numinosity in terms of Eriuganean dialectic, and Eriugena gives a definition when seeking to locate some 'thing' in its own proper terminology: "place is nothing else but the boundary by which each thing is enclosed within fixed terms." He states that there are many kinds of places, and even that there are incorporeal places which bound incorporeal things. The boundary, limit or form of all rational and intellectual spirits is the Word of God; the boundary of irrational spirit is sensible things; the boundary of bodies are the four elements. He goes further, in that "place is constituted in the definitions of things that can be defined."[31] The definitions of all things are contained in the knowledge *(scientia)* of the liberal arts, therefore the liberal arts are the places of things which can be defined. Eriugena concludes that place is in the mind, since the arts are in the mind. His purpose is clear: he is arguing in respect of place what Augustine and Plotinus hold in respect of time, namely, that it exists in the mind, and through it the mind measures things. Thus Eriugena now rejects as foolish those who say that earth is the place of animals, water is the place of fish, air is the place of birds and ether is the place of the planets. The true place of everything is its essential definition, which is changeless, and which as *logos* or 'rationale' is preserved in the mind, but whose mind? Clearly Eriugena means the human mind, since he has just been discussing the liberal arts as containing the definitions of all things. The human mind has the power to define, hence all things which it defines are set in their proper place. It can be inferred that, if the true place of everything is its essential definition and is changeless, and the human mind has the power to define, then whatever a thing is—as it presents itself

---

28. Carpenter, *Biography*, 163.
29. Heaney, *Beowulf*, 31.
30. Bates, *The Real Middle Earth*, 218.
31. Eriugena, *Periphyseon*, 1.474b.

to us phenomenally—is governed by the mind and, as Eriugena postulates, the mind creates the body. Of course, the human mind, since it transcends definition and place, cannot define itself, and hence it is located in no place. God, the angels and human minds all escape being defined and hence none of these is in a place. Human nature itself is without place, and indeed has a kind of omnipresence, similar to that of God. In this respect, the body can/could be what the mind desires it to be. Only when it truly *is*, when it is manifest in materiality, can it be assigned a particular place. In terms of place, the deification of finitude is evident at key points in Tolkien's myth. When the messengers of Manwë tell the Numenoreans, "it is not the land of Manwë that makes its people deathless, but the Deathless that dwell therein have hallowed the land."[32] True nature is not a 'what,' but a 'whom' in early Christian cosmology, as in Middle-earth.[33]

That Beren/Lúthien are mortal/immortal is a key factor in the narrative, and their intermarriage would be improper and discouraged, and yet Tolkien sets up an almost insurmountable sequence of events for Beren in which to win his Lúthien.[34] For Beren, the quest to retrieve a single Silmaril would cost him both a hand and later his life, and yet in the deed we see an extraordinary freedom exercised at a number of levels (or layers): First, Beren, whilst bound by his past oaths, upon discovering Lúthien Tinúviel dancing and singing in the woods, was free to move undetected in the 'Hidden Kingdom' of Doriath. Secondly, despite his corporeal particularity, he and Lúthien were not limited to their 'forms': they were shapeshifters. They became like orcs; Sauron (a Maia) took the shape of a werewolf, then serpent, then vampire; Huan (the dog) and Lúthien become giant fell bats; before the gaze of Morgoth Lúthien was 'stripped of her disguise.'[35] Thirdly, and most significantly, the concept of 'doom' as it presents itself to Tolkien is introduced. In *The Tale of Tinúviel* it is used fifteen times, even of the dog—Huan. In all these instances it has a sense of 'proper place' or 'order,' marked by a governing higher power. The degree of freedom within the plenitude of order is a key debate within the greater theme. Fourthly, the undoubted greatest 'degree of freedom,' exercised by deliberate will, is the giving up of immortality by Lúthien upon the death of Beren. It is a singularly moving narrative, whereby the elf-maiden sang before Mandos and gained one of two choices: to depart Middle-earth for Valinor, where she could dwell forever free from her grief, but eternally separated from Beren; or to return to

---

32. Tolkien, *Silmarillion*, 317.
33. Siewers, *Cosmic-Christian Ecology*, 148.
34. Tolkien, *Silmarillion*, 201.
35. Ibid., 204, 210.

Middle-earth with Beren, but as a mortal. She freely chose the latter 'doom,' thus sealing her own fate, and yet became the "forerunner of many in whom the Eldar yet see."[36] The progeny of Beren and Lúthien extend through to the Third age in the tale of Aragorn and Arwen, whose own fate is mirrored in the Appendix to *The Lord of the Rings*.

Given the particularity of the Two Kindreds—elves and men, amidst the Vala (Morgoth/Melkor), Maiar (Sauron), wolf, dog, etc., Tolkien takes great pains to weave a tale wherein there is a constant dialectic between what is real and proper, and what is 'assumed' in a quasi semi-permanent form, but only for a particular purpose and with an equally specific act of the will. The phenomenon of shapeshifting in this *Tale* is one striking example of this quasi semi-permanent form. Nothing happens here by chance, but by rational deliberation. The whole, constituted of the collective entities, appear uncertain as to their 'outward' and corporeal nature: "in Middle-earth, this back-and-forth lends a sense of permanent instability to human constructions and objectifications of nature."[37] This reaches a zenith in the final transformation of Lúthien to a mortal, and the restoration/resurrection of Beren, to dwell once again upon Middle-earth. There is no *prima facie* resolution in an Eastern patristic hope for *deification*, but given that, nature in its essential and ontological participation in the Creator as first principle, is 'hallowed' and deified in its return, beyond what it had in its *exitus*.[38]

Tolkien is seen repeatedly using borrowed traditions in both the construction and subject development of his *legendarium*, and one such borrowed tradition became a personal and professional obsession of Tolkien, and that was the Anglo-Saxon poem *Beowulf*. He unashamedly utilized key ideas from this tale as it emerged out of Europe's pagan past, into an ordered but pre-modern world. Tolkien's own reading of the poem is well documented, and his personal store of notes and unpublished sketches provide a valuable source in which to further develop my argument.

3.2 Beowulf as an Anglo-Saxon Paradigm of Myth-as-Truth

There is insufficient scope here to fully explore the totality of this significant Christian poem, and its influence on Tolkien's self-understanding.

---

36. Ibid., 224–25.
37. Siewers, *Cosmic-Christian Ecology*, 146.
38. This is assessed in relation to Eriugena's philosophy of being in sections 4.1.7 and 4.1.8.

Therefore, I shall focus this investigation on the poem's *Exordium*, lines 1–64, and how it relates to the whole work in relation to the nature of life as 'being and gift' as it is lived out within the proximity of a growing sense of Christian hope—both in life and death. For Tolkien, this opening passage is unique, and "nothing exactly parallel to the genealogy and setting of the Beowulf *Exordium* can be found elsewhere," and as such it deserves special consideration.[39] Tolkien's extant published works (chiefly his *Beowulf: The Monsters and the Critics* essay, and *Old English Exodus* commentary and notes) are a key source in helping us to develop and digest his 'Northern' sense of 'being and gift.' Set alongside his extensive unpublished works, I have been able to piece together both a 're-formed' pagan outlook, juxtaposed with an emergent Neoplatonic Christian one.

In creating such an opening to the poem, "it is legitimate to suspect at least that the poet has been at work here [. . .] using and reshaping old material to his special purpose."[40] In the commentary of his posthumously published *Old English Exodus,* Tolkien speaks of the Exodus narrative as transcending a "mere tale of victory."[41] It is at once a historical poem about events of extreme importance, but it is also an allegory about the soul, or the Church of militant souls, "marching under the hand of God, pursued by the powers of darkness, until it attains to the promised land of Heaven."[42] Tolkien was adamant that he never stooped to allegory as a literary form, but he did borrow from others. He openly acknowledges this to be an acceptable practice in Old and Middle English literature, where work was borrowed almost as if it were a common property:

> there was a traditional style, vocabulary, and phraseology, much less modified by the individual [. . .] that was not in fact not felt any worse for being traditional.[43]

It would appear that upon this 'common fund,' not only words but phrases also might draw in common: "they would not hesitate to do so—to breathe the common air of fine speech and solemn utterance was no more plagiarism than to use the formulae of everyday courtesy."[44] Here is a clear justification, written in the 1930s and 1940s, of a man whose own sources draw from that 'common air,' and so it is unsurprising that he displayed at the

---

39. *Bodleian SC-MSS* A31 folio13/1.
40. Ibid.
41. Tolkien, *Old English Exodus*, 33.
42. Ibid.
43. Ibid., 34.
44. Ibid., 35.

same time a striking dependence and debt to the Old and Middle English traditions of Northern Europe.

Like the *Old English Exodus*, therefore, the period in which *Beowulf* was written and edited was characterized by literature possessing a narrow range, and "less diversified stock and themes" than later ages.[45] Instead one is left with the challenge of recapturing the "deep pondering and profound feeling that they gave to such as they possessed."[46] This is precisely how literary critics of Tolkien assess his whole project (especially Shippey and Siewers): by using the overlay manuscripts of antiquity, he creates a world which speaks and overlaps with our world. As we move beyond the first instances of written sources, we can then embrace a literary legacy which is free from the encumbrances of philological and scientific analysis, and thus free our minds to enter that world. There is an inexorable exchange of being across these layers of myth/reality in which we can explore the true natures and purpose of our own existence.

3.2.1 Life and Being in the Twilight of European Paganism

Tolkien's unpublished *Lectures and Notes Relating to Beowulf* (dated October 1933) note that his university studies were intended primarily for specialists, or for the student who "is presumed to possess sufficient enthusiasm to carry them over the bogs and arid places."[47] In terms of literary invention, Tolkien's professional reading of *Beowulf* betrays his own melding of legend and tradition, suggesting how it may inform and influence his own ideas of sub-creation. A case in mind is the founder of the House now presided over by King Hrothgar: the legendary figure *Scyld Scefing* becomes, in line 4 of the poem, *Shield Sheafson*. Tolkien notes curiously that "legends are not logical" and that "Scyld has an unhistorical look," though "there can be no doubt that a real Danish dynasty once existed [...] yet he was sufficiently remote from the days of written history."[48] The first historical name in that family is that of *Healfdeane*: "Scyld was a mere eponym, a fiction of dynastic historians and alliterative poets."[49] As the name moves to England, and *Beowulf* was written in England,[50]

---

45. Tolkien, *Monsters*, 10.
46. Ibid.
47. Bodleian SC-MSS A31 folio5/1.
48. Ibid., folio10.
49. Ibid.
50. Heaney, *Beowulf*, x.

> Scyld gets mixed up with mythology much more poetic and suggestive, but much more difficult to unravel—leading in fact far far away into the forgotten realms of imagination and belief.[51]

This ambiguity suited Tolkien as a translator, interpreter and writer of fantasy. The less that we are able to locate key characters in time and space, then the more these characters and their topology become located in myth. As such, the layered texts of historical truth and mythical usage can become a foil for the writer of fantasy, using the substance of a genre such as *Beowulf*, and adapting its essential themes for his own use. Tolkien's professional and personal interest in *Beowulf* are therefore *the* keys to unlocking his method of writing fantasy from these multi-layered texts and borrowed traditions, and how they portrayed a worldview with which he was confronted throughout his life.

In line 26 *Scyld/Shield* dies, "when his time came, and he crossed over into the Lord's keeping."[52] Tolkien notes that this "allotted hour" was "perhaps a vestige of his originally divine or miraculous nature," but "in the legend as it is shaped in Beowulf is Christianized," and is a clear allusion to his death.[53] Tolkien further notes that in describing the rich and fitting manner of his sea-burial, "in the Germanic manner, that somebody was expected to receive the cargo, whether in this world or the realm of shadows [. . .] that cargo came to strange harbours men have never seen."[54] Things and people have an Otherworld transcendent quality, as the passage from life to death is to move beyond the phenomenal to the noumenal, to the realm of mystery and hope, but not beyond the providence of God (line 27). Tolkien's ideas of things 'coming into being' is dependent on the *Beowulf* text here: there is a dislocation at the end of the *Exordium*, where legend (*Scyld*) becomes reality and located in space/time:

> The miraculous house—already partly humanized by the dynastic setting and the expression 'on Frēan wāere'—becomes a kingly line, if one of noble and heroic structure.[55]

---

51. *Bodleian SC-MSS* A31 folio11.

52. Ibid., folio12/2. There is a similar allusion to this use of 'crossing' at the end of the poem *Pearl*, where the father sought to cross the river to join his daughter (see below).

53. Ibid., folio12/2.

54. Ibid.

55. Ibid., folio13/1.

Whatever else we can say about his origin, there is the transition from the metaphysical to the physical, myth to reality, and this is seen as much in his use of Old Norse and Anglo-Saxon texts, as it is of Neoplatonic philosophy.

Tolkien has a unique mastery of the *Beowulf* text, its origins and derivatives, and notes that the Scandinavian sources of the *Exordium* show "no trace of any connexion with Sheaf—there is also no trace of any supernatural arrival or strange departure."[56] Whatever claims Tolkien may have about the de-Christianization (or re-paganism) of the Christian poem, there is still sufficient evidence of a Christian 'Otherworld,' such as we find in *Pearl*. Tolkien here observes that,

> the account in Beowulf is even at first glance seen to be of complex origin. It is not merely a piece of mythology, or symbolic ritual (cf. the Sea–burial), not merely the necessary complement to his mysterious arrival in a boat, although the Old English poetic account is plainly tinged with mystery and glimpses of the Otherworld.[57]

That such actual burials took place is supported and confirmed by archaeology, and

> burial at sea is said in Scandinavia to belong to a period covering the 4th, 5th, and 6th centuries AD. It was sometimes accompanied by burning. It was followed, after c.AD 600 by ship-burial on land (cf. in England the great mound-covered ship and treasure of Sutton Hoo).[58]

The manner in which these two divergent lines meet—historical tradition and mythology—is here well illustrated: "yet that ceremony (of sea-burial) was itself bound up with the beliefs, vague or explicit, of sea peoples in an 'Otherworld,' on far unvisited shores."[59] Whilst our being and existence is located in space/time, there is always a shadow cast by our identifiable transcendent nature, as yet unknown, but as sure a reality as our realized materiality. In this respect, Alfred Siewers provides a profound and persuasive insight into Tolkien's intention and method. If Tolkien followed this mode of writing, and we can now see the deep impression that it made upon

---

56. Ibid., folio15/1.

57. Ibid.

58. Ibid. We find this phenomenon in *The Return of the King*, prior to the death of Denethor, as he prepares to take his son Faramir to their joint funeral pyre: "We will burn like heathen kings before ever a ship sailed hither from the West." *LOTR*, 857.

59. *Bodleian SC–MSS* A31 folio15/1. It is very difficult not to read out of these excitable lines Tolkien's own ideas of the distant and inaccessible island of Valimar.

him as a professional, then where Tolkien is impressed by the juxtaposition of overlaying textual and mythical traditions, Siewers will be seen to focus upon the overlay landscapes that arise out of this method, without access or reference to these Bodleian manuscripts. Yet the shadowy mantle of our transcendent nature opens a door to the possibility of an Eriuganian mode of being/non-being, and the even more enticing prospect of a melding of medieval Neoplatonism and Anglo-Saxon mythology.

Tolkien, in his lecture notes, here observes that the *Beowulf Exordium* now looks more complex, having identified these multi-layered cross-over themes: "I think we can [. . .] gain a few lights on the processes of legend-making in the process, as well as catching a glimpse of northern antiquity."[60] Here we see these cross-over themes at work, each supporting and enhancing the other within the whole. He follows in that, "the English were concerned to equate and harmonize the inherited traditions (which were loved and prized) with those of Christian and classical learning," and having reached the limit of native northern tradition we then pass to scriptural traditions leading back through Noah to Adam. He continues in his assertion that,

> it cannot be doubted, I think, that this link between native tradition and scripture was made at this point and in this way the name Sceaf was associated with a journey from a distant land in a boat: hence the Ark.[61]

This is clearly very important to Tolkien, evidenced by the text being both underlined and starred in the manuscript. He concedes that this link between the northern and scriptural traditions, alongside overlay landscapes of history and myth, can be seen in sources easily overlooked: "thus we see that even behind the dry genealogies lies the mythological boat-legend, although it is not there explicitly mentioned."[62] There is a further, but more speculative piece of evidence which demonstrates this admixture of the pagan and Christian aesthetic mind, which Tolkien would have undoubtedly been aware of. Tolkien visited Lancashire on many occasions, as his son—John—was training for the priesthood at Stonyhurst College, Hurst Green, given that English seminarians could not study in the occupied countries of Europe during the Second World War. Five miles from Hurst Green lies Whalley Abbey, the site of the hanging of the Abbot during the Pilgrimage of Grace in 1537. Given Tolkien's lifelong support of English Catholicism, he would have undoubtedly been aware of the Abbey grounds, and the

---

60. Ibid., folio31.
61. Ibid.
62. Ibid.

three stone crosses that lie therein. They are typical of those dating from the tenth to the eleventh centuries, and are often referred to as being Anglican, though two of the crosses display what is probably Norse influence. The three crosses are often thought to be associated with St Paulinus who came to Whalley in the seventh century AD and used them as preaching crosses, but this is thought unlikely. He may, however, have established the first wooden church here on this very site, though the present-day church is largely a medieval structure, dating from the beginning of the thirteenth century (Appendix C). In Harrison Ainsworth's romantic gothic novel, the crosses are described, in that:

> They say those are runic obelisks, and not Christian crosses, and that the carvings upon them have a magical signification. The first, it is averred, is written o'er with deadly curses, and the forms, in which they are traced, as serpentine, triangular, or round, indicate and rule their swift or slow effect. The second bears charms against diseases, storms, and lightening; and on the third is inscribed a verse which will render him who can read it rightly invisible to mortal view.[63]

The crosses bear the marks of Christian symbols, but those also of an earlier pagan past. The ancient northern traditions brought to Britain by the Angles, are typified by mythical stories derived from old cultural legends connected with agricultural religion and ritual.

These legends contained the figures *Sceaf* or *Sceafa*, a personal 'sheaf,' and *Beow* a 'corn-spirit,' the genus of barley: "kingship and priesthood in the primitive culture-religion was closely allied," and Tolkien notes that in England these two quite different themes were blended.[64] Tolkien is careful to acknowledge in the very language of the poem that the noumenal and phenomenal worlds overlap, and that what is historical (or real) is juxtaposed to that which has its origins in mythology. The word 'real' has Middle English roots in what is 'royal,' 'majestic' and 'kingly,' and Winterson highlights this link such that "in both Greek and Hebraic tradition, the one who is royal is one who has special access to the invisible world. [. . .] Royalty on earth is expected to take its duties on earth seriously but the King should also be a bridge between the terrestrial and the supernatural."[65] Therefore, if we detect a particular pagan temper in his work, then it is a continuation of that tradition which he identified in the composition and redaction of the received

---

63. Ainsworth, *Lancashire Witches*, 122.
64. *Bodleian SC–MSS* A31 folio33.
65. Winterson, *Art Objects*, 140. The word *rial* derives from Old English : "Belonging or appropriate to a king; of or relating to a king."

text of *Beowulf*. What Tolkien is clearly not prepared to do is make clear and obvious allusions to biblical texts and/or events in his own writings. In folio 39 of the A31 Bodleian manuscript, Tolkien postulates that the compiler of the final text combined three different traditions: first, an historical tradition, showing a primary interest in dynastic legend; secondly, a treatment that blended dynastic legend with mythology (Barley<Shield<Sheaf); thirdly, a written source of learned origin—probably in Latin—the object being to 'rationalize' native northern legend, harmonized with Scripture.

Returning to the constant revisions and changes, which typified the evolution of *The Tale of Tinúviel*, and the interweaving of themes such as doom, freedom, and physical ambiguity, they can now be seen in the light of how Tolkien read the narrative of *Beowulf*, how his own works may be viewed as a multi-layered text containing real-world history, intertwined with Otherworld and mythological tropes. Thus, the whole point of the *Exordium* as poetry (not merely history) was to glorify *Scyld* and his family, and so enhance the background against which the struggle of Grendel and Beowulf takes place. In constructing his own *legendarium* in like manner, Tolkien allows the possibility of the immanently tangible (history) to merge with an Otherworld source (myth), often using motifs and disguised language from his own Catholic Christian life. Once again, in one of his perhaps most obscure and philosophical works—*The Notion Club Papers*—Tolkien writes of the link between myth and history:

> Sometimes I have a queer feeling that, if one could go back, one would find not myth dissolving into history, but rather the reverse: real history becoming more mythical—more shapely, simple, discernibly significant, even seen at close quarters. More poetical, and less prosaic, if you like.[66]

3.2.2 The Repaganizing of a Christian Poem

One can all too easily read certain characteristics of *Beowulf*, as a historio-mythological narrative of a pagan tale, with glimpses of Christianity breaking into the narrative at key moments. As such, it bears the hallmarks of the Northern sense of fate (*wyrd*), rendered by a determinism which tends towards unmerited fatalism. This theme is discussed below in a comparison of the Latin and (King Alfred's) Anglo-Saxon texts of Boethius' *Consolations*. The *Beowulf* text offers little that is positive about human nature in its relation to the Creator, and ultimate salvation is uncertain. Memories of virtuous

---

66. Tolkien, *Sauron Defeated*, 227.

men are instead anchored in the songs of minstrels, and whilst the present may be insecure, thus their immortality is secured. In Line 83, we read that "Heorot was still glorious, but it was doomed to be burned."[67] The present lies under a constant pall of the threat of Grendel, and Tolkien is quick to note here that the work is ultimately the product of the tradition of 'minstrelsy' (of oral recitation), and it uses old material.[68] In its written form he concedes that the work "is an 'amalgam,' not wholly perfect, but one made with a purpose, [. . .] it also allows that here and there the poem may have attracted the itching hand of a late writer."[69] Themes of immanent doom are noted elsewhere in the earliest *Commentary on Beowulf*, dated in the 1920s where, in the 'Finnsburg Episode' (Lines 1070–1158), Tolkien translates Line 1075 as "They fell according to their destiny," and this is clearly read in a deterministic sense: it was bound to happen.[70]

In seeking a resolution, and a redemption motif, we find instead a motif of 'doom' which is largely inconsistent with the analysis of Augustine's doctrine of redemption 'in Christ' and through the sacramental mysteries.[71] Neither the author of *Beowulf* nor Tolkien offer such a systematic doctrine of salvation, but Tolkien again weaves Christian mysticism and elements of salvation history into his *legendarium*, such that the reader may take from it more general themes of both doom and hope: fall and restoration. This doom is a concept carried over from these studies of *Beowulf*, wherein he accepts and embraces the inevitability of death (from a human perspective): "He is a man, and that for him and for many is sufficient tragedy [. . .] life is transitory [. . .] light and life together hasten away."[72] For Tolkien, however, morality is not a curse imposed on men for disobedience, but something proper to their particularity and genus. Shippey's observations that the Old English 'Doomsday' has no sense of 'luck' or 'chance' about it, but more of 'fate'—the idea of a power sitting above mortals and ruling their lives by its sentence or by its speech alone—may be too narrow a reading of this limitation of human freedom.[73] I argue below that whilst Tolkien as a medievalist may have been aware of this usage, he need not necessarily have interpreted it as such, and therefore need not have written with such a hard deterministic outlook of

---

67. Bodleian SC-MSS A28/C-D folio 5v.

68. Ibid., folio 6r.

69. Ibid., folio 7r.

70. Bodleian SC-MSS A28 folio 122. Heaney, *Beowulf*, 71, translates it as "foredoomed, cut down and spear-gored."

71. See discussion on *Pearl*, in section 3.4.3.

72. Tolkien, *Monsters*, 18.

73. Shippey, *Road to Middle Earth*, 288.

life and being. Tolkien explains that "the doom of the Elves is to be immortal [. . . ,] the Doom (or the Gift) of Men is mortality, freedom from the circles of the world."[74] Whilst the kindreds of Middle-earth may be ordered in their natures, they can still be free in their actions.

In a further unpublished manuscript, *Commentary and Notes on Cruces in Beowulf,* Tolkien takes up the theology of the poem, and asks of the reader that s/he use "justice and common sense," as the author is both competent and intelligent."[75] The author—*Hearrenda,* Tolkien calls him—was a Christian, having knowledge of the works of Caedmon, but also had a working knowledge of poems belonging to the ancient English tradition. He knew also that Hrothgar and Beowulf were 'heathens,' and that Offa of Mercia was not.[76] The poet would have had an 'attitude' towards northern paganism, "and looked at its own past with new eyes, but it looked carefully, and pondered what it saw with much thought."[77] He was in no way intimidated by old European paganism: "Ancient England was in fact as a whole aflame with missionary zeal, engrossed in the work of evangelizing Frisia and Germany, and revivifying Gaul."[78] One might imagine, therefore, that the writer would have written the poem in a more polemical tone, and Tolkien's own response to this sets into focus one clear reason why he was reticent to incorporate an overt Christian (allegorical) message into his own works. Again, we can remind ourselves that:

> The Lord of the Rings is of course a fundamentally religious and Catholic work; unconsciously so at first, but consciously in the revision. [. . .] I have cut out practically all references to anything like 'religion,' to cults and practices, in the imaginary world. For the religious element is absorbed into the story and the symbolism.[79]

In not condemning the worship of the 'old gods' (Lines 175f),

> the real reason for his silence is because he thought these details unimportant. He believed that the pagans of noble temper had a natural and inherited knowledge of Almighty God, the Maker

---

74. Carpenter, *Letters,* 147.
75. Bodleian SC–MSS A28/C-D folio 7r.
76. Ibid.
77. Ibid.
78. Ibid.
79. Carpenter, *Letters,* 172.

and the universal beneficent Providence of the world. But they were cut off from access to Him.[80]

The pagan worldview did not have the optimistic hope that emergent Christianity claimed and looked to in times of difficulty, and certainly when faced with death. According to Tolkien, "the mood of such men was a dark one [...] they had no certainty, except of evil. Hell and shadow was ever close to them." For emphasis, 'shadow' is underlined in the manuscript, and is a theme taken up in *The Lord of the Rings* at many levels.[81] If the poem has pagans as its central characters, and monsters as their chief adversaries, then it could be argued that either, *Beowulf* is a Christian poem re-paganized to suit an older temper, against the backdrop of a more secure and Christian theological framework, or it is a pagan poem, with hints of Christian hope.

Tolkien asserts at the time of his now famous lecture, *Beowulf: The Monsters and the Critics* (1936), whilst we have no surviving English pre-Christian mythology, the heroic legacy of ancient England and Scandinavia must have a common convergence.[82] The defeat of the gods in Norse mythology—and the men allied to them—whilst on the right side, are defeated by Chaos and Unreason, viz the mythological monsters. Defeat is of little consequence: absolute resistance is perfect, and precisely so because it is without hope.[83] "The paradox of defeat inevitable yet unacknowledged" is a theme to which the poet has devoted the whole poem of *Beowulf*.[84] Man is at war with the hostile world and his inevitable overthrow in time, "the particular is on the outer edge, the essential in the centre."[85] If this is the manner in which Tolkien reads *Beowulf*, then we may begin to read Tolkien's mythology in that same 'temper.' The sense of doom that we see in regard to his early characters such as Beren and Lúthien is not so much out of divine judgment upon men being weak in the face of a superior adversary, but a right sense of ordering or natural principle in his own mythology. We see this sense of hopeless valor echoed in Tolkien's *The Two Towers*, after the fall of Gandalf in Moria. Aragorn, Legolas and Gimli chase the orcs of Isengard despite the lack of hope in success. The three kindreds are united in the paradox of "struggle towards defeat." The exclamation of Aragorn when Gandalf the White appears—"Beyond all hope you return to us in our need!"—has a deeper meaning than the emergence of a substitute for the

80. *Bodleian SC–MSS A28/C-D* folio 8v.
81. Ibid. folio 8v.
82. Tolkien, *Monsters*, 21.
83. Ibid.
84. Ibid., 18.
85. Ibid.

team: the order of 'doom' is unravelling in a strange way. Even before the Black Gate, Aragorn holds to this principle.[86]

As the composition of *Beowulf* came under the joint influences of the pagan imagination and Christian scriptures, then Tolkien remarks that one does not have to wait for the Christian to replace the pagan, so that in time the latter would be forgotten, "for the minds which still retain them are changed, and the memories viewed from a different perspective [. . .] at once they become more ancient and remote, and in a sense darker."[87]

In *Beowulf*, the Christian is like his forefathers, "a mortal hemmed in a hostile world."[88] The monsters remained the enemies of mankind, "the infantry of the old war, and became inevitably the enemies of the one God."[89] The old monsters become images of the evil spirits, rather than 'good' creatures, marred and disfigured by demonic or spiritual possession. Tolkien makes an interesting remark in his *Appendix* to the lecture, in that the poet knew an already existing body of Christian poetry, thus making *Beowulf* more intelligible then the religious language initially presents itself, being partly re-paganized rather than Christianizing a pagan lay.[90] The poet assumes knowledge and an understanding of Old Testament and New Testament themes, and motifs of salvation, and it is against this backdrop that he writes into the poem the themes of despair and hopeless determinism. A good example of this is the funeral of Beowulf: it is not Christian, and his reward is the earthly recognized virtue of his kingship and the hopeless sorrow of his people. The poet was not ignorant of a theological 'heaven,' or of the use of *heofon* as the Anglo-Saxon equivalent of *caelum* in the Scriptures.[91] Therefore, we can assume that its omission in respect of Beowulf's funeral is deliberate, in a poem dealing with the pagan past. However, Tolkien's *Monsters* lecture is by no means his last word on the matter.

Tolkien notes that, "Providence is the half-realized purpose and ordinance that governed the ineluctable events in history: wyrd."[92] This is seen especially at Lines 1055–59, whereby,

> had not mindful God
> and one man's daring prevented that doom,

---

86. Tolkien, *LOTR*, 516 and 919, 921.
87. Tolkien, *Monsters*, 18.
88. Ibid., 22.
89. Ibid.
90. Ibid., 41.
91. Ibid., 38.
92. *Bodleian SC–MSS* A28/C–D folio 16v.

> Past and present, God's will prevails.

The "one man" (Beowulf) can, if Tolkien reads the text correctly, be working in a kind of free 'symbiotic' relationship with God, whereby the former acts freely in space/time and the latter acts from the perspective of eternity. It will be seen that 'doom' in fact requires us to see God's will—*Metod eallum wēold,* at Line 1057—as the arbiter of fate: Providence, who can control *wyrd* 'events' in space/time, but from eternity. If Tolkien views *Scyld* as a figure of uncertain progeny, then he holds no such doubts as to the central character, Beowulf. Being of great physical strength and courage to match, he was in early youth, "suitably adventurous, even rather wild, though he showed from the first a noble temper."[93] These attributes he used for good and chivalrous ends. Tolkien registers his character as "ofgeorn, and preferred to suffer and to triumph by his own efforts."[94] Here in his marginal notes, Tolkien adds the noun *ofermōd*, giving a sense of self-reliance, but also hints at 'pride,' 'arrogance,' and even 'over-confidence.'[95] Combining these two attributes, we see a character not too far removed from Beren, who uses his freedom and self-determination to carry out his self-appointed task of recovering the Silmaril, even at great personal cost, and in the face of near impossible odds.

In the case of Grendel, Tolkien notes that amidst the 'hope-less' fatalism of the pagan outlook of Beowulf, there is a Boethian sense of both providence and free will attached to his nature. Grendel "could not touch (or approach) the gift-throne (sc. whence came royal gifts to loyal thanes), the precious things because of Providence (sc. because God did not allow it?)."[96] In this instance, the word "Providence" is underlined for emphasis in the Manuscript. In translating lines 168–69 in this way, Tolkien betrays his Boethian bias and Neoplatonist outlook on the apparent paradox of divine order and freedom of the will, and his concluding note on this section is entirely pragmatic and comic: "There seems to have been no magical or divine protection over the throne [. . .] and Grendel may well have sat upon it and gnawed bones!"[97] Beowulf's monsters, like Tolkien's, are rooted in the real world, and their habitation is spoken of in the basest and simplest terms: "Grendel eats the flesh and blood of men; he enters

---

93. Ibid., A31/2 folio 104.

94. Ibid. *A-SD* renders *georn* as 'zealous' or 'desirous.' Therefore, *of-georn* has in it the sense of 'too eager' or 'elated,' 427.

95. *A-SD,* 736.

96. *Bodleian SC-MSS,* A28/C-D folio 11v.

97. Ibid.

their houses by the doors."[98] In Beowulf, we have the great pagan leader on the threshold of the change of the world, and the Christian imagination is just over this threshold. The character of Grendel, and the constant references to the biblical (Old Testament) character Cain, is a demonstration that early Anglo-Saxon poets could not "keep Scandinavian bogies and the Scriptures separate in their puzzled brains. The New Testament was beyond their comprehension."[99] Amidst the Northern and pagan religious outlook of the early medieval period, the poet of *Beowulf*, and Tolkien as his acolyte, are keen to emphasise the possibility of freedom as a primary category of human 'being.' The determinism of the pagan past may break through as a scripted device, but Beowulf and Tolkien's world are alive to new possibilities, freed as they are from the chains of doom and determinism of old European fatalism.

3.3 Freedom's Optimistic Turn in an Anglo-Saxon World

3.3.1 Doom and the Anglo-Saxon Provenance

Catastrophe—the counterpoint to his invented idea of *eucatastrophe*—is never randomly encountered in Tolkien's writings, but is always the direct effect of a previous cause. Tolkien renewed a current of magic and metaphysical delight in children's and adult literature that demonstrates a skilful juxtaposition between hope and doom. In his important essay *On Fairy Stories*, he acknowledges the importance of the "Consolation of the Happy Ending," the sudden and joyous "turn" which he calls "Eucatastrophe":

> it does not deny discatastrophe, of sorrow and failure: the possibility of these is necessary to the joy of deliverance; it denies universal final defeat and in so far is evangelium, giving a fleeting glimpse of Joy, Joy beyond the walls of the world, poignant as grief.[100]

And yet instances, such as the punishment of Númenor, sinking like Atlantis, have a moral, rather than a geological origin.[101] There are complex

---

98. Tolkien, *Monsters*, 23.
99. Ibid., 19.
100. Tolkien, *Tree and Leaf*, 69.
101. This story is told in the *Akallabêth* (*Silmarillion*, 311–39), and paraphrased in his own *Letters*, 154–57; 206. In the Second Age, the men of (the island of) Númenor became increasingly jealous of the immortality of the elves, and turned their back upon the 'Ban of the Valar' to sail near to Valinor—the Undying Lands. Tempted by their power and wisdom, they turned instead to occupy and subjugate Middle-earth.

issues which relate Tolkien's mythological world with our own, and hence the simultaneity of the problem of evil, freedom, and chance, in both. John Rateliff makes a strong case for accepting in a fairly literal sense Tolkien's insistence that his *legendarium* is about the lost history of *our* world, in an imagined prehistory. Middle-earth will ultimately become *our* earth: that is its (and our) tragedy.[102] This sense of 'doom' demonstrates a chastening rebuttal to the accusation of mere escapism into a better (or bygone) age. Tolkien's world is very dark, and Rateliff's essay recalls the Appendix to *The Lord of the Rings*, where Arwen freely chooses to surrender her Elvish immortality in order to marry Aragorn, wherein the adjectives 'hard' and 'bitter' resonate throughout. The 'Gift' or 'Doom' of death to men which comes to Aragorn finds him ready, after a long life. But not so Arwen: "to Arwen the Doom of Men may seem hard at the ending [. . .] Arwen has become as a mortal woman, and yet it was not her lot to die until all that she had gained was lost."[103] Her sense of bereavement is overwhelming, and she returns to the now deserted Lothlórien to await death alone. Until the world is changed "all the days of her life are utterly forgotten by men that come after."[104] This is one example of how Tolkien's mature work exudes a powerful sense of loss, and his decision to locate his tales in the imagined prehistory of *our* world has a necessary consequence:

> Every wonder he creates is predestined to be destroyed, every race and creature he invents doomed to fade into extinction, every race and culture to pass away utterly, leaving no discernible trace. Only a word or two, a few vague legends and confused traditions.[105]

If this is fatalism, then it is fatalism of a particularly melancholy kind, and may be influenced by events in his own traumatic early life: the loss of both parents at a young age, and the personal losses resulting from the Great War. In this latter respect, and in the Foreword to *The Lord of the Rings*, he wrote:

> One has personally to come under the shadow of war to feel fully its oppression; but as the years go by it seems now often

---

Tempted by Sauron's council, the King raised an Armada to sail west to the 'Blessed Realm.' As they approach, the Valar call upon the One (Eru), who creates a seismic wave to engulf Númenor, destroying their race, save but a small remnant. The story is reminiscent of the story of Noah, and is the only occasion when Eru intervenes in Middle-earth directly.

102. Rateliff, "All the Days of Her Life," 67–68.
103. Tolkien, *LOTR*, 1074–1075.
104. Ibid., 1077.
105. Rateliff, "All the Days of Her Life," 68.

forgotten that to be caught in youth by 1914 was no less hideous an experience than to be involved in 1939 and the following years. By 1918 all but one of my close friends were dead.[106]

He was then only twenty-six years old. Despite difficulties in locating Middle-earth into the exact geography of Europe, Tolkien locates his tales in an imaginary time, but keeps his feet on his own mother-earth for place:

> The name 'Middle-earth' is not an imaginary world. The name is the modern form of 'midden-erd' [. . .] an ancient name for [. . .] the abiding place of Men, the objectively real world, in use specifically opposed to imaginary worlds (as Fairyland) or unseen worlds (as Heaven or Hell). The theatre of my tale is this earth, the one in which we now live, but the historical period is imaginary.[107]

In respect of these collective events which unfold, we have a language whereby this fatalism—or doom—in the temporal sphere of space/time of Middle-earth is linked to the nature and providence of God. The Anglo-Saxon word—*Dōm*—has a broad variety of meanings and nuance: A "statute, ordinance, decree, judgment or decision." Whilst often used in a mood of 'sentence' issued adversely, in Tolkien's early writings it takes on a more ontological meaning, pertaining to a thing's 'proper nature' or 'order.' It can pertain also to a person or a thing's fate or proper (irrevocable) destiny, with strong overtones of determinism. Whilst this can be problematic at first reading, it need not be so if it is conjoined with the rule of statute. It can thus be seen as the will of God in the sense of a thing's proper order, and there is ancient usage to support this. Bosworth's *Anglo-Saxon Dictionary* states a broad interpretation of the word's derivatives, but also highlights an important link not just to the mere fact of statute/law making, and passing sentence, but also to the character of the sentence-maker: the origin of the order and juridical decree. In this it takes on a further function of "might, power, dominion, majesty, glory, magnificence, honour, praise, authority."[108] The Anglo-Saxon usage is pressed further to include ideas of "will, free will, choice, and option." In Tolkien's linguistic panorama, infused with Anglo-Saxon and Northern European cultural ideals, 'doom' need not be read in a deterministic sense, but with a degree of relationality to a dignity and honour

---

106. Tolkien, *LOTR*, 9.

107. Carpenter, *Letters*, 239 and 283. See also Tolkien, *Sigurd and Gudrun*, 187, note.

108. *A-SD*, 207.

proper to its own nature, whilst at the same time existing in an ordered world which still has in it a sense of freedom and even arbitrariness.

Examples of this variety of readings of *dōm* predominate in texts that would have been familiar to Tolkien:

'Daniel had much <u>honour</u> in Babylon.'

'No little <u>glory</u> sprang to Sigemund.'

'May the Lord ever have glory, bright <u>praise</u>.'

'That he might enjoy the ring-horde of his own <u>free will</u>.'[109]

The use of the word *dōm* can even be used as a noun, giving the sense of 'dwelling place, state, condition,' as opposed to time. This becomes significant when we consider Alfred's translation of the *Consolations*. This originates in Sanskrit *dhāman*, where the *dhā* prefix is rendered 'to put or place.' When used in the sense of wis-dōm, it refers to the state of being free, holy, or wise.[110] Given that Tolkien's *legendarium* was skillfully woven around the creative and accurate use of ancient words, it would not be too speculative to interpret the use of 'doom' in the *Tale of Tinúviel* in this latter sense of 'being': a thing or person's doom is their proper glory, wisdom, correct order. It is uncertain as to how this 'doom' rests in the freedom and self-determination of God to order a thing 'as it is,' and the subject's own freedom in and of itself.

That human freedom and culpability are central pillars of Tolkien's ethical approach to his philosophy, the basis upon which he is then prepared to defend this claim is significant. Following my exposition of Tolkien's own reading of themes in *Beowulf*, and the above linguistic analysis, I can safely assert that for an author after the Anglo-Saxon *temper*, 'Doom' has less to do with determinism and impending judgment, and instead has as its key focus the divine ordering of society within a wider cosmogonical hierarchy. Given my earlier assertion that Boethius was amongst his most significant philosophical influences then, just as in the case of the *Beowulf* poet, his works are given special consideration.

3.3.2 Boethius, Alfred and the Timelessness of God

There is no clear documentary evidence that Tolkien relied on, or had as a dependency for his own *legendarium*, the works of Boethius. It is reasonable to assume that Tolkien would be aware of at least his *Consolations of*

---

109. Ibid.
110. Ibid.

Philosophy, being one of the most popular and influential works in Western Europe from the time of authorship in 524 AD until the end of the Renaissance.[111] Tolkien would have known the text if only for the purpose of his study of King Alfred's translation. For Tolkien, who avoided unnecessary and deliberate use of Christian language, Boethius also provided a framework in which to present his own heavily nuanced ideas about providence, free will, chance, and necessity in a philosophical perspective. It is worth noting that Boethius also omits overt theological references in his *Consolations*, and instead couches his ideas and enquiry in the form of an extended dialogue. In this he was able to free himself from reliance of biblical texts and motifs—something which Tolkien was also keen to do. For Boethius, providence is the divine reason itself, the unfolding of temporal events as this is present to the vision of the divine mind. Fate is the same unfolding of events as it is worked out in time, as we perceive it in the temporal world.[112] Some events seem to us discordant or chaotic from our temporal and phenomenal perspective, yet our limited perception leads us to recognize the order which lies behind the apparent disorder.[113] All things have a purpose, such that

> the best possible ordering of the world exists only in the divine nature which abides in the divine Mind, and inaugurates an unvarying sequence of causes, and this sequence with its own immutability constrains the world of change which would otherwise float away at random.[114]

The question remains, therefore, whether or not there is any free will within a teleological universe, or even the possibility of chance, for "we can define chance as the unexpected outcome of a conjunction of causes in actions carried out for some purpose."[115] Chance defined as a random or non-consequential activity cannot exist in a teleological universe, but chance defined correctly implies:

> whenever something is done with a particular purpose in mind [. . .] and as a result of certain causes something other than was intended occurs, it is called chance.[116]

---

111. Dubs, "Providence, Fate and Chance," 133.
112. *Consolations*, 4.6.9.
113. Ibid., 4.6.21.
114. Ibid., 4.6.20.
115. Ibid., 5.1.18.
116. Ibid., 5.1.13, commenting on Aristotle's *Physics* 2.4–5.

Boethius presents a universe created and governed by a benevolent providence, where everything—including fate and chance—has purpose, even if that purpose transcends human perception and understanding. He develops his enquiry with regard to freedom of the will: "in this sequence of interlocking causes, do we have any free will, or does the chain of fate constrain the movements of men's minds as well?"[117] Lady Philosophy answers emphatically that "there is free will, for no rational nature could exist if it did not possess freedom of will."[118] When Boethius inquires about the relationship between freedom of will and divine providence, he elicits a lengthier response:

> You will respond that if it lies in my power to change my course of action, I will deprive Providence of her role when I happen to change and act which she foreknows. My response will be that you can indeed divert your course of action, but the truth of Providence observes in the present your ability to do this, and whether you are doing it, or in what direction you are changing it. So you cannot evade the divine foreknowledge, just as you cannot escape the gaze of a person's eye which observes you at this moment, even though you vary your actions by use of your free will.[119]

We see this turn of fate in several key moments in Tolkien's mature works. In *The Fellowship of the Ring* Frodo 'marvels' that he escaped the Black Riders with only a slight wound, Gandalf replies, "yes, fortune or fate have helped you [. . .] not to mention your courage."[120] To this we may add that a will for survival also played its part. Furthermore, at the Council, Elrond introduces the proceedings and the problem of the One Ring:

> That is the purpose for which you are called hither. Called, I say, though I have not called you to me, strangers from distant lands. You have come and are here met, in this very nick of time, by chance as it may seem. Yet it is not so. Believe rather that it is so ordered that we who sit here, and none others, must now find counsel for the peril of the world.[121]

There is implied here a 'mind' behind this turn of chance meeting of strangers and kindreds, yet it could be read straight out of the *Consolations* Books 4

---

117. Ibid., 5.2.2.
118. Ibid.
119. Ibid., 5.6.37–38.
120. Tolkien, *LOTR*, 238.
121. Ibid., 259.

THE CONCEPT OF LIFE AS 'BEING AND GIFT' IN TOLKIEN'S LITERARY *CORPUS* 133

and 5. Chance may have a part to play, but it is never independent of a higher, overarching mind, which directs or orders its many causes.

When Gandalf cautions Bilbo about using the Ring, and explains its origin and history, he asserts that the Ring has a power of determination linked to the will of its creator—Sauron. The Ring 'decided' to leave Gollum, and was trying to get back to its master.[122] Yet there was more than one power at work. This idea reaches its zenith when Gandalf explains that Frodo's 'appointed' task is ordered by 'providence' (though he does not use the word), and has a clear purpose. As Gandalf continues to describe what he knows about the Ring, there is a thoughtful turn to optimism:

> Behind that there was something else at work, beyond any design of the Ring-maker [. . .] Bilbo was meant to find the Ring, and not by its maker. In which case you were also meant to have it. And that may be an encouraging thought.[123]

It would appear from this reading that Sauron does not have complete mastery over the Ring, making free the choices of those who choose to use it, for good or ill. At the end of the conversation over the Ring, Frodo's options become clear, but it still implies a free choice amongst other options. Tolkien speaks with clarity in a Boethian mode, that despite the possibilities of chance and fate, "the decision lies with you."[124]

There are here, therefore, a compelling collection of key moments in Tolkien's later and mature mythology, where there are clear references to a Boethian psychology of freedom of the will, despite an overarching ordering of events. Indeed, prior to leaving Lothlorien, the Lady Galadriel acknowledges that a plan exists, and that Frodo's offer of the Ring was generous (implying freedom as a naïve but virtuous 'ring-giver'): "In the morning you must depart, for now we have chosen, and the tides of fate are flowing."[125] At unexpected turns in *The Lord of the Rings*, we see this freedom exercised, alongside the proper ordering of nature. When Samwise Gamgee becomes for a short time a ring-bearer, he has delusions of grandeur which the One Ring affords, that of being a mighty warrior. As he is as yet unaffected by the Ring's power to subjugate, he shrugs off the notion and accepts his fate—his particular 'doom' in the wider scheme of things.[126]

122. Ibid.
123. Ibid., 69.
124. Ibid., 75.
125. Ibid., 385.
126. Ibid., 935. Sam's 'doom' entails, "The one small garden of a free gardener was all his need and due, not a garden swollen to a realm; his own hands to use, not the hands of others to command."

These ideas of fate and free will are not statements of incompatibility or paradoxical when viewed from the dual perspective of both eternity and temporality. Free will operates within the order of the universe, fate being the (Middle) earthly manifestation of that order. In this instance, it is free will and its extension in time that decides the contingency of future events: hard determinism does not necessitate here, even if the 'mind' of providence perceives the choices from eternity.

3.3.3 Alfred's Anglo-Saxon Reading of the *Consolations*

One of the significant movements of late antiquity and the early medieval period consists in the translation and spread of significant texts. A demonstration of the importance of Boethius' *Consolations* is its translation by Alfred the Great, Chaucer, and Elizabeth I, but it is to the former that I wish to focus my analysis. Alfred's translation of the *Consolations* into Anglo-Saxon took place between AD 887 and 899,[127] and it would appear that both Alfred and Boethius had similar concerns in their respective lives. Both were charged with heavy responsibility; both engaged in scholarly pursuits in their leisure time; both were determined to create and rebuild amidst civilizations that were crumbling around them; they were both translators of the works of others.[128] They both sought to find something permanent in the "flux of decay that gives their works a relevance to ages beyond their own."[129] Boethius, in seeking to preserve the works of others, as well as writing his own, demonstrates his pressing desire to preserve the "old images"—an intellectual and philosophical tradition—that were slipping away. His chief aim was to preserve a body of work of such substance as to give future (Roman) leaders a sound intellectual pillar on which to lean. His arrest upon accusation of treason brought a swift end to this project.[130] It could be argued with some force that, as Tolkien was aware of the works of Alfred, and taught on other Old English texts, alongside Alfred's *Consolations*, this aim was also at the heart of Tolkien's project. He was not merely writing fantasy, or developing the genre, but addressing some of the pressing concerns of his own day.[131]

---

127. Payne, *King Alfred and Boethius*, 4.

128. Boethius in his *De Interpretatione* first translated some works of Plato and Aristotle, prior to his attempt in reconciling their teachings.

129. Payne, *King Alfred and Boethius*, 4.

130. Ibid., 8.

131. Tolkien taught on Alfred's *Cura Pastoralis*, and his lecture notes can be found

Alfred's translation departs significantly from Boethius' Latin text, one of which is the discussion in Book 5 on God's foreknowledge and human freedom. As this is the case, as I shall demonstrate, then this modified rendering of a Boethian philosophy of human freedom would be problematic for Tolkien's adoption of humans as being essentially free moral and psychological agents. Boethius' solution rests on his differentiation of time and eternity: the former is the dimension in which men experience as the sequence of continually moving present moments; the latter pertains to the eternal state of God,

> that which grasps and possesses simultaneously the entire fullness of life without end; no part of the future is lacking to it, and no part of the past has escaped it.[132]

God's sight in his eternal present no more restricts human freedom than man's sight, in the finite present, imposes any restriction or necessities on those whom he sees walking before him. Therefore, for Boethius, the standpoint of (finite) humanity can only observe that their freedom lies in the future, in a moment which has yet to arrive. For God, that free decision or act is already a limitless present for God, which embraces the future and past in an infinite/eternal present. Alfred retains very little of this key argument in his adaptation. He instead substitutes his own discussion of freedom (ch. 41) and a description of God (ch. 42). Alfred omits completely Boethius' Neoplatonic explanation about the states of time and eternity:

> Every creature, however, both reasoning and unreasoning, declares that God is eternal, for never would so many creatures and so mighty and so fair have bowed themselves to a lesser creature and a lesser power than they all are, nor even to one equally great.[133]

This key text does not place God in the Boethian state of an eternal present, but serves only to designate God's separateness from, and superiority to other beings who revere Him because He is more powerful than they. The Boethian distinction between the world and eternity cannot be maintained unless it is made evident that there is a 'place' or 'existence' which a being without beginning or end occupies, as an indication of the inalienable separateness from time. Because Alfred does not describe such a 'place,' then the third category (below) means again only that God is superior to any part of creation:

---

in the *Bodleian SC-MSS A27/1*.

132. *Consolations*, 5.6.8.

133. Quoted in Payne, *King Alfred and Boethius*, 18.

> Do you know that there are three things on this earth? The first lasts for a time only; it has both beginning and end; [...] The second thing is eternal; it has beginning and no end; [...] such are angels and men's souls. The third thing is eternal, without end without beginning; [...] that is God.[134]

In two further passages concerning the nature of God, Alfred once more mention's God's 'apartness' from time, but also that which God has 'within' the realm of space and time man can never hope to attain. The implication here from Alfred's own real world concerns only secures God from "the doubt, the struggle, the fear, and the toil of men."[135] The conclusion—in contrast to Boethius—serves a different purpose: differentiating between the uncertainty of man and the wisdom and beauty of God. Both are played out largely within the sphere of similar states of being. Because Alfred never posits a state of eternity either in his version of *Consolations Book 5* or before, Wisdom (unlike Philosophy) has not proved by the end of 5.1 that man's destiny is a part of the inflexible order of the universe which ends in the Onenness of God, a proof which finally challenges the (Latin) prisoner's pride (5.2), and makes him demand to know whether there is such a thing as freedom. In the Old English text (ch. 41) God does not always choose to foreknow, hence it is not logically necessary to reconcile foresight and freedom—not in the elaborate sense of the (Latin) Boethian dialogue.

A second major departure from Boethius is Alfred's rejection of the Neoplatonist rendering of *Ordo* that we find in the Latin text. In the latter, there are many phases of order: order as the natural world; as the compelling force in the universe; as the thought of God; as the structure of human government. All of these are entirely dependent upon the concept of eternity and time apparent in the last prose in the *Consolations*. Alfred, in contrast, adopts only a single concept for his purposes: order in relation to nature. This contrast can be seen most markedly in the use of 3.9.33, where after a debate on false and true happiness, Lady Philosophy sings a hymn taken largely from Plato's *Timaeus* 27c–42e:

---

134. Ibid., 19.
135. Ibid., 20.

Latin	Old English
Yourself most beautiful, you likewise bear in mind a world of beauty, and You shape our world in like appearance. You command its perfect parts, to form a perfect world. (3.9.33)	Just as you yourself planned, you made this earth and rule it just as you desire and you yourself distribute all good just as you desire. And you here made all creatures like each other and also in some things unlike. Though you named all creatures separately with one name, you named them all together and called them world. (79:29–34)

In this, Boethius echoes Plato; Alfred echoes Genesis.[136] For Boethius, the world of time—past, present, and future—has a simultaneous existence within the eternal mind of God. For Alfred, the world is the result of a plan which God formed and then carried out; God's present relation to the world is that of ruler. The Old English version of the *Consolations*, insofar as it has any direct part in human affairs, depicts the natural order as the means by which the thinker may know the strength of God who has the power to hold in harmony what would otherwise be the chaos of the struggling elements. Boethius' text depicts the natural world instead as a symbol of the order of the cosmos, and his aesthetic projection of beauty and order is a projection of materiality out of the mind of God.

If, given my speculation of Tolkien's 'dependency' on the mature works of Eriugena, and that Tolkien moved from a Boethian Neoplatonism of being to the position held by Eriugena, then he did so without adapting his works in line with Alfred's interpretation of the former. Alfred lacks the originality and mystical elements of Plato, and instead promotes a muscular robust image of God as a driver, the horseman, guiding the universe. It is a series of images that emphasizes physical strength and skill. Where Boethius is impressed by the unity (*unam formam*) and order of nature (*naturae ordo*), then *Mod*—the prisoner of the Old English text—is impressed by physical strength required to create and hold such diversities in peaceful coexistence.[137]

In *Consolations* 4.6.39–42, Boethius links fate and order, passages in which this order become a synonym for fate, time, and the thought of God. Alfred omits these important texts, in particular the one above:

---

136. Ibid., 23.
137. *Consolations*, 3.12.15–24.

Thus when this arrangement of the temporal order is a unity within the foresight of the divine mind, it is Providence, whereas when that unity is separated and unfolded at various times, it is called fate.

Boethian order has a static phase called Providence and a dynamic phase called Fate, but for practical purposes the three words—order, fate, providence—describe the same reality, "a reality whose projection into the multiplicity of time and retraction into the oneness of eternity contains no immediate loophole for the contrariety of freedom."[138]

Alfred's departure from Boethius here is not so much in his denial of order, fate, or providence, but in the manner of their translation into the Old English meaning: fate (*wyrd*) becomes associated with God's power:

Latin	**Old English**
Fate is the order imposed on things that change, through which Providence interlinks each and every object in their due arrangement. Providence indeed embraces all things alike, however different and however boundless. (4.6.9)	But what we call wyrd is God's work which he does each day, both what we see and what is invisible to us. But divine forethought restrains all creatures, that they may not slip from their order. (128:18–22)[139]

In this context, *Wyrd* is limited to the work of God, and Alfred anthropomorphizes God's activity in space and time only. The infinite and eternal in Boethius instead becomes dangerously immanent and restricted in Alfred's rendering of the dialogue.

It is in this (Latin) Boethian sense that Tolkien understood the concept of *wyrd* in later Anglo-Saxon literature. In his unpublished notes on *The Wanderer*, he pairs the work with *The Seafarer*, but can discern no immediate context for the work.[140] The general mood of the Old English poem is that of "an apprehension of Divine Mercy contrasted with the background of the inexorable world; hope of final deliverance from impermanence."[141] However, in dating it around AD 1050—some 150 years later than Alfred—we see that the word *wyrd* occurs in lines 5, 15, 100 and in particular 106. For Tolkien, *wyrd* is history: "The ineluctable series of events that has marched, and will march on and over Man."[142] When asked, "are these forces necessarily

---

138. Payne, *King Alfred and Boethius*, 32.
139. Ibid., 33.
140. *Bodleian SC-MSS* A38 A&B.
141. Ibid., folio 9.
142. Ibid.

opposed to the ideas of God?" Tolkien responds with a resounding, 'No!': "wyrd is becoming, happening, that is its etymological sense, and that is its fundamental sense, whether remaining abstract or personified."[143] It may well be looked on as an ineluctable series in Time. Tolkien later describes *wyrd* as "the devastator of weorold (the generations of Men), and this by a poet who refers to 'The Father.'"[144] For Tolkien, there is clearly some inconsistency between what is implied in the term *wyrd*, as a harbinger of doom in the Anglo-Saxon pagan sense, and what is ordained by God as providence. In the case of the poet of *The Wanderer*, this is not just being 'muddle-headed,' but that the poem as it presents itself is a "fortuitous blend of a pagan and a monkish redactor."[145] For Tolkien, this poem and others of its kin lived in a kind of 'twilight' between paganism and Christianity. In this, he aims a caution at both the 'confusion-mongers' and 'discrepancy-hunters' of his day in that "there is a real difference between a period not far removed from a pagan past, and one in which a genuine pre-Christian paganism is very remote." *The Wanderer* was composed, Tolkien observes, at the juncture of the emergence of Christianity and near paganism:

> past beliefs cast their shadow behind: the mind long outlives them. The dominant note of paganism is regret, or indeed despair. It may have fair gods, or foul gods (or both); but at any rate it has little hope.[146]

If the Anglo-Saxon 'temper,' originating out of this material sense of *wyrd*, is one which infuses regret or despair, then we are indeed a long way from Boethian fate, order, and providence. Furthermore, if Tolkien's understanding of *wyrd* is similar to that of Alfred, then it can accommodate a divine 'architect' and sustainer of the universe, but one whose actions are revealed in time, and not *ordo*, as in the overlaying ideas of Boethius.

In a further passage of comparison between Alfred and Boethius, *fatum* (fate) is simply omitted in the translation: 'order' is associated with God's care for material things.[147] In the four remaining passages where Boethius mentions fatal order (or fate and order), Alfred drops *ordo* and writes instead about *wyrd*. So in *Consolations* 4.6.11, "though the two are distinct, the one depends on the other, for the order of Fate emerges from the indivisibility of Providence" becomes in Alfred: "for wyrd comes from

143. Ibid.
144. Ibid.
145. Ibid.
146. Ibid.
147. *Consolations*, 4.6.55.

the intelligence and from the forethought of Almighty God."[148] Alfred's alterations and simplification of ideas implies that *wyrd* is the only aspect of what occurs in time, and that the reduction of fate and order to *wyrd* limits the scope of his view of God's activity. Where fate and order become separate in the Alfredian universe, they remain aspects of creation, but not the totality of God's projected thought. The Alfredian universe consists of a number of planes extending in various directions into the darkness, where God operates in mysterious ways. Such a universe poses problems for man, but not primarily the problem of freedom.[149] For Boethius, the universe is "a kind of brilliantly lighted, translucent pyramid projecting from the mind of God," even if that projection implies from the human vantage point a crushing determinism.[150] *Consolations* 4.6.53 posits that,

> some sort of order pervades all things. If something forsakes the planned order assigned to it, it slips back into some alternative pattern, admittedly different but none the less a due order, so that nothing in the realm of Providence may be left to chance.

This passage supports the ontological relationship between providence and the fatal order. Read in this light, the turn of evil from good is only a part of that fatal order which serves God's greater purposes, and "the only force which transforms evil things into good is that of God, when he aptly exploits them to draw out of them an element of good."[151] Alfred does not associate *wyrd* with either mutability or earthly goods; nor does he associate *wyrd* with order, the guiding principle behind fortunes in Boethius' comprehensive vista. In *Consolations* 4.6.30, the prisoner is told that fortune is an aspect of fate—the force which men take to be mutability itself. This is merely a single aspect of the divine order of the cosmos for Boethius. His *fatum* is a term inseparably linked to the words *ordo* and *providentia*. The prefix 'pro-' means 'in front of' rather than 'beforehand': it is reference to position rather than time.[152] Hence its links to order: the corresponding terms in Old English have an entirely different relation to one another, and hence correspond to the Latin terms only superficially. The 'fore-' prefix in Old English describes a relationship to time and not position, since Alfred nowhere describes Boethian eternity, "Alfred's God does not sit in front of the projection of his thought, the tableau of time and space; his state of existence moves along

---

148. Payne, *King Alfred and Boethius*, 34.
149. Ibid., 35.
150. Ibid.
151. *Consolations*, 4.6.52.
152. Ibid., 5.6.17.

with human time"—a model of a God for whom eternity is everlasting, and who is in danger of mutability if human freedom is to be preserved.[153] Alfred's presentation of the divine can think about the future beforehand, make decrees about it, but he does not—as in Boethius—shape it from an eternal present. As a result of these Old English variances, the three terms—order, forethought, wyrd—are not compelled to refer to the totality of all that exists, as are the corresponding Latin terms—order, providence, fate. Instead, each refers to a single phenomenon that occurs in time.

If the Anglo-Saxon meaning of *wyrd* compromises both God's eternity and human freedom, then we can assume that *if* Tolkien was aware of this important text, then his philosophy of divine providence and human freedom were more akin to the Latin Boethian model. Despite his skill at weaving Anglo-Saxon motifs into his mythology, there lies at the heart of human anthropology a perception of doom which is best read in terms of 'order' within a framework of providence, even if at times it leaves an 'aftertaste' of deterministic fatalism. The only sense in which Tolkien may have translated the Anglo-Saxon concept of *wyrd* out of documents such as Alfred's (or indeed *The Wanderer*), is so that he can write into his mythology a 're-paganized Christianity' such as he highlights in the poet of *Beowulf*. The Bodleian Library manuscripts have indeed revealed this to be the case, but not for this reason. This is a critical distinction: the philosophical enquiry of the prisoner in Boethius' *Consolations* is searching for hope in what presents itself as a situation of despair. Whilst it appears as one of deterministic doom, or mere chance, Boethius can move forward in the knowledge that "every fortune, pleasant or harsh, is bestowed on the one hand to reward or to exercise the good, and on the other to punish or correct the wicked, they are all of them good, for it is clear that they are either just or useful."[154] These effects which impinge upon us are therefore not of any kind of necessity (or doom), but part of both God's ordering and providence from a timeless eternity, allowing for an exercise of human freedom in temporality.

Was Tolkien's 'Northern' outlook therefore rejected by his following Boethius in matters of providence and the fatal order? Not necessarily. John Holmes reminds us of the importance of the *Consolations* in the Anglo-Saxon period, and that the Latin phrase popular in later medieval poetry—*ubi sunt que ante nos fuerunt* ('who were those who were before us')—originates in Boethius' discussion of the goddess 'Fortuna' in the *Consolations*. This is a good example of Boethius' concern over his mixed fortunes on life, whereby his interlocutor reminds him of Fortune's fickle ways: "Having entrusted

153. Payne, *King Alfred and Boethius*, 87.
154. *Consolations*, 4.7.3.

yourself to Fortune's dominion, you must conform to your mistress's ways. What, are you trying to halt the motion of her whirling wheel?"[155] Holmes notes that the Old English poets cribbed the *ubi sunt / ubi nunc* nostalgic phrasing at the beginning of poetic lines *from* Boethius, and translated it as *Hwaer com* in *The Wanderer* and other elegiac passages. Indeed, Miranda Wilcox identifies this poetic tone, reminiscent of this lyric-elegiac quality of Old English poetry, displaying a profound sadness of time and change in certain passages in *The Lord of the Rings:*

> Where now the horse and the rider? Where is the horn that was blowing?
>
> Where is the helm and the hauberk, and the bright hair flowing?
>
> Where is the hand on the harpstring, and the red fire glowing?
>
> Where is the spring and the harvest and the tall growing corn?[156]

Here, Aragorn speaks of the forgotten poet of Rohan who, like the minstrel in *Beowulf*, tells the coming of the ancestors to the present King of the Golden Hall (Heorot/Meduseld).[157] The narrative continues, as they "passed the silent mounds" typical of burial sites of the later Anglo-Saxon period:

> They have passed like rain in the mountain, like a wind in the meadow;
>
> The days have gone down in the West behind the hills into shadow.
>
> Who shall gather the smoke of the dead wood burning,
>
> Or behold the flowing years from the Sea returning?[158]

These reminiscences of the Anglo-Saxon temper are more subtle in Tolkien's episodic and stylistic borrowing of certain phrases, linking his own works with *Beowulf*, for example.[159] Wilcox postulates that *The Wanderer* influenced Tolkien to at least the same extent as *Beowulf* and *The Battle of*

---

155. Holmes, "Dustsceawung," 45; *Consolations*, 2.1.18.
156. Wilcox, "Exilic Imaginings," 133; *LOTR*, 530.
157. *Beowulf*, lines 308 & 311; *LOTR*, 529.
158. Tolkien, *LOTR*, 530.
159. In both *The Hobbit* and *Beowulf* we read of a cup being stolen from the dragon-hoard, thus enraging the mighty 'wyrm' (lines 2216–20); in both we read of the King's 'Golden Hall' (lines 308 & 311). He even borrows the name of "Eomer [...] his warrior's mainstay and master of the field" (lines 1960–62).

Maldon.[160] However, if, as I have stated above, Tolkien is more dependent on Boethius than Alfred in his philosophy of human freedom, then it need not be a 'Southern' turn, as it should be noted that Boethius was a contemporary of the ancient kings cited in the *Beowulf Exordium* (above), insofar as they are historical, and that the king whom Boethius served—Theodoric—had as many Germanic as he had Italian influences.[161] What we read in Aragorn's recitation in the passage above is the Anglo-Saxon sense of *Dustsceawung*— "a contemplation of dust"—how present images contain both shells of their past and seeds of their future.[162] If, therefore, Tolkien's treatment of time—a lament for an irretrievable past—may be read as a 're-paganised' Christian tale, then whilst it may be called 'elegiac' by the Greeks and Romans, it is in point of fact borrowed from the Boethian tradition, and recast as a fusion between the *ubi sunt/ubi nunc* of late Roman antiquity and an even later Anglo-Saxon conceptual idea. In choosing a Boethian model for timelessness and freedom, based on divine providence, the fate of human endeavour cannot rest entirely on pagan ideas of 'doom,' but one which is both at the same time optimistic and coexistent within the dual landscapes of both God's eternity and human temporality.

3.4 Grace in Human Realization and Destiny

It shall be seen that Eriugena speaks of the return into mystical and uncertain terms, and has none of the precision evident in the works of Aquinas. In addition, Eriugena tends to both pantheism and universal salvation; whereas Aquinas maintains a clear distinction between Creator/creature and addresses the means by which we experience existence and salvation with more clarity. In my exposition of Tolkien's use of the Middle-English poem *Pearl*, and his short story—*Leaf by Niggle*—it can be seen that the means of salvation derives from a Christian Neoplatonism which has resonances with both Augustine and Boethius, and places the incarnation at the epicenter of God's salvific activity. This section develops the previous analysis of Tolkien's use of participatory language of the giftedness of created being, in terms of the *reditus*—and how it is expressed in his own writings and professional studies. Given the previous hypothesis, that Aquinas would have been very much at the heart of Tolkien's self-understanding, then we may read these texts in light of Aquinas' teaching on life as a participation in God, and the return into God upon death. It is hardly surprising that we

---

160. Wilcox, "Exilic Imaginings," 133.
161. Holmes, "Dustsceawung," 45.
162. Ibid., 45.

find in Tolkien's works a metaphysics of life as 'being and gift' and I have already demonstrated how, in his metaphysics of music, he tends towards a reworked Thomist approach, influenced also by the works of Maritain. Whilst it may be seen that Tolkien's account of life and being are at times couched in the mystical language of Eriugena's dialectical method, I can now assert with certainty that it was also influenced by the Thomist revision of a participatory ontology. This section expounds this Thomist approach, and we may read Tolkien's use of Eriugena (below) through the sharper lens of the metaphysics of Thomas Aquinas.

3.4.1 Grace and the Metaphysics of Participation in the Thomist Revision

Alongside other recent Thomist scholarship,[163] the contributions made by those who place themselves within the *Radical Orthodoxy* movement have reasserted the Neoplatonist influences in writers such as Aquinas. The movement asserts to reclaim the original early church idea that Theology is the 'queen of the sciences.' This means that if the world is to be interpreted correctly, it must be viewed through the lens of theology. Consequently, science, ethics, politics, economics, and all other branches of study may be interpreted and informed through theology.[164] Their *raproachment* of theological and philosophical inquiry, I shall demonstrate, offers profound insights in relation to what it means to be 'gifted' human. Within the philosophical *zeitgeist* of Radical Orthodoxy, John Milbank, Catherine Pickstock, and Simon Oliver, following other Platonic and Neoplatonic readings of Aquinas, highlight a crucial building block in his overall thought: the metaphysics of participation. Rziha uses the simple illustration of water: It is not hot by nature, it can be cold, but is only hot by receiving heat from something that is hot by nature (e.g., fire). The water is hot by participation. The one participating (i.e., water) can be said to share or take part in something. That in which one participates is said to give and communicate something. For example, God gives his being, goodness and truth to creatures that are said to participate in his being, goodness, and truth.[165] Indeed, these

---

163. Notably, Burrell, *Aquinas: God and Action*; Oliver, *Philosophy, God and Motion*; Te Velde, *Aquinas on God*; Hibbs, *Aquinas, Ethics, and Philosophy of Religion*; De Young, et al., *Aquinas' Ethics*; and Rziha, *Perfecting Human Actions*.

164. Especially in the work of John Milbank, Catherine Pickstock, Graham Ward, and Simon Oliver. This is claimed explicitly in Simon Oliver, "Introducing Radical Orthodoxy," 18.

165. Rziha, *Perfecting Human Actions*, 6–28.

commentators see a Neoplatonic participatory ontology at the heart of not only Aquinas' writing on language, but of his whole theology.[166] This basic concept can be seen to have its philosophical origins in Plato, but Radical Orthodoxy's emphasis on participation promotes a non-dualistic reading of Plato's thought, and provides a crucial model for Aquinas' view of creation's analogical relation to God.[167] This non-dualistic concept in Plato could be seen as a direct antecedent of the viewpoint of overlay landscapes of medieval literature, and the mutual integration and interpenetration of fantasy and reality in respect of this world and Otherworlds. That being is always in relation to something prior to itself on a cosmological scale, then its true nature or essence can only be known to the extent in which it participates in its origin. In terms of Plato, it is the unchanging Forms or Ideals; in terms of Eriugena and Aquinas, it is always in respect to God.

Following Aquinas, Milbank and Pickstock claim that there are substantial entities in creation, but only insofar as they participate in the gratuity (grace) of God's gift of being. They describe this relationship as if we were considering our recognition and appreciation of trees:

> For to know such a thing is not to know an isolatable fact or proposition; it seems more to be the knowing of a kind of manner or operation of life. But in knowing the treeness of a tree we are knowing a great deal more besides. Since the tree only transmits treeness—indeed, only exists at all—as imitating the divine, what we receive in truth is a participation in the divine. To put this another way, in knowing a tree, we are catching it on its way back to God.[168]

God bestows upon creation a finite participation in his own substantiality: creation does not have existence by its own virtue and merit, but only and always in the gratuity of God. It may be inferred from this that creation has no autonomous existence, and hence all activities and qualities that are

---

166. Oliver, *Introducing Radical Orthodoxy*, 18. Rziha, *Perfecting Human Actions*, 9, observes that there is no simple way to characterise Aquinas' thought, since he had thoroughly synthesized the best elements of many different traditions (Plato, Aristotle, Augustine, Boethius, Avicenna, etc.).

167. De Young, et al., *Aquinas' Ethics*, 33–34, 40–43, note that Aquinas rejects the kind of 'substance dualism' present in Plato due primarily to his belief that the human being is essentially 'one thing.' In following a broadly Aristotelian metaphysics, the rational soul is the substantial form of the human body. The soul is what organizes and structures matter into a living, organic human substance with specific biological processes and functions. Matter on its own is in potentiality to be anything whatsoever (*ST* 1a.75–89; *QDV* 8.6).

168. Milbank and Pickstock, *Truth in Aquinas*, 12. See also Te Velde, *Participation and Substantiality*, 279.

existent within it.[169] This interpretation of Aquinas postulates that knowledge is God's perpetual return to Himself, not as a movement from 'known' to 'unknown,' but a kind of 'encircling,' always already completed from the beginning of eternity, "for God, in knowing His own essence, also knows other things in which He sees a likeness of Himself, since He grasps Himself as participable, and so He returns to His essence."[170] For Aristotle and Aquinas there is a qualitative hierarchy of motion, whereby

> circular motion has a complete quality, being unitary, lying within its own bounds, and having an almost motionless quality [. . .] such motion seeks nothing beyond itself [. . .] being complete at every moment, without discernable beginning or end.[171]

Creation does not stand 'alongside' God, as another focus of existence; neither does it lie 'outside' God:

> Creatures, for Aquinas, beneath the levels of patterns of granted relative necessity and subsistence, are radically accidental. But not thereby, of course, accidents of the divine substance: rather they subsist by participation in it.[172]

Te Velde summarizes Aquinas' teaching in that, because God's knowledge *is* His divine nature, He can produce diverse and limited effects by His nature. God creates by means of emanation, and that this creation as a planned limitation of diverse beings is based on the notion of participation, since it is by participation in the *esse* of God that something has a likeness of God, and God's wisdom determines the diverse ways that each creature participates in God's *esse*. Hence, Te Velde can say that: "the notion of participation expresses at the same time the intrinsic value and meaning of a creature which is a 'being' as well as its essential imperfection inasmuch as it has only a part of being."[173]

Christian theology introduces the notion of creation as a gift of grace, whereby, at every moment, creation is *ex nihilo*. A corollary of this is that *creatio ex nihilo* does not refer to some kind of primordial temporal instant where God willed everything into being and stood aside (deism).

---

169. Oliver, *Introducing Radical Orthodoxy*, 18.

170. Milbank and Pickstock, *Truth in Aquinas*, 12. Here it may be said that Aquinas is modifying Aristotle in the direction of combining Aristotle with Neoplatonism in an entirely new way.

171. In respect to this perfect 'encircling' motion, see Oliver, *God, Philosophy and Motion*, 46, and Oliver, "Sweet Delight of Virtue," 55.

172. Milbank and Pickstock, *Truth in Aquinas*, 35.

173. Te Velde, *Participation and Substantiality*, 105–6, 118.

At every moment, creation is 'ex nihilo,' "and does not privilege any particular moment as being 'the moment of creation.' At every moment, creation is 'suspended over nothingness.'"[174] Its existence is a continuous and gratuitous divine donation in the form of an improper participation in God's own substantiality. Timothy McDermott's own summary of Aquinas' teaching on God's eternal omnipotence and gratuity draws on Thomas' own use of Augustine:

> Whatever actually possesses form exists, given the influence of God. God can no more confer on a creature continued existence without activity on his part, than he can confer on it uncausedness. The activity by which God maintains things is no new activity, but the continued activity of giving them existence, an act which is not a process in time (just as light in the air is maintained by the continuous shining of the sun).[175]

Aquinas deploys the Neoplatonic legacy and the metaphysics of participation to show that he regards human capacity for thought as a partial receiving of divine intellection. Just as for Aquinas we exist by participation in being, which is also 'accidental' to our essence, we do not 'have' to be, since 'being' alone gives us our determinate essence. Te Velde is apposite here, in that he stresses the *analogia entis*—analogy of being—as the formula of the metaphysical continuity-in-difference between the world and God as necessary, since we cannot easily overcome the immanence of human language and the transcendence of God. God, being the eminent source and principle of creation, manifests himself in the world through a diversity of perfections, such as 'being,' 'goodness,' 'wisdom,' etc. These perfections flow from the divine source into the created effects, whereby creatures participate in them:

> the sun may be regarded as a universal cause extending its powers to many and diverse effects in lower nature, each of which may be said to participate a diminished likeness of the full and undiminished perfection of the sun itself. [. . .] Analogy is meant to designate the intelligible connection between cause and effect. The effect may be said to be 'differently the same.'[176]

---

174. Oliver, *Introducing Radical Orthodoxy*, 18 and note 34.

175. McDermott, *Summa Theologiae*. In paraphrasing *ST* 1.104.1resp, he brings our attention to a quotation of Augustine (*Gen ad lit.* 4.12): "If at any time, the ruling power of God were to desert what he created, his creation would immediately lose its form, and all nature would collapse," 154–55.

176. Te Velde, *Aquinas on God*, 95–118, esp 110.

Therefore, we only exist 'humanly', that is, according to a higher kind of life, exercising our intellects, by participation in knowledge.[177] It may be shown that what is therefore 'extra' to us most defines us:

> The gifts of grace are added to nature in such a way that they do not destroy it, but rather perfect it [. . .] since what is imperfect bears a resemblance to what is perfect, what we know by natural reason has some likeness to what is taught to us by faith [. . .] just as sacred doctrine is based on the light of faith, so philosophy is based on the natural light of reason. So it is impossible that the contents of philosophy should be contrary to the contents of faith, but they fall short of them [. . . ,] nature itself is a preamble to grace.[178]

John Montag summarizes this claim in light of his reading of Henri de Lubac on *The Mystery of the Supernatural*, and identifies two key issues in support of Lubac's *ressourcement*. First, there is the lack of appreciation of the relationship between God and creation as one of 'radical giftedness' in which no autonomous stance before God is possible. Secondly, there is the confusion between nature as inert matter, and nature as a proper kind. Such people may think of the supernatural as 'unnatural' in the material sense. Montag thus proposes that 'supernature' denotes a super-matter on top of the matter accessible to us; it is imposed on us by God, added to our 'pure nature': "a 'supernatural' direction and finality indicate the openness of a nature to becoming what is not only beyond the realm of its own origin and end, but beyond the whole of all origins and ends."[179] Intellection is akin to grace, because the most important part of us is not part of our animal essence, but is super-added to us, properly and yet accidentally. Following Pseudo-Dionysius and Augustine, Aquinas surpasses the Aristotelian and Neoplatonist ideas of the Prime Mover as *nous* (self-identical thought thinking itself), but unlike Aristotle and the Neoplatonists, he introduces a certain role of relationality and difference into God. He speaks of God's knowledge of all the modes in which he can be participated. God knows all things fully in knowing their ends, their perfection, which includes all that they are.[180]

---

177. Milbank and Pickstock, *Truth in Aquinas*, 12. For a more detailed linguistic analysis of this concept in relation to how we speak about God, and Analogy, see David Burrell, *Aquinas: God and Action*, 62–67.

178. *SBT*, q2 a3 resp.

179. Montag, "Revelation," 46.

180. Milbank and Pickstock, *Truth in Aquinas*, 12.

This participation is improper in the simple sense that it is not 'proper to creation' in that there is no sense in which creation has a self-subsistent 'right' to existence. At all times, creation 'is' only because of the gratuity of God. Participation, therefore, avoids what might otherwise be a risk in understanding creation's relation to God through the analogy of attribution, namely the pantheistic view that the only really subsisting thing is God.[181] In this sense, participation asserts that creation is real, but it also asserts that creation's reality is not autonomous, but is a constantly arriving gracious gift of self-subsistent being, namely God. Creation is not simply a 'given,' it is 'gift.'[182] Although there are analogies between things in the universe and God, Aquinas stresses the gap repeatedly, in his reflection on the divine life, commenting on how our attempt to think about how that life inspires wonder in us: "Metaphysics thus begins and ends in wonder, an avowal of human ignorance about the highest things."[183] Our knowledge of God and the life of God are reflected in this analogous relationship as we are known by God, and in creation. Given, therefore, that participation in creation and the 'things of God' is in entirety a gift of God's free grace, this opens up the possibilities that the good life, as expressed in the virtuous life is equally by participation in this gift of grace. For Tolkien, the acquisition and gift of *virtus* has an extension beyond (and below) rational being, and is shared also with the artifacts of sub-creation (e.g., art, armor, food and drink).

That human dignity resides in a projection of grace, then its *modus operandi* is creation and createdness as gift—gift willed by a deliberate act of benevolence when none is required. This realization in the Thomist resolution of the Neoplatonic locus moves the debate towards a solution comprising human *telos* and the interdependent modes of being alongside other creatures. Grace in the metaphysics of participation truly defines what it is 'to be' in relation to the Creator and yet distinct, and is a 'tidier' resolution than what we shall find in Eriugena. In either case, the gift of 'being' does not subsist in human autonomy, but extends from the 'being' that is located in divine *quidity*—even if God's being/non-being is from our perspective, ineffable. In contrast, however human nature is defined within its radical giftedness; it has a familial and formal link to its origin and source. This

---

181. Oliver, *Introducing Radical Orthodoxy*, 18.

182. Ibid.

183. Hibbs, *Aquinas, Ethics, and Philosophy*, 10. However we speak of God, we naturally and instinctively refer to things within creation, and we name God from creatures (*ST* 1.13.1). Oliver, *Introducing Radical Orthodoxy*, 13, asserts that this is not entirely problematic for Aquinas, as 'effects resemble their causes.' Because God is the cause of creation, then creation will express *something* of the character of God—something of its divine origin.

discussion, therefore, needs to move a step closer to that human realization in the return, as both a free and mutable agent within a wider metaphysics of freedom, chance, and the providence of God.

3.4.2 Towards a Theology of Redemption in the *Reditus*

All creatures are said to subsist by grace in the sense that they only subsist in their constant return to full divine self-presence, whilst intellect simply is the consciousness of this return:

> God is said to be in a thing in two ways; in one way after the manner of an efficient cause; and thus He is in all things created by Him; in another way he is in things as the object of operation is in the operator; and this is proper to the operations of the soul, according as the thing known is in the one who knows; and the thing desired in the one desiring. In this second way God is especially in the rational creature which knows and loves Him actually or habitually. And because the rational creature possesses this prerogative by grace, as will be shown later (Q[12]). He is said to be thus in the saints by grace.[184]

Thus, not only is the intellect grace; it is in a sense simply the site of manifestation of the creature, and so of grace. Because we are mind, humans specifically are destined to be deified.[185] Here it is maintained that for Aquinas, in a post-lapsarian economy, the incarnation is the sole ground for the restoration of our participation in the divine understanding. Consequently, for us, not only are things true as participating in God; they are also only true as conjoined to the body of the incarnate *logos*. If God is to infuse grace into human nature, then he would come so close to that nature so as to join it to his own. For Aquinas, this is what we find in the incarnation. In communicating redemptive grace by which humanity might be moved to its ultimate end, Aquinas sees that it is most fitting that human nature should be joined to the divine nature fully in one person.[186] Christ, therefore, is both the sole-bearer of grace to humanity, and its reliable teacher, who restores for us also truth and knowledge in respect of his *potential absoluta*.[187]

---

184. Milbank and Pickstock, *Truth in Aquinas*, 37–38; *ST* 1a.8.3 resp.
185. Milbank and Pickstock, *Truth in Aquinas*, 60.
186. Oliver, *God, Philosophy and Motion*, 66.
187. Ibid.

God might have redeemed and reinstructed us without the incarnation of the Son.[188] His omnipotence and omniscience could have affected a simple cancelling of our sins by decree, allied to an act of positive re-creation. By this approach to the atonement and reconciliation, Aquinas assures us that God had no need to be appeased in order to be reconciled to us, and that, in him, he always and eternally was so reconciled. The incarnation, therefore, does not bring about this reconciliation of God, but instead mediates it to us, making it effective for and in us, thereby ensuring that we too are reconciled. It would seem that whilst truth necessarily is participation in God, only 'accidentally' and by appointment is it participation in Christ. Whist this 'mode' of redemption and reconciliation was not 'of necessity' in the incarnation, it must thereby have been the 'fitting' or 'convenient' manner of which this reconciliation is mediated to humanity: *Sed ei quod est necesse-esse sua necessitas essendi convenit inquantum est hoc signatum*.[189] Thus, Milbank and Pickstock can claim that

> this thematic of 'convenience' as applied to the divine economy of creation and redemption signals, in Aquinas, an aesthetic construal of participation: God creates, and is partially disclosed within, appropriate proportions which radiate according to their inherent 'integritas.'[190]

If *convenientia* is supremely and exhaustively shown in the incarnation, then this must be because within creation the analogical resemblance to God becomes transparent to the mode or 'way of being' of the divine *persona* of the logos. *Analogia entis* becomes *analogia Christi*, and the former, for Aquinas, is only available for fallen humanity through the latter.[191] Tolkien, in so far as he understood the Catholic theology of salvation, subscribed to this analogical 'exchange of being' in his daily attendance at mass, and its attendant merits for the faithful. In the belief that God is truly present 'in Christ' via an *alter Christus*, his own devotion to the Blessed Sacrament is well documented (below). His mythology reveals no developed messianic theology of atonement, even if there are several allusions which have led many down a

---

188. *ST* 3.1.2 resp; *SCG* 4.55.4.

189. *Convenientia* in *SCG* 1.42.13: "Again, nothing that belongs to this designated thing as such can belong to another, for the singularity of some thing belongs to none other than to that singular thing. But its necessity of being belongs to the necessary being so far as it is this designated being. Therefore, it cannot belong to another, and therefore there cannot be several beings of which each is a necessary being. It is, consequently, impossible that there be several gods."

190. Milbank and Pickstock, *Truth in Aquinas*, 61.

191. Ibid.

blind alley (e.g., Aragorn and Kingship; Gandalf's 'resurrection'; Sam carrying Frodo up the slopes of Mount Doom).[192]

Through the incarnation, God draws near to humanity in a most unexpected and extraordinary fashion. God is infinite, replete, and cannot be rivalled, and can therefore give of himself entirely—even his own divine nature to human nature.[193] In reflecting upon the text of John 1:17—"Grace and Truth came by Jesus Christ"—Milbank and Pickstock summarize these aspects of the *Convenientia* as follows: whilst according to the bare logic of his omnipotence, God could have redeemed us another way. The aesthetic fittingness of the way actually chosen reflects the way in which the eternal divine *logos* itself is most adequately characterized as the eminent realization of beautiful *proportio*. The means appointed, in the very freedom of this appointment, manifest the heart of divine 'necessity.' Since the 'hominization' of the Son is 'appropriate' as restoring the deification of humanity, this shows that what it restores is analogical ascent through various degrees of *esse ipsum*. Thus, not only is truth conveniently displayed in Christ, it is displayed as convenience. In order to remedy the fault of human sin, something 'in excess' of this occasional use of the incarnation is brought about, namely a new ontological state for the creation, the causing of a human creature directly to subsist in a divine hypostasis. This new 'circumstance' realizes a mode of divine self-sharing more absolute than the most absolute giving of the infinite to the finite according to its capacity for reception: this 'more absolute than the absolute' is the utter fusion of the finite with the infinite, and opens up the way for humans to receive the means by which they may attain to their ultimate *telos*: reconciliation with God, and the restored beatific vision.[194]

Here Aquinas exploits to the full the Dionysian paradox of God, 'existing outside of himself.' Just because there is no outside to God, then God can entirely externalize himself; just because he cannot share anything he can share everything.[195] Adam was created to enjoy the beatific vision, and to share without reserve, but to the measure of human personhood, in the divine nature.[196] Humanity has a natural kinship with the supernatural, bearing the *imago Dei*—albeit somewhat remotely—as the Son bears a

---

192. Many popular commentators ascribe to Tolkien a false intention that he was promoting in, an 'apologetic' sense, a Christian gospel. Whilst his works are suffused with Christian themes and motifs, one can read them independent of any such intention, given that he denied such obvious interpretation of his works.

193. *SCG* 4.55(3), and Milbank and Pickstock, *Truth in Aquinas*, 63.

194. Milbank and Pickstock, *Truth in Aquinas*, 63.

195. *ST* 1.20. Resp2.

196. Ibid., 1.20. Resp2; *SCG* 4.55(2); *ST* 1.97. Resp1.

resemblance to the Father, and since human beings as intelligent creatures already possess close kinship with the divine substance. This Thomistic understanding of the manner in which the *reditus* is effected, at least for the developed Neoplatonism of Aquinas, is assumed in Tolkien's understanding of the sacramental realities, and the self-understanding of how 'creatureliness' is an extension of both 'being and gift.'

3.4.3 *Being and Gift*: Pathways of Freedom to God's Eternal Present

There is no tidy solution to Tolkien's presentation of the return, or his presentation of life after death. There is no *Götterdammerung*, no real 'eucatastrophe' or catastrophic ending in which, though much is destroyed, good totally triumphs. There is no event in Tolkien's work comparable to Christ's dyscatastrophic death, issuing in his eucatastrophic resurrection. In this sense, it is very un-Augustinian, where the dualism of good/evil exerts itself beyond what may be proposed as privation. If Tolkien is presenting a solution to the complex problems of freedom, chance, and determinism, then he avoids the formulas of Catholic orthodoxy, and from within the mysterious undertones of his own faith, he is without doubt informed and influenced by wider ranging sources. In *The Hobbit*, the respite of safety and comfort is Beorn's house. As Beorn is a 'shapeshifter'—and thus a dangerous entity—his home nevertheless has a table which literally flowed with milk and honey. It was in this rich imagery that God spoke to Moses, recounted in Exodus 3:8, ratifying the covenant and promise to his descendent, Abraham. The elves, being immortal, give of their food for the journey—*Lembas*—which provides both sustainability and healing, metaphors rich in Christian Eucharistic theology, and upon which Tolkien was unashamedly orthodox:

> Out of the darkness of my life, so much frustrated, I put before you one great thing to love on earth: the Blessed Sacrament. [. . .] There you will find romance, glory, honour, fidelity, and the true way of all your loves upon earth, and more than that: Death: by the divine paradox, that which ends life, and demands the surrender of all, and yet by the taste (or foretaste) of which alone can what you see in your earthly relationships (love, faithfulness, joy) be maintained, or take on that complexion of reality, of eternal endurance, which every man's heart desires.[197]

---

197. Carpenter, *Letters*, 53–54.

In the posthumously published *Children of Hurin*, we read that Lembas is the gift to men of the (elf) Queen, a rare gift without which Frodo and Sam could never have reached their journeys' end, "the greatest gift that one who loves you still has to give [. . .]. Here is Lembas [. . .] the way-bread of the Eldar that no man has yet tasted."[198]

The theme of doom is notably a positive aspect of the fate of men:

> Death is their fate, the gift of Ilúvatar, which as time wears even the powers [Valar] shall envy. But Melkor has cast his shadow upon it, and confounded it with darkness, and brought evil out of good, and fear out of hope.[199]

However, as the mortality of men is but a part of Tolkien's particular 'degree of measure'—their 'doom'—then death may be embraced with good virtue and in due course. If the example of Arwen (above) is not proper to her (original) nature, but by free will born out of love, then Aragorn's death in the Appendix to *The Lord of the Rings* hints at a hope beyond life: "In sorrow we must go, but not in despair. Behold! We are not bound for ever to the circles of the world, and beyond them is more than memory." William Mann distinguishes between a diachronic and synchronic assessment of this particular aspect of the problem of mortality and mutability: one who laments the passing away of ephemeral things should realize that to wish that they might last forever is to wish that not they, but some other kind of being existed—yet that is precisely what Lúthien did.[200]

Another example of this misunderstanding of 'being' is the jealousy of the Númenoreans of the elves' immortality. They failed to accept their place in terms of their particular measure and order which differentiates the two kindreds. In the tale *Of Beren and Luthien*, Lúthien pleads the life of Beren before the Vala, Mandos, who in turn consults Manwë—having in his mind the 'will' of Ilúvatar (The One).[201] Two choices are set before her, and it is significant here that they are laid out as free choices with dire consequences: either, that she should be released from Mandos, and dwell in her rightful place as an elf—Valimar—where the memory of her grief is erased; or, return to Middle-earth with (a resurrected) Beren, wherein they both take their chances for good or ill.[202] The former choice ensures her material immortality, but separation from Beren: the latter forfeits her immortality, but ensures

---

198. Tolkien, *Children of Hurin*, 140. This 'gift-giving' is a persistent accolade directed at virtuous kings in the text of *Beowulf*.
199. Tolkien, *Silmarillion*, 48.
200. Mann, "Augustine on Evil," 45.
201. Tolkien, *Silmarillion*, 225.
202. Ibid.

an extended time in Middle-earth with Beren, as it is not permitted for the gods to change the essential and proper doom of humans. They may neither dwell in the Blessed Realm of Valimar, nor can they be transfigured to an earthly immortality, such as the elves experience. This passage is clear in that "Death [. . .] is the gift of Ilúvatar to Men." The deathlessness of elves is not true immortality, but simply the prolongation of life. In Tolkien's view, the real escape from death is *through* death to eternal life.[203] Tolkien is careful to inculcate a belief in the afterlife, and what hints he gives presuppose a Neoplatonist and Catholic understanding.[204] What is not clear is how the future will develop and enfold, because Tolkien's sense of uncertainty is always to render a humble sense of 'chance,' that all may yet be lost: "The Quest stands upon the edge of a knife. Stray but a little, and it will fail, to the ruin of all. Yet hope remains while the Company is true."[205]

3.4.4 Grace and Participation in *The Pearl of Delight*

In order, therefore, to reconcile the Tolkinian sense of 'being as gift,' insofar as I am able to extrapolate from this complex cycle of tales, I now turn finally to another source of great importance to both Tolkien and his contemporaries, and that is the Middle English poem "Pearl." The poem is contained within the 2006 edition of *Sir Gawain and the Green Knight*, and Tolkien began its translation soon after 1925, as a collaboration with E. V. Gordon. It exists in several forms in the unpublished Bodleian Library manuscripts. In this published edition Christopher Tolkien notes that of the author nothing is known, save that he was a major poet of his day (circa 1400), originating in the West Midlands of England, and with an 'amateur' knowledge and interest in theology: he was not a scholar of the day.[206] The poem contains two important biblical allegories, and may be read as an allegory itself as a whole. It is generally accepted as an elegy on the death of a child (not yet two years of age) by her father, though other readings are possible.[207] What is clear from the text is that whoever wrote the poem was acquainted with grief and real sorrow, and was attempting

---

203. Tolkien, *LOTR*, 1076.

204. Tolkien, *Silmarillion*, 64. Here we read of the death of Miriel, whose "spirit departed her body and passed in silence to the 'Halls of Mandos.'" Her body was 'incorrupt'—'unwithered'—a rare privilege claimed of certain Christian saints (e.g., Cuthbert, John Southwell, Bernadette of Lourdes).

205. Tolkien, *LOTR*, 376.

206. Tolkien, *Sir Gawain and the Green Knight* (including *Pearl* and *Sir Orfeo*), 1.

207. "Pearl," 7–13.

to reconcile this mental and emotional struggle alongside a profound late medieval Christian faith. In this investigation into the philosophy of being in Tolkien's rich oeuvre we gain as much from how he treats and speaks of death as he does of life. It is here that we can find parallels with the grief and choices of Lúthien when faced with the death of her Beren, and again Tolkien almost hides his own beliefs in life after death, presents them as a mere susurration, contracted in the choices which fate their own ends— given his own profound and deep Catholic faith.

In the poem "Pearl," there is a sense that life in its abundance is good, and comes from 'the good,' and using the biblical imagery of 1 Corinthians 15:35–41 the poet concedes that,

> For all grass must grow from grains that are dead,
>
> No wheat would else to barn be won.
>
> From good all good is ever begun, and fail so fair a seed could not,
>
> So that sprang and sprouted spices none
>
> From that precious pearl without a spot.[208]

However, given this acceptance of the *ordo* of life, in relation to the resurrection of Jesus, the grief of Lúthien could be read straight out of the opening lines of *Pearl*, in that Stanza 2, line 5 reads "But my heart doth hurt now cruelly," but is rendered in Tolkien's own manuscript notes as "That my heart now pierceth cruelly," and has strong Marian overtones via the *Stabat Mater* prophecy of Simeon to the Blessed Virgin in Luke 2:34–35.[209] Human life is inter and intrapersonal, and the loss of one so 'pure and clear' is a great personal tragedy. Yet in this grief, we see a consistent if not grudging compliance with human *doom* in its proper sense, whereby:

> what you lost was but a rose
>
> That by nature failed after flowering brief;
>
> [...] And yet you have called your fate a thief
>
> [...] you grudge the healing of your grief.[210]

We see that the phantasm of the poet's daughter berates him for his lack of faith, and disregard for the promise of Jesus:

> Who believes our Lord would speak a lie.

---

208. *Pearl*, Stanza 3, lines 5–10. References here and below reflect both his published version, and the unpublished texts extant in the Bodleian Library, Oxford. Where they vary markedly, then they are referred to separately.

209. *Bodleian SC–MSS* A33/2, folio1.

210. *Pearl*, Stanza 23, lines 6–11.

> He promised faithfully your lives to raise
> Though fate decreed your flesh should die;
> His words as nonsense ye appraise
> Who approve of naught not seen with eye.[211]

His grief and lack of acceptance of her 'heavenly estate' is a good example of Mann's analysis above, that we sometimes wish that things were other than what they are by design or *ordo*. If this is true of Lúthien, and we have no reason now to suppose the contrary, then her dialogue with Mandos is no different in principle between the poet of "Pearl" and his (deceased) daughter. What is at odds, and where Tolkien departs from the poem's conclusion, is that the poet capitulates to the accepted order, whereas Lúthien pleads her case and is given the grace of two choices, thus unfolding the natural order of the two kindreds. Interestingly, where the poem uses the word 'doom' in relation to the Adamic fall, "by Eden's grove and stream," it is in the sense of judgment, and that being death. Stanza 54 has a simple view of the fall, but one which appeared in time, and the food (apple) is objectified as a harbinger of that doom. 'Fate,' as we encounter it in the Boethian usage, is the unfolding of events as it is worked out in time, as we perceive them in the temporal world.[212] The dialogue between poet and his "Pearl" is reminiscent also of those between Boethius' prisoner and Lady Philosophy, and could in some sense be inspired by Alfred's own translation. His own 'doom' is his particular fate, shared with all humanity, and in the passing of loved ones, "to mourn once more. [...] Must bereavement new till death be mine?" is an ever-present reality.[213] In the poem there is no escape from this inevitability of death, and whilst each believer may not be graced by such a vision of heaven, or have a similar heavenly visitation, the poet accepts his grief and looks to a life of grace, in that:

> May He that in form of bread and wine
> By priest upheld each day one sees,
> Us inmates of His house divine
> Make precious pearls Himself to please. Amen Amen.[214]

What is of particular interest is that, as this theme of death and doom develops into the middle stanzas of the poem, we read of the means whereby

---

211. Ibid., Stanza 26, lines 4–8.
212. *Consolations*, 4.6.9.
213. "Pearl," Stanza 27, lines 2 and 4.
214. Ibid., Stanza 101, lines 9–12.

the 'curse' of the fall is undone, and the return becomes possible. In this simplified account of the fall there is no mention of either Eve or the deceiving serpent: it is the feeding upon the apple—the deed—which caused our lapse from grace. There is here something 'counter-sacramental,' that the objectification of one kind of fruit is undone by the reception of another—the sacred host. If *omnis natura bonum est*, then the apple here becomes the 'participation in evil,' whereas references to the mass and baptism (Stanza 55, line 5f) are means of divine grace:

> Water and blood from wounds so wide:
> The blood redeemed us from pains of hell,
> Of the second death the bond untied;
> The water is baptism, truth to tell,
> That the spear so grimly ground let glide.
> It washes away the trespass fell
> By which Adam drowned us in deathly tide.

These lines are very Johannine and rich in Eucharistic imagery, and follow on from a related phrase referencing the blood of the cross:

> But soon a healing hither sped:
> Rich blood ran on rough rood-bough,
> And water fair. In that hour of dread
> The grace of God grew great enow.[215]

There is a developed theology of atonement here, mediated through the sacraments of baptism and the Eucharist. It is not those who plead their rights before God who are redeemed (via the Parable of the Vineyard, in Stanzas 42–51), but those who "are tried, By innocence and not by right."[216] There is in the theology of the poem a sense of *reditus* and hence completeness in the restored state of purity, which the poet's daughter had never lost, dying so young. Amongst all the creatures of heaven, she is one of the great and blessed company, for "Of all the realm is queen or king" and each "Hath a virtue of its own being."[217] In "the court where the living God doth reign" Mary—"Mother immaculate, and fairest maid"—has a pre-eminent place by virtue of being "Blessed beginner of every grace!"[218] The poem reinforces the

---

215. Ibid., Stanza 54, lines 6–10.
216. Ibid., Stanza 59, lines 11–12.
217. Ibid., Stanza 38, lines 4 and 2.
218. Ibid., Stanza 37, lines 3–4.

inter-personal sense of community in heaven, referring to St Paul's teaching on the Body of Christ, again from 1 Corinthians 12:12–27, each part having its own usefulness and purpose.[219] Whilst her father doubts her suitability to be in "God's domain," she pleads her own baptismal grace:

> But enow have the innocent of grace
>
> As soon as born, in lawful line
>
> Baptismal waters then embrace;
>
> Then they are brought unto the vine.[220]

Within the precarious dialectic of father/daughter: earthly/ethereal there is in the backdrop a broadly Boethian view of God who is both unmoved by human suffering, and immutable, through "your prayer His pity may excite, so that Mercy shall her powers expend," and "Tis His to ordain what He might may deem."[221] God is timeless and without place, and lines 3 and 4 of Stanza 42 bear witness to this Boethian sense of God's essential goodness mediated in both reward and punishment, health and suffering:

> For just is all that he doth assign,
>
> And nothing can he work but right.

So begins his exposition of the Parable of the Vineyard, and the justification of heavenly rewards being meted out from "the first to the last." The second biblical exposition in the poem recalls Jesus receiving the little children (Matt 19:13–15). We read in Stanza 60 that:

> And people pressed their babes Him nigh,
>
> For joy and health from Him did pour.[222]

However, there is a note in red in the unpublished manuscript of the poem, which reads:

> And their babes the people pressed Him nigh,
>
> "Pray touch our children!" they implore,
>
> For from him flowed both health and joy.[223]

Again, we read strong sacramental language in this red section, different to that eventually published, and reminiscent of the Johannine crucifixion

219. Ibid., Stanza 39.
220. Ibid., Stanza 53, lines 1–4.
221. Ibid., Stanza 30, line 7 and 12.
222. Ibid., Stanza 60, Lines 5–6.
223. *Bodleian SC-MSS* A33/2, folio 18.

scene and Stanza 55, lines 2 and 7. We have here both Eucharistic and baptismal motifs of 'touch' and 'flowed'. The developing objectification of the sacraments in the late medieval period was based on both proscribed actions and words by the bishop or priest, and are all present in the poem. It is by the immanent gratuity of God that things can be restored and transformed. There is a further marginal note to the red text above, which gives this sacramental sense even greater clarity: "For the health and joy he did supply."[224] Here is an account of a true 'gift-giver,' explained in words (Stanza 60, line 1) and realized in the "overlay landscapes" where earth and heaven coincide. A yet further marginal note renders line 5 as, "For the health and joy that in Him lie."[225]

Tolkien clearly struggled with his translation here, as to what sense he was going to promote. Whatever attributes of God can be known in heaven are known perfectly (Stanza 62, line 5), and are mediated by word and touch, by analogy in relation to how we have kinship with that source—the One. Following this latter marginal note, if we can enjoy "health and joy"—as does this "Pearl"—it is linked to our participation in the attitude of Christ (in the imagery of the Lamb), and his acceptance of mere children. This heightened sense of participation is entirely sacramental, and we see that it is the Lamb himself who is the subject of that participation, mediated in the participation in the mass:

> The Lamb us gladdens, and, our grief redressed,
>
> Doth at every Mass with joy us bless.
>
> Here each hath bliss supreme and best,
>
> Yet no one's honour is ever the less.[226]

This Eucharistic and participatory theology is reinforced in the strongest terms as the poem draws to its conclusion, as the phantasm moves to a description of St John's apocalyptic vision:

> No church was there the sight to greet,
>
> Nor chapel nor temple there ever abode:
>
> The Almighty was their minster meet;
>
> Refreshment the Victim Lamb bestowed.[227]

---

224. Ibid.
225. Ibid.
226. *Pearl*, Stanza 72, lines 9–12.
227. Ibid., Stanza 89, lines 5–8.

In the marginal notes, Tolkien renders the last line as "The lamb as sacrifice food bestowed," thus making clear the ontological participation between subject/object.[228] In departing from his translation of the poem, Tolkien further adds his own reflections on these last few lines in the context of their biblical and eschatological context, making clear the spiritual/earthly conjoining of the heavenly temple and the New Jerusalem with the earthly church and cathedral:

> It was not in any earthly sense a church or cathedral. There was no altar: for God himself sat there. But it occupied the position of a great city [...] and Mass was celebrated there, in that the Lamb offered Himself as the host to the Father. It seems to me that the poet, with the freedom that he often shows in adapting Scripture to his vision and purpose, has taken Apocalypse xxi, 22 and 25 in close connexion, and according to his pictorial vision.[229]

In this, God could be said to pour into both humans and nature his goodness and virtue, just as for Tolkien an 'evil person' may impart their particular and deliberate malice into their own creations.[230] For "Pearl," the Lamb to whom she is now a bride is both "immaculate" and her "final end."[231] The previous Stanza mentions "Aristotle's love" and we see here a deliberate use of Middle-English poetry acknowledging the legacy of Greek classical philosophy, well into the fourteenth century AD. From the perspective of the "Pearl," God as both the efficient cause (by participation) and final cause (by deification) has by his own desire and grace,

> In his blood he washed my weeds in state,
>
> Crowned me clean in virginity,
>
> And arrayed me in pearls immaculate.[232]

The 'phantasm' has achieved its natural end or *telos*, the end to which all things pertain. The marriage of the Lamb has been enacted in language which is strong in biblical metaphor, and in terms of Aristotelian (and Thomist) metaphysics.

---

228. *Bodleian SC–MSS* A33/2, folio 27.

229. Ibid.

230. This is seen in the case of the One Ring, but also in other weapons of destruction, such as *Grond*—the cruel battering ram used in the siege of Gondor: "Long had it been forged in the dark smithies of Mordor, and its hideous head, founded of black steel, was shaped in the likeness of a ravening wolf; on it spells of ruin lay." Tolkien, *LOTR*, 860.

231. "Pearl," Stanza 64, line 1.

232. Ibid., Stanza 64, lines 10–12.

In a further manuscript, Tolkien creates a diversionary discussion on how the poet of "Pearl" sees the nature and work of Christ's atonement, alongside a Middle English etymology of sin.[233] It centres around the word *clem*, and is a form of *claime/claim*. Tolkien states emphatically that the common usage is "to demand, sue for, something as proper to the claimant."[234] With respect to 'sin,' this is entirely inappropriate, as sin is improper and alien to Christ (as the poem is at pains to explain).[235] He—Jesus—never "claimed it": it is laid upon or attributed to him. After his prayer in Gethsemane to be released from forthcoming suffering, he submitted, and so became a voluntary sacrifice.[236] He might thus be said to take upon himself, to attach to himself, the sins of the world, but not to 'claim' them, whether in the sense to assert a right to them, or to 'clamour' for them. He had actually 'deprecated' them.[237] Tolkien notes here that, "the construction and senses of CLEAM (OE claeman) do seem to me to fit."[238] This verb means "to daub or plaster something" (with some adhesive stuff)—to stick such a stuff onto something. The latter use is the one that appears in "Pearl," "The use of a verb with regard to sin that is in familiar life applied to adhesive and often soiling things is entirely apt."[239] These things are not often repulsive, but they are often felt to be. The fact that the daughter in paradise is now free of all actual and original sin, and the father has yet to be cleansed of the former, is reason enough why, when he plunges himself in the watery gulf that separates them, he cannot cross to her side of the shore.[240] The father/poet now has to return to his life, and work out his own salvation, but like the prisoner in Boethius' *Consolations*, does so with a renewed sense of hope. His 'doom' is fixed, but the passage beyond life is now mapped out before him in rich metaphor and aesthetic beauty.

---

233. *Bodleian SC–MSS* A11, folio 38.

234. Ibid.

235. Especially Stanza 71: "Jerusalem's Lamb had never stain, of other hue than whiteness fair; There blot nor blemish could remain, so white the wool, so rich and rare."

236. In *Bodleian SC–MSS* A11, folio 38, Tolkien notes in the margin the Latin text of Isaiah Liii.6, "*posuit in eo Dominus iniquitatem omnium nostrum* (and the LORD has laid on him the iniquity of us all)."

237. Here again Tolkien quotes from the Latin text of Isaiah Liii.7 in the margin, and the phrase "*oblatus est quia ipse voluit* (A victim? Yet he himself bows to the stroke)" takes on himself something which is entirely alien and inappropriate.

238. *Bodleian SC–MSS* A11, folio 38.

239. Ibid.

240. *Pearl*, Stanzas 97–98.

3.4.5 Grace and Participation beyond the Grey Havens

We see yet another sense of the return in another of Tolkien's lesser works. In spite of their respective labours, Bilbo and Frodo found great respite in the elven stronghold of Rivendell—the Last Homely House—and yet it was insufficient for the weariness and agitation in the two hobbits. As the elves began to depart from Middle-earth at the end of the Third Age, Bilbo and Frodo made that same journey to the Western Isles via the *Grey Havens*: "No temporal dwelling, no matter how paradisical, answers to the ultimate needs of our spirits."[241] For Michael Treschow, this point is further stressed in Tolkien's 'allegory' *Leaf by Niggle*. In painting his 'leaf,' Niggle develops the theme to a great tree, and desired to add a great background of mountains and waterfalls. Despite his obsession to complete the painting, he is constantly disturbed by the urgent needs of his neighbor, Parish, and is then required to leave his picture and home—unfinished. Treschow interprets this sudden departure as Niggle's death, and that the ensuing regret over his treatment of Parish is viewed as purgatorial.[242] Niggle is sent to the very place that he was painting. The tree and settings now become real, and yet unfinished, so he sets about the task of completing his cottage and garden, as if he were co-creating his own art work, assisted by his old neighbor.[243] This is what I shall demonstrate in Alfred Siewers' understanding of *non-being* in relation to Tolkien, whereby that which exists in the mind—and here we discern a strong Eriugenian strand—comes into being, and the spiritual and numinous are both and at the same time same and distinct.[244] Prior to completing this new task, Niggle is once again invited to move on by a shepherd and finds that he does, leaving behind Parish who is now waiting for his wife to join him. Following Treschow's reading of this 'allegory,' each stage of Niggle's life and work is only a single but interconnected stage in his journey to the mountains. Unsurprisingly, this theme of quest—medieval in origin—is present in most of Tolkien's works, and all of his Middle-earth writings at some stage. There is no settling in one place, and the ultimate (and sometimes urgent) need for return and final rest is ever-present. If this is so of Bilbo and Frodo, then it is equally so of Beren and Aragorn. Life cannot hold them, even for a second time as in the case of Beren. Like the biblical characters of Lazarus, Jairus' daughter, and the widow of Nain's son, life after death in Tolkien's world involves a body, yet this resurrection

---

241. Treschow, "Wisdom's Land," 280.
242. *Tree and Leaf*, 103–4. Tolkien also saw it in this sense, in his *Letters*, 195.
243. *Tree and Leaf*, 112–15.
244. Siewers, *Strange Beauty*, 6.

upon Middle-earth is only transitory. If Jesus is a model here, then for him it was but a forty-day sojourn in a reanimated body. The return beckons to the source. The New Testament is strangely silent about the fate and second death of those whom Jesus raised from the dead, and as such, so is Tolkien's account of Beren and Lúthien.

Ad locum unde exeunt flumina revertuntur.

All streams run to the sea,
but the sea is not full;
to the place where the streams flow,
there they flow again.[1]

---

1. Ecclesiastes 1:7.

4

Tolkien, Eriugena, and the Conjoining of Borrowed Traditions

In this chapter I shall discuss the sophisticated use that Tolkien made of early medieval Welsh and Irish texts, alongside suggestive parallels with the mystical Neoplatonism of the ninth-century Irish philosopher John Scottus Eriugena. There is a pursuasive link between Tolkien's co-creation and Eriugena, and it is the latter's philosophy of being, and Tolkien's possible use of it, which provides one further model of how life and being are inextricably linked to the Creator via the Neoplatonic model of participation. These insights offer a significant development from those previously encountered in the medieval period up to Aquinas, and this only serves to strengthen the claim that Tolkien did not rely solely on one strand of the Christian Neoplatonic tradition.

There are three stages to this investigation: first, I have charted Eriugena's understanding and analysis of freedom in *The Periphyseon*, presenting nature generally, and human nature in particular, as both optimistic and free from a fall as can be read out of Genesis chapter 3. In this regard, it may be seen just how Tolkien's own ideas of 'fallen' nature have strong resonances with Eriugena's philosophy. The return of fallen human nature to the source in God is not presented as a redemption and/or bodily resurrection, such as we find in a literal reading of the Gospels and St Paul, but a *theosis*—a transformation in being—whereby our nature is assumed in a turning around of temporality, to one of timelessness and eternity. Eriugena explains human nature in terms of its correspondence to the divine nature by participation, and yet seemingly indistinct in the *reditus*. This has already been raised when considering Tolkien's philosophy of finite being in *The Tale of Tinúviel*, given the uncertainty of form of the chief protagonists on the one hand, and the whole of Middle-earth as it evolved and changed over time, on the other. Secondly, I shall expound Eriugena's understanding of human freedom, in contradistinction to his contemporary Gottschalk, in that it largely accords with those of both Augustine and Boethius. This is significant in the development and resolution of Chapter 5. Finally, I shall explore the concept that, alongside Middle-earth's quasi-physical evolutionary landscape, and Tolkien's repeated interplay between his own co-creation and the reality of our world, there can be seen to exist a complex and unfolding overlay landscape drama, similar to those we find in early medieval Irish and Welsh mythological narrative. This is a development of the work of the American medievalist Alfred K. Siewers, who, while his writings focus on environmental and literary landscapes, offers a compelling framework for a cosmic dialectic, such as we read out of *The Periphyseon*.

4.1 Tolkien's Neoplatonism, and the Mystical Paths of Christian Mythology

Eriugena's influence on Tolkien is persuasive in helping make sense of some mystical aspects of his *legendarium*, but I suggest this is only a part of the whole Neoplatonist well from which he drank deeply. At the conclusion of this part of the investigation, it will be seen that, at least within *The Tale of Tinúviel*, an Eriugenean philosophy emerges. Eriugena's Neoplatonism is at times consistent, and otherwise divergent from earlier forms of the Neoplatonic tradition, and here I develop his ideas from primary sources, and trace step by step his philosophy of being, and how Tolkien's own human anthropology and psychology of freedom may be seen to fall within its embrace.

4.1.1 Eriugena and his Sources

Eriugena had no direct knowledge of the early Neoplatonists Plotinus, Porphyry or the later philosopher, Proclus. He appears to have known Plato's *Timaeus*, in Calcidius' translation, and the Pseudo-Augustinian paraphrase of Aristotle's *Categories*, Rufinus' Latin translation of Origen's *De Principis* (On First Principles), and Boethius' *Consolations of Philosophy*. Eriugena was eager to show this knowledge of Platonism, gathered from Macrobius, Calcidius and the Latin translation of Plato's *Timaeus*, in terms of the principles of the liberal arts. He believed that these principles were innate in human beings, but not easily recovered, and not properly captured by their sensory manifestations—like the dual existence of Plato's ideals/forms and the sensory world of shadows.[1] His chief authorities, however, were Augustine,

---

1. Marenbon, *Medieval Philosophy*, 73–74.

Ambrose, Hilary of Poitiers and Jerome, among the Latin Fathers, but he more often expresses a preference for the Eastern Church Fathers, in particular Dionysius (whose entire corpus he translated into Latin) and the Cappadocians, Basil, Gregory of Nazianzus and Gregory of Nyssa. It was the latter's work, commonly entitled *De Hominis Opificio* (The Creation of Man), that he translated under the title of *De Imagine* (On the Image of Good). He also translated Maximus Confessor's *Ambigua* (Difficult Questions of Interpretation) and *Quaestiones ad Thalassium* (Questions to Thalassius). Given the available sources, Eriugena was exceptionally learned, but his true genius lay in being able to bring all these authorities together in a new cosmological framework. Eriugena, by his translation of the Greek Fathers, as well as his own works, despite his own very considerable debt to Augustine, provided a kind of window through which for the last time for many centuries the West could gaze on the theological landscape of Byzantium.[2] The Greek Fathers he translated were precisely those who worked out a Christian version of the ancient cosmic understanding of humanity.

4.1.2 God as the Utterly Unknowable and Unknown Ground of Being

Eriugena's dialectical approach is developed in *The Periphyseon*—Division of Nature—his major philosophical treatise, which is built upon an all-encompassing definition of its subject matter: nature is the general term "for all things that are and all things that are not," and these include both God and created effects.[3] His approach to the terms 'Creator' and 'created' differs from the idea that they are usually understood as two distinct and differentiated entities. God is uncreated, yet in the act of creating, God creates God's self (*a se ipso creatur*). God, as Cause, is the essence of all things,[4] and outside of God there is nothing.[5] Therefore, the second and third divisions of nature are eternal since they are God, and they are made since they are not God. All things are bound together in the unity of their cause:

---

2. Louth, "The Body," 120.

3. *Periphyseon*, 1.441a. Nature is divided into four 'species,' echoing similar divisions in Augustine and Victorianus: (1) That which creates and is not created (i.e., God); (2) That which is created and creates (i.e., primary causes or Ideas); (3) That which is created and does not create (i.e., temporal effects, created things); (4) That which is neither created nor creates (i.e., God as non-being and nothingness, as to that which all things return).

4. Ibid., 1.454a.

5. Ibid., 1.452c.

> The beauty of the whole established universe consists of a marvellous harmony of like and unlike [...] and ineffable unity.[6]

In the tradition of Alcuin, influenced by both Augustine and Boethius, as to whether or not any of Aristotle's *Ten Categories* are predicable of God, Eriugena demonstrates that none of the *Categories* apply to God—not even 'being.' At the commencement of *The Periphyseon* he proposes a division even more fundamental than the four-fold one: into what exists and what does not. God does not exist in the sense that he is 'beyond being,' and it is God—and God alone—who does not exist in this way. Here Eriugena separates himself sharply from Augustine and almost all the Latin thinkers. They had preferred to speak of God in the terms associated with Plotinus' second *hypostasis*, as 'intellect.' In distancing themselves from Plotinus' view that the One, the ultimate ground of explanation, is not a being, but beyond being, the Christian Neoplatonists were able to reconcile their philosophical 'model' alongside the active role that God plays in creation, salvation, and final judgement.[7] Not having direct knowledge of Plotinus, Eriugena uses a distinction taken from Pseudo-Dionysius' *Mystical Theology*, and proposes two ways of speaking about God: affirmative/cataphatic, and negative/apophatic.[8] The former affirms attributes of God which are true in so far as they are understood causatively. God is not 'literally' good or just, nor does He literally even exist. God's existence is understood in terms of being the cause of goodness, justice, etc., and these attributes may be said of Him metaphorically. Eriugena's apophatic approach—like other Neoplatonists—speaks of what God is not, stating that in each case God is beyond that attribute. However, in the Eriugenean model, apophaticism is taken to a further extremity, in that not even God *knows* what *He* is, and does so on two grounds.[9] Firstly, if none of the *categories* (above) can be properly understood to be applied to God, then there is no answer to the question, 'What is she/he/it?' Any such reply would give Him substance: God is not a substance to be known, so cannot understand Himself. Secondly, if God is 'infinite,' then He lacks all bounds, and so cannot be defined, and is therefore unknowable as to what He is. God is therefore nothing, and the nothing from which God creates *ex nihilo* is simply the nothing which is God himself.[10] Moran posits that Eriugena's departure from the Dionysian tradition, regarding non-being as equally important as being, then he develops a negative dialectic

---

6. Ibid., 3.638a.
7. Marenbon, *Medieval Philosophy*, 75.
8. *Periphyseon*, 1.458a–d.
9. Marenbon, *Medieval Philosophy*, 76, commenting on Periphyseon 1.586–90.
10. *Periphyseon*, 3.681a–c.

which counterbalances ontological affirmations and constructions, with a radical meontology. This is perhaps the most creative analysis of non-being since Plato's *Sophist* and *Parmenides*.[11] For Eriugena, there are not two beings—God and the universe. God is 'no thing' in the universe, but becomes manifest in the universe, and only by means of theophanies. The whole of creation is therefore a theophany.[12]

In Tolkien's use of this infusion, God is present in creation in two ways: first, and transcendently, by the command of His voice—*Eä*—which both defines the universe, and also names it; secondly, as immanent semi-divine beings—Valar. Tolkien writes, "they were the agents and vice-gerents of Eru (God). They had been for nameless ages engaged in demiurgic labour completing to the design of Eru the structure of the universe (*Eä*); but were now concentrated on earth for the principal Drama of Creation."[13] *Eä* was achieved mediately by the Valar: created effects themselves create in a more earthly and immanent manner than Eriugena's divine theophanies. These are not merely parallels to what Eriugena as a Neoplatonist is defining nature in relation to God: Tolkien is doing the same thing, but after a different *modus operandi*.

The second division of nature—that which is created and creates—consists of the primordial causes, rather like the Platonic Ideas in the mind of God, and the 'seminal reasons' in Augustine's *De Genesi ad Litteram*. Eriugena postulates that humans have a highly favoured position in the *schema*. Eriugena's description of the primordial causes is very broad, ranging from Greek ideas of *prōtotypa* (primordial exemplars); *proorismata* (predestinations, or predefinitions); *theia thelēmata* (divine volitions); and are even commonly called *ideai*—species or forms in which the immutable reasons of things that were to be made were created before (the things themselves) existed.[14] As man is made in the *imago Dei*, then the human intellect shares with God the inability to know itself for what it is in essence, though the human intellect is knowable by God alone.[15] In respect of the human soul, and following Maximus often verbatim, Eriugena describes its three motions—the Intellect, the Reason, and the Sense. The motion of the *Intellect* is motion around God Himself, which is beyond the nature of the soul itself, and knows God 'according to what he is.' This knowledge, according to Eriugena, results in the knowing that God is not

11. Moran, *John Scottus Eriugena*, xiii.
12. *Periphyseon*, 3.681a.
13. Tolkien, *Morgoth's Ring*, 330, 336.
14. *Periphyseon*, 2.529b.
15. Ibid., 2.585a–b.

any sort of thing and cannot be defined for what He is. The motion of the Reason (the activity of the third hypostasis, soul, according to the usual Neoplatonic scheme) knows God as the Cause of all things. Eriugena's dualism is complete in that to experience sense, the soul requires a body, but is both distinct from it, and creates its own body.[16]

In a discussion on the true nature of men, Tolkien discusses this process of 'ensoulment' by clarifying that there are incarnate creatures (elves and men) who are made of a union of *hröa and fëa*, roughly equivalent to body and soul.[17] The two were made for each other, to abide in perpetual harmony. *Fëa* is indestructible, "a unique identity which cannot be disintegrated or absorbed into any other identity." *Hröa* can be destroyed and dissolved, though its separation from *fëa* is unnatural, and does not accord with the design of Arda. It would appear that Tolkien's anthropology is more Platonic than Eriugenaean, though as the *fëa* was held to be created directly by Eru, then it would have a self-knowledge of God rather akin to Plato's account of the soul's descent/return to the world of the Forms. It would have an innate knowledge of its source, otherwise it would have neither a participatory nor teleological existence in relation to God. This is further evidenced by a note concerning *fëa* and the passage of time: "Since Men die, without accident, and whether they will to do so or not, their *fëar* must have a different relation to Time."[18] Furthermore, Tolkien is clear not to imply an account of human reincarnation, in that "the *fëar* of Men, if disembodied, left time (sooner or later), and never returned." It was the belief of the elves—though never asserted—that "No *fëa* of a dead Man ever returned to life in Middle-earth."[19] Since it is "sent into Eä," and one assumes embodiment, then there is no scope to hold to any dependency here upon Eriugena, who makes no clear distinction between God and immanent humanity, and there is no evidence that a descent into materiality for Tolkien is a lapse from a prior unfallen perfect state.[20] In these more obscure texts of Tolkien, we find him not simply engaged in the process of writing a co-creative mythology, but engaging in metaphysics, expounding his own philosophy of life as 'being and gift' in relation to its source and material existence. This is cross-referenced to the case study (above) concerning the return for Beren in that, whilst there is an ontological prohibition in terms of reincarnation, there are notable exceptions such that, whilst "Beren returned to actual life,

16. Ibid., 2.572c–573b; 2.580b.
17. Tolkien, *Morgoth's Ring*, 330.
18. Ibid., 331.
19. Ibid., 340.
20. Ibid., 336.

for a short time; but he was not actually seen again by living Men."[21] As the creation of Arda unfolds from the mind-music-vision reality procession, the gift of *fëa* is a particular gift to men and, like death, is a universally defining aspect of their essence.

The procession of God into all things as created effects means for Eriugena that all things have the one primordial cause, the same beginning, and ultimately will have the same end. In the procession from God, the nothingness from which all things are created is actually God's self, because there can be nothing coeternal and coexisting with God. This 'nothing' becomes 'something' through the creative process, in that the unknowable reveals itself through creation, and in so doing becomes something that both itself and created effects can know. God's fullness above being is the 'nothing' that is the negation of something, but through its becoming, it becomes the negation of the negation. The divine nature becomes 'other than itself': God becomes not-God through the process of 'ex-stasis,' literally God's going out from God.[22]

In *The Periphyseon*, creation means God's movement from nothingness into something, indeed into all things—a 'self-negation.' Paradoxically, there is no 'self' to negate until the movement into the causes begins, "for as yet there is no essence."[23] Creation, therefore, does not refer to the making of things that exist outside of God, because in the very act of creating, the divine essence actually causes itself. Outside of God there is nothing, "since all things are from Him and through Him and in Him and for Him."[24] In theological fashion, Eriugena cannot compromise God's simplicity and infinity by acknowledging that God existed before God created, for creation,

> while it is eternal it does not cease to be made, and made it does not cease to be eternal, and out of itself it makes itself, for it does not require some other matter which is not itself in which to make itself.[25]

Creation has both 'being' coeternal and coessential with God.

To make sense of any Tolkinian reading of Eriugena, we are bound to consider how Eriugena reads the Genesis text in light of his own literary legacy and that of antiquity. There is no mention of the creation of angels in Genesis, but we find this in Augustine's mature reading of the 'Hexameron'

---

21. Ibid., 340–41. The reincarnation of the elves is discussed in this section.
22. Carabine, *John Scottus Eriugena*, 35.
23. *Periphyseon*, 3.683a.
24. Ibid., 3.679a; 1.452c.
25. Ibid., 3.6768d–679a.

(six days) in the *De Genesi ad Litteram*. Written when Augustine was over sixty years of age, it is an extremely measured and reflective document, free from earlier controversy and dogmatism, and is open to a variety of interpretations.[26] The imperative command, *Fiat lux*—let there be light—for Augustine, refers to the creation of the angels:

> Immediately after the word spoken by God, light was made [the angels], and this created light was united with the creating Light, God, beholding Him and beholding in Him itself, that is, the form according to which it was created.[27]

This has its origin in Plotinus' *Enneads*,[28] wherein the *nous* is a radiance of the One, and looks towards the One from which it has its being, recognizing that it was separated from the One, saw reflected in itself the potentiality of the One, and moved in love towards its origin. Thus had the *nous* emanated from the One. In interpreting the Genesis 1 account of the creation of man and woman, Augustine regards them as being equal in the image and likeness of God, yet differentiated in sex: "*And God made man to the image of God.* For the nature of this creature is intellectual, as is the light previously mentioned, and so its creation is identified with its knowing the Divine Word through whom it was made."[29] St Paul in 1 Corinthians 11:7 preceding Augustine would appear to stress a different precedent: "the male is the image and glory of God, but woman is the glory of the male": man and woman may be said to be differentiated in their causal reasons.

Eriugena's treatment of the *Fiat lux* demonstrates a departure from both St Paul *and* Augustine: the general procession of the primordial causes into their effects is one creation.[30] Following Dionysius, darkness signifies the incomprehensibility of the eternal reasons in God as well as God himself; and light signifies the *de-claratio*, manifestation or theophany of those reasons in the effects that we can see.[31] The difference between Augustine and Eriugena is fundamental: Eriugena interprets Augustine as understanding that the 'reasons' or causes of things are eternal in God and, in being created, from being light become darkness. O'Meara is correct in stating that it would be unjust to describe Augustine's approach as more philosophical/intellectual, and Eriugena as more theological/mystical. There is a profound

---

26. O'Meara, *Augustine and Eriugena*, 233.
27. *De Gen ad Lit*, 4.32.50.
28. *Enneads*, 3.8.3; 3.8.8.
29. *De Gen ad Lit*, 3.20.30–32.
30. *Periphyseon*, 3.691a–693c.
31. O'Meara, *Augustine and Eriugena*, 271.

difference between looking at darkness as a symbol of something transcendently superior to light or greatly inferior to it. It would appear, therefore, that Tolkien's anthropology of life, both angelic and human, is largely Augustinian, in that he uses anthropomorphic images to bring into being created effects from the primordial causes—which are the Ainur/Valar. There is no inherent apophaticism in Tolkien's approach: instead his readers are aware of the direction of his narrative.

4.1.3 The Meaning of Human Nature

Eriugena's starting point is the anthropology of the Pauline Epistles and Augustine. As in Augustine, Eriugena is concerned to define or situate human nature with respect to the divine nature, rather than the rest of the created cosmos. Again, he is especially influenced here by Augustine's conception in the *De Genesi ad Litteram* of an ideal 'ratio' of human nature, which is almost an 'undescended' part of the soul, and by his concept of human introspective self-awareness: a 'cogito.'[32] Eriugena's theory of human nature understands humanity under two aspects: perfect human nature, as it might be understood prior to the fall, and present-day fallen nature.

Eriugena asserts that the Greeks maintained that there are two creations of man: an indivisible and universal humanity, similar to the angelic nature, but without differentiation of sex, and a secondary nature, "which was added as a result of the foreknowledge of the Fall of the rational nature, and in which sex is established."[33] He consistently ranks original humanity as at least equal to the angels, in so far as they are *imago Dei*, unique amongst all of creation. His concept of fallen human nature is consistent with that of many late Greek writers: "the limits of human nature are the limits of paradise."[34] If human beings had not departed from paradise, then they would enjoy the kind of being which Christ himself enjoys. For Eriugena, paradise is merely an allegorical way of expressing what humans 'might' have been. Paradise is perfect human nature,[35] and is here spiritualized in contrast to Augustine's understanding of an actual place.[36] Eriugena is not interested in paradise as a place, since place for him is mind-dependent and has no external corporeal reality. In relating paradise to a possible perfect state of being, and the kind of being which is enjoyed by Christ, then that

32. *De Gen ad Lit*, 4.4.9–10.
33. *Periphyseon*, 4.817A.
34. Ibid., 4.825c; Steel, *The Unchanging Self*, 132–41.
35. *Periphyseon*, 4.809 b–d.
36. *Civ. Dei*, 14.26.

unique being pertains to him outside all place and time. Humanity, in its essence, is independent of spatio-temporal and corporeal restrictions:

> For in the world it is not the corporeal and spatially extended masses and the manifold varieties of its diverse parts that right reason contemplates and venerates, but its natural primordial causes, united in themselves and most beautiful, to which, when [its] end comes, it shall return and abide for ever [in them].[37]

Paradise is at once enjoyed by Christ and desired by man as the perfection of human nature. One can see how, if Tolkien used Eriugena as an influence, there is no need for a physical place called heaven/paradise for humanity, because it can be everywhere at once when man is liberated from the desire and effects of the fall. A virtuous man such as Aragorn, and by his act of self-sacrifice, the Maia Gandalf in Moria can die, because the perfection and attachment to physicality need not be experienced spatio-temporally. When Gandalf was seized in Moria by the Balrog they entered into mortal combat, and as victor, Gandalf experienced a metamorphosis. The process did not take place in time, nor in normal space but, "we fought far under the living earth where time is not counted. [. . .] Then darkness took me, and I strayed out of thought and time."[38] The transformation of Gandalf, from Grey to White, was accompanied by a sort of resurrection body which defied the normal constraints of corporeality. Gwahir the eagle describes Gandalf's new status as being, "Light as a swan's feather in my claw you are. The sun shines through you. Indeed, I do not think you need me any more: were I to let you fall, you would float upon the wind."[39] Through this experience Gandalf becomes more than Gandalf: "Indeed I *am* Saruman, one might almost say, Saruman as he should have been."[40] Gandalf's new actualized state is mystical—like the risen body of Jesus—in that he was not immediately recognizable; his ontological being is still Maiar, but within that genus he has assumed the mantle of another. Life and being here are, once again, uncertain and in a state of moral and material fluidity. Even so, that temporal life has both a beginning and an end is a common thread in Christian Neoplatonism, and I shall offer a theory—albeit a speculate one—of how Eriugena's account of its *exitus* and *reditus* has a particular resonance with that of Tolkien's developed (and more mystical) human anthropology.

---

37. *Periphyseon*, 2.539c.
38. Tolkien, *LOTR*, 523–24.
39. Ibid., 524.
40. Ibid., 516.

In Eriugena, paradise is a special form of knowing, and gaining this knowledge gives the seeker entrance to this spiritual domain. He stresses the intellectual rather than moral aspects of this *gnostica virtus*, and the cherubim with flaming swords as guards of the gates of paradise are to be understood as the symbol of the fullness of human knowledge and wisdom—philosophy is the gate of heaven.[41]

4.1.4 Perfect Human Nature

Human nature is essentially immaterial, eternal, omniscient, omnipotent and has being which transcends above all created being, while also immanent in all being. Human nature will move to a state beyond the paradox of being and non-being: human nature in its perfection is not merely eternal in the sense of having no end—it is more accurately timeless. In this it could be said that Eriugena is assimilating a Boethian divine attribute into the anthropology of human nature in its undifferentiated form. Perfect human nature is contained neither by space and time, nor by any other category which limit human existence in the created realm. So just as God by his nature transcends all the Aristotelian categories of quality, quantity, place, time, position, etc., so also human nature is not bound within these limits.[42] Here he speaks of the corporeal body of Jesus on earth, and its conjoining with his eternal existence in paradise: "there is one (natural) reason, (and) uniting the world and paradise in Himself."[43] He then extends this concept to the 'substance' of human nature: "so the human replica of the Divine Essence is not bound by any fixed limit any more than the Divine Essence in whose image it is made."[44] There are no ontologies or spiritual barriers imposed on the 'march of the spirit,' and Eriugena goes much further than merely asserting the incorporeality and unboundedness of perfect unfallen human nature: "Man and God are paradigms/exemplars of each other." The term 'paradigm/exemplar' here is borrowed from Dionysius: "We give the name 'exemplar' to those principles which pre-exist as a unity in God and which produce the essences of things,"[45] and refers to the Dionysian concept of 'being itself' (*to auto einai*), 'life itself,' etc.[46] Similarly, all of God's attributes can also be found in human nature, the distinction being that God

---

41. *Periphyseon*, 5.865c.
42. Ibid., 2.539c–d.
43. Ibid.
44. Ibid., 4.772a.
45. *Div Nom*, 5.824c
46. See also *Periphyseon*, 2.615d, and 2.559a–d.

is Himself *per essentiam*, whereas man is God *per participationem*. In this regard, Eriugena goes much further that Nicholas de Cusa, for example, who likes to emphasize the finitude of human nature and the inseparable gap between finitude and infinity.[47] For Cusa, only the single man can attain to the maximum—that is Christ himself. For Eriugena, man and God are mutually self-defining: just as God is incorporeal and spiritual, so human nature is incorporeal and spiritual. Human nature is an incorporeal essence (*ousia*), which can be identified with pure intellect (*nous*), and human nature is interpreted to be, in its essence, an incorporeal spirit. In this, the human self is neither male nor female, but sexless, hence Eriugena's understanding of Galatians 3:28—"there is neither male nor female." *The Periphyseon* has a striking ultra-optimistic view of un-fallen human nature, in that,

> if human nature had not sinned but had adhered to unchangeability to Him who had created her, she would certainly have been omnipotent. For whatever in nature she wished to happen would necessarily happen, since she would wish for nothing else to happen save that which she understood her Creator wished to happen.[48]

Therefore, the freedom of the will is incorporated within this heightened intellectual participatory relationship with the Creator. God's will is not causal in terms of human will, but that the two are reflexive: in its unfallen state, the human will is both boundless and co-terminus with the Creator from whom it originates.[49]

By association with God's stated omnipresence,[50] Eriugena frequently expresses the idea of human omnipresence—"Man being everywhere a whole in himself"—and that human nature is whole throughout all the parts of its nature, which in fact encompasses all the parts of created being, "since human nature is so in itself, it goes beyond its whole."[51] There is a danger in understanding the whole of the *Tale of Tinúviel* in terms of their respective natures, in that too much is made of the affinity between elf and man, given their ontological difference. An Eriuganian interpretation might lead us to read the *Tale* not so much in terms of these natures, but more of what they can be, given the freedom which exists in their undifferentiated ontologies as 'being.' Tolkien alludes to the basic ontological relationship between the two kindreds, in that "Elves and Men are evidently in biological terms one

---

47. *Da Docta Ignoranta*, 3.3.200.
48. *Periphyseon*, 4.778b. See also 4.777c–778a.
49. Ibid., 2.539c–d; 4.772a.
50. Ibid., 3.683c–684d; 3.677c; 4.759a.
51. Ibid., 4.759b.

race, or they could not breed and produce fertile offspring—even as a rare event."[52] They are still essentially in their essence and being a union of *hröa* and *fëa*, and in this sense share a common 'nature.' According to Eriugena, if man, therefore, is able to 'transcend' his bodily self in his true nature, then he could (theoretically) take on the form of another, because "man participates in (these) together with all other animals."[53] "These" refers to the motions arising out of irrational creatures, which man participates in as a rational creature. Eriugena goes on to assert that,

> man is all animals, and all animals in him, and yet he transcends them all [. . .] the same man is a species of the genus animal and also transcends every animal species, and thus admits an affirmation and a negation: for it may rightly be predicated of him—'man is an animal'; and 'man is not an animal.'[54]

Where Eriugena is speaking of human anthropology in relation to non-rational creatures, then in the sense of Beren and Lúthien (and Sauron) being 'shapeshifters,' it may be extrapolated from this transcendental and yet incarnational reading of Eriugena, that man as genus is omnipresent in all things, and could therefore be represented in all creatures, of whatever species within this common genus. This anthropology accords with that of Aquinas' later ontology, in that man is a microcosm, assuming and summing up all other levels or orders of their respective natures. Man is

> altogether an animal [. . .] in his higher nature, which consists in reason and mind and the interior sense, with all their rational motions, which are called virtues, and with the memory of the eternal and divine things, he is altogether other than animal.[55]

If Tolkien is influenced here by Eriugena, then he is engaging in more than metaphysics. Tolkien is developing a mystical philosophy of being which has an affinity with Eriugena's sources (especially Gregory of Nyssa and Maximus the Confessor), where the ontological difference within the category of genus is uncertain, and subject to the free agency of the subject. This freedom has both an ethical and material aspect, as these shape-shifting characters carry out their tasks in relation to their respective quest: Beren and Lúthien for good, and Sauron in relation to his nemesis, Morgoth.

52. Carpenter, *Letters*, 189.
53. *Periphyseon*, 4.752b.
54. Ibid., 4.752c.
55. Ibid., 4.752d.

4.1.5 Human Nature as Absolute Freedom

The Periphysion 4.796a–b is a statement ascribing to human nature both absolute goodness, and by extension freedom of the will. If God is the plenitude of all good things, and human nature has a participation in every good, then there is in us every form of good, every virtue, every wisdom and everything whatever that is best. It can be seen (below) that Eriugena defends human freedom from double-predestination, and hence hard-determinist theological ideas. He emphasizes the voluntaristic side of human nature, free from all necessity: "That which is constrained under duress cannot be a virtue."[56] In fact, Eriugena differentiated the good and free natures of God and man as those whose natures are uncreated, whilst man obtains his being through creation. In this sense, he interprets St Paul in 1 Corinthians 3:15–16, that the spiritual man is subject to no law but gives the law to himself: "Man in his spiritual nature judges all things, but is himself judged by none."[57] The superior (spiritual) man is free to give himself any law, or operates according to no fixed law, since there are no fixed limits on his nature and conduct. In this, Eriugena follows Maximus' *Ambigua*, for whom Adam before the fall enjoyed complete freedom because he had *apatheia*—a stoic detachment from all things.[58] Just as God and the causes are without origin and obey no fixed law or order, so also human nature, when it contemplates God and the causes need obey no fixed order or progression:

> And be it noted that this sequence of the primordial causes which you ask me to set out distinctly in a definite order of precedence is constituted not in themselves but in the aspects, that is, in the concept of the mind which investigates them, [. . .] for in themselves these causes are one and simple and none knows the order in which they are placed or are distinguished one from another.[59]

The causes are ordered by the mind, which can proceed any way it likes: "Man is boundless, anarchic, self-transcending contemplation or subjectivity," and therefore can reasonably take on form as he desires, or is able.[60]

---

56. Ibid., 4.796b.

57. Ibid., 4.753a.

58. Ambigua 42.4: "In embracing creaturely origin just as it was before the transgression of Adam, and in being formed as man He naturally assumed, through the inbreathing, the condition of sinlessness."

59. *Periphyseon*, 3.624a.

60. Ibid., 3.624c–d.

4.1.6 Fallen Human Nature

I have shown that following Maximus and Gregory, Eriugena asserts that perfect human nature is not differentiated by sex: maleness and femaleness are not an essential attribute of human nature:

> If human nature had remained in that blessed state in which it was created it would not have needed sexual intercourse for its propagation, but would have multiplied as the angels multiply, without the use of sex.[61]

The fall is a symbol of the descent of intellect into reason and sense, the descent of the soul into the body—the shift from a timeless world to a world governed by space, time, and corporeality. It is caused through human free will which is distracted from spiritual to carnal pleasure, but also due to too much self-love or preoccupation with the self—a turning to self instead of God.

Plotinus explains human descent from the One in terms of *tolma* (audacity) at *Ennead* 5.1.1 and 2.9.11, which carries overtones of 'wilfulness.' It is not identical with Augustine's *superbia* (pride), but is its nearest Greek neighbor.[62] Plotinus paints a portrait of a growing restlessness of the soul and a kind of audacity by which it overreaches itself. In some of his *Enneads* he emphasizes the more voluntary and necessary nature of this movement.[63] Eriugena speaks of the human soul creating the mortal body.[64] The body, the result of sin, but not being evil, is "moved to create our nature [. . .] not only does He bring men from non-existence into generation, but ordains that he shall not lack goodness."[65] In interpreting the story of the fall in Genesis 3, Eriugena turns to the situation out of which the Parable of the Good Samaritan (Luke 10) arises: a man journeying from Jerusalem to Jericho, whereby Jerusalem is identified with paradise, and Jericho with the descent

---

61. Ibid., 4.812c.

62. O'Connell, *Augustine's Early Theory of Man*, 173–74; Rist, "Augustine on Free Will," 441 : "The difference between the two would seem to lie in the fact that Plotinus is still dualist enough to associate the weakness of the individual soul not with its material element viewed strictly as an element of nonbeing, but viewed as material. Thus Augustine, who recognizes that the weakness in created things lies in the fact that they are ex nihilo, pushes Plotinus' position to its logical conclusion. For Plotinus, sin which is tolma arises for the soul because it is associated with matter (ultimately equal to non-being) as its cause; for Augustine sin, which is *superbia,* may arise for the soul because it is *ex nihilo.*"

63. *Enneads*, 4.3.13. O'Connell, *Augustine's Early Theory of Man*, 155–83.

64. *Periphyseon*, 2.580b.

65. Ibid., 4.795c–796a.

to the weakness and instability of temporal nature.[66] Tom O'Loughlin points out that, had the man remained in Jerusalem then he would not have encountered the thieves: "this only happened because he *went* out from there, and down to Jericho."[67] Jerusalem stands for paradise and a state of human nature which, once it has abandoned paradise, is characterized by being open to the weakness and instability of temporality. In this descent, Adam was "already wounded by his fall and despoiled of all those natural goods in which he had been created."[68] The implication for Eriugena is that man fell himself before he was tempted by the devil, and here we recognize a striking parallel with Tolkien's own understanding of what it means to be fallen human nature. In Tolkien's presentation of a fall it is not human but, like Augustine, it is quasi-divine creatures who fall. Tolkien says as much in relation to Morgoth, but not directly in relation to humanity:

> I suppose a difference between this myth and what we may perhaps called Christian mythology is this. In the latter the Fall of Man is subsequent to and a consequence (though not a necessary consequence) of the 'Fall of the Angels': a rebellion of created free-will at a higher level than man. [. . .] In this Myth the rebellion of created free-will precedes creation of the world (*Eä*).[69]

We thus encounter humans as already differentiated, male and female:

> When the human mind in its perfection resided with God, it was a formless non-being: when it appears in this world it does so only clothed in the garb of reason and sense.[70]

In this splitting of the original unity of *nous*, its 'becoming' is enveloped in a male/female *aesthesis*, cloaking its original nature. The unformed and formless perfect mind now has form and is formed by the act of thinking and expressing itself in sound and script. Formally it was 'known only to God and ourselves,' now it knows itself only through images of sense and memory, which Eriugena calls collectively *phantasiae*.[71] He speaks of the mind producing reason and sense as 'making' or 'creating,' or as the mind 'exteriorizing' itself.

---

66. *Periphyseon*, 4.811b–c.
67. Tom O'Loughlin, "Imagery of the New Jerusalem," 246.
68. *Periphyseon*, 4.811c.
69. Carpenter, *Letters*, 286–87.
70. Moran, *John Scottus Eriugena*, 175.
71. *Periphyseon*, 1.454d.

4.1.7 The Mind Creates the Body

In its descent into corporeality, pure intellect can no longer operate on its own in a timeless way: it must proceed via the temporal processes of reason and sensation, becoming enveloped in irrational passions. Pure intellect possesses spiritual or 'true bodies'; whereas fallen humanity possesses a real and corporeal body, which is in fact an illusion created by fantasies of sense.[72] In this manner, the human body is created by the mind in the manner that the body is its own self-manifestation. The mind expresses itself through the motions of the body, and thus the body is something the mind makes.[73] Moran notes that Eriugena uses the terms *facere* ('make') and *creare* ('create') interchangeably—a confusion not cleared up until Aquinas.[74] For Eriugena, the creation of the body is not a making from nothing, but is a self-manifestation and a movement from the incorporeal to the corporeal.[75] It is one small part of the cosmic process of creation. Here Eriugena blends an Augustinian account with that of Dionysius at 1.500c–501a, that "formless matter is the mutability of mutable things which is receptive of all forms."[76] For Eriugena, matter is itself not circumscribed by any place or form, and can only be defined by the *via negativa*.[77] The human mind therefore produces the impression of corporeal matter by mingling together the incorporeal qualities into which the four elements of fire, water, earth, and air permeate and infuse.

Eriugena's interpretation of the Genesis text (chapters 1–3) in Books 2–5 of *The Periphyseon*, is strongly influenced by Augustine and Ambrose, and the Greeks: Origen, Basil, Gregory of Nyssa, and Maximus.[78] The biblical text is meaningful in an almost magical way for Eriugena, in that there are an infinite number of ways in which it can be interpreted, and even the shortest passage could have numerous meanings, "just as the smallest part of a peacock's feather contains an innumerable variety of colours."[79] The idea of multifarious interpretations derives from Eriugena's use of the Johannine motif of 'one house and many mansions' (John 14:2). One truth but many revelations and understanding is recurrent in the dialogue at 1.448c–d. He

---

72. Ibid., 5.993d.
73. Ibid., 2.580a–b.
74. *ST*, 1.45.7; Moran, *John Scottus Eriugena*, 177.
75. *Periphyseon*, 2.580b.
76. *Conf*, 12.6.6 and *Div Nom*, 4.729A
77. *Periphyseon*, 1.495d–496a.
78. Marenbon, *Medieval Philosophy*, 77.
79. *Periphyseon*, 3.749c.

relates this multiplicity to the infinitely diverse 'plenitude' of humans, who exist in and return to the One.

> Hence it may be seen in that which all men participate is one and the same nature which is redeemed in Christ and free from that servitude under which in this life it still groaned and suffered, so that in it all are made One, the qualities and quantities of their deserts [...] are variously and infinitely large and manifold. But all those things are in due order comprehended in that one spacious house in which the state of the Universe created in and by God is displayed in many diverse mansions, that is, in many degrees of merit and grace. And that house is Christ.[80]

As Tolkien avoids the direct Neoplatonic language of 'participation' in his *legendarium*, I can therefore safely make the claim that, if he incorporated an Eriugenean Neoplatonism into his philosophy of being, beyond that of the precise language of the Neo-Thomism of Maritain, then the 'divine in nature' is as a result of the *theophanies* or 'unfoldments' in the various modes of being.[81] The second mode of being/non-being is seen in the orders and differences of created natures, whereby as one level of nature is said to be, those above or below it in the hierarchy are said 'not to be': Lúthien is an elf, and therefore has non-being as a human or anything else; Beren is mortal, and therefore in terms of immortality has 'non-being.' In reversing these 'proper natures' at the conclusion of *The Tale of Tinúviel*, Tolkien shifts the *modus operandi* to the third *mode*, which contrasts the being of *actual* things with the non-being of *potential* or *possible* things still contained in "the most secret folds of nature." This is commonly understood to distinguish actual things which are the effects of the causes, having being, whereas those things which are still virtual in the Primary Causes are said 'not to be' (e.g., the souls of the unborn). If he does so, then

---

80. Ibid., 5.984a–b.

81. At the commencement of his *Periphyseon* (1.443c–1.446a), Eriugena defines and describes five modes of being/non-being : first, those things accessible to the senses and intellect are said to be, whereas anything which transcends our cognitive faculties are said not to be; secondly, regarding the order and differences of created natures, if one level of nature is said to be, those orders above or below it are said not to be; the third mode contrasts the being of actual things, with the 'non-being' of potential or possible things contained in "the most secret folds of nature." The fourth mode offers a roughly Platonic criterion for being: those things contemplated by the intellect alone may be considered to be, whereas things caught up in generation and corruption do not truly exist. The assumption is that things cognitive to the intellect alone belong to a realm above the material, corporeal world, and hence are timeless. The fifth mode is essentially theological, and refers to those humans which have been sanctified by grace and are said to be, whereas sinners who have renounced the divine image are said not to be.

he has creatively applied the Eriugenean psychology of 'the mind creates the body' to anything which it potentially *may be*, in a carefully crafted narrative, reminiscent in subject to Northern tales of borrowed traditions.[82] Even if the stylized form of the text has parallels with Norse mythology, its ontological foundation may reside in perfect human nature, if dependency upon Eriugena could be established.

There is further evidence for this in that Melkor, when he sought the spider Ungoliant, in order to destroy the two trees of Valinor, "put on again the form that he had worn as the tyrant of Utumno: a dark Lord, tall and terrible. In that form he remained ever after."[83] There is deliberate malice in this choice, and his act of the will/mind reduced his shape still further from what it had been in the opening sequence of *The Ainulindalë*. This is not a declension in being, in the Neoplatonic sense, but an act of freedom in order to demonstrate that liberation from form: the mind creating the body. If this were not so, then Tolkien would be charged as reducing Melkor's being according to the fourth mode—one of mutability and corruption. Eriugena's presentation of fallen human being is a descent into form and materiality, from formless non-being, cloaking its original unfallen nature. If Tolkien is influenced by Eriugena here, then Melkor's transformation—like those of Beren, Lúthien, Sauron and Huan—is possible because the body in a fallen state is *phantasiae*, uncertain and yet governed by intellect.

4.1.8 The Return of Human Nature

Eriugena is not a dualist in the Classical sense, but he does describe two conditions of humanity in nature: spiritual/eternal and temporal/material. These two orders are radically distinct, and yet not entirely irreconcilable. They are not two states, but one, seen under two aspects: *causaliter* and *effectualiter*. Using his dialectical method, he is able to say that man is not a corporeal body just as he is able to say that he is. The total unity of humanity is not destroyed, even by the fall. This allegorical event for Eriugena does not dissolve or splinter the integrity of human nature: instead

---

82. Anderson, *The Saga of the Völsungs*. The *Völsungasaga* contains many shape-shifting characters. Siggeir's mother changed to a wolf to help torture his defeated brothers-in-law with slow and painful deaths. When one, Sigmund survived, he and his nephew and son Sinfjötli killed men wearing wolfskins; when they donned the skins themselves, they were cursed to become werewolves. (61–62, 65–66). Fafnir was originally a dwarf, a giant or even a human, depending on the exact myth, but in all variants he transformed into a dragon—a symbol of greed—while guarding his ill-gotten hoard (81, 163).

83. Tolkien, *Silmarillion*, 86.

it merely cloaks and hides our true nature from our own understanding. Human nature is a whole and a unity:

> To one thing I hold most firmly, that the soul is simple and lacks no composition of parts [...] it is a whole in itself and its wholeness pervades the whole of its nature. [...] As a whole it perceives the sensible species through the whole of its senses [...] as a whole it extends beyond and above every creature, including even itself in so far as it is itself reckoned above the numbers of the creatures and, purged from all vices and all phantasies, revolves about its Creator in an eternal intelligible motion.[84]

Eriugena extends this unity to include the body. The original spiritual body which was totally united to his soul is now identified with an 'animal body,' merely as a result of free choice: a co-mingling of fantasies, and hence not really a true body. In 4.759a–c, it has already been seen that the absolutely unified, omnipresent, and transcendent nature of man includes the unity of the body, and of the body with the soul, since "it could not otherwise cleave to its Creator if it did not go beyond all the things that are beneath it and beyond itself."[85]

Eriugena reunites fallen human nature with its perfect self through his account of the return, relying on the writings of Maximus' *Ambigua* 37: "All things are from Him, and to Him all things return,"[86] and this return is a natural stage in his dialectic. This outgoing and return are eternal and timeless in God, though from the human perspective this return takes place in and through human temporal activity.[87] It is, in fact, a turning around of the temporality to one of timelessness and eternity. He distinguishes between the return which he calls *restauratio*[88] and *recursio*[89], and the return which goes beyond it, as a distinction between general and special. The former is the return of all effects to their causes—a return to paradise—which can be seen to be a type of *henōsis*, a unification with God.[90] The latter, *deificato* is a return through the causes into the Godhead itself—a return to complete identity with God. In his own words, "For it is one thing to return to paradise, another to eat of the Tree of Life."[91] For Eriugena, deification is

---

84. *Periphyseon*, 4.754b–c; cf Plato, *Timaeus*, 34a.
85. *Periphyseon*, 4.759b.
86. Ibid., 5.893a.
87. Ibid., 5.890c–d.
88. Ibid., 5.979c.
89. Ibid., 5.979d.
90. Ibid., 5.979a.
91. Ibid.

entirely gratuitous, different according to the merits of individuals, whereas resurrection is a gift that is implied in the creation of human nature, for all nature has proceeded from God in order to return to him. Christ is the first to be resurrected and, by his resurrection, started off the whole process of return.[92] Because in his incarnation he adopted human nature, in which the whole world is comprehended, then he took upon himself every creature: "The Return of the whole of human nature into its first condition shall be in Him Who took that whole nature upon Himself, namely, in the Incarnate Word of God."[93] Thus through his resurrection also the whole sensible world in all its manifold effects is saved from destruction and brought home to its causes.[94] It is to the plenitude of this perfect man that we will all return at the resurrection, in "a body containing no sensible qualities, without gender, mass, occupying no space or time, present everywhere because it is fully united to the divine cause."[95] This is beautifully expressed in the Concilliar document, *Gaudium et Spes,* in that "Human nature, by the very fact that it was assumed, not absorbed, in him, has been raised in us also to a dignity beyond compare. For by his incarnation, he the son of God, has in a certain way united himself with each man."[96]

Joseph Ratzinger (or more correctly, Pope Emeritus Benedict XVI), makes an excellent distinction between the notions of *exitus* and *reditus* between Plotinus and the (Greek inspired) Johannine writings of the Fourth Gospel:

> For Plotinus and his successors, the 'going out,' which is their equivalent of the divine act of creation, is a descent that ultimately leads to a fall: from the height of the 'One' down into ever lower regions of being. The return then consists in purification from the material sphere, in a gradual ascent, and in purifications that strip away again what is base and ultimately leads back to the unity of the divine. Jesus' 'going out' [. . .] presupposes that creation is not a fall, but a positive act of God's will. It is thus a movement of love, which in the process of descending demonstrates its true nature—motivated by love for the creature, love for the lost sheep, and so in descending reveals what God is really like. On returning, Jesus does not strip his humanity away again as if it were a source of impurity. The goal of his

92. Ibid., 5.896a; 894a. *cf* 1 Corinthians 15
93. Ibid., 5.978d.
94. Ibid., 5.910a; 913a–c. On the resurrected body of Christ see 5.894a–896d.
95. Steel, "Return of the Body," 607.
96. *Gaudium et Spes*, 22, in *Vatican Council II: The Concilliar and Post Concilliar Documents*, 923.

descent was the adoption and assumption of all mankind, and his homecoming with all men is the homecoming of 'all flesh'.[97]

This is a Christology carefully crafted in the language of Neoplatonic dialectic. So too, in his assimilation of this model, and avoiding a theological framework for his philosophy of being, Tolkien is able to sidestep the accusation of simple biblical allegory. Instead he formulates his locus of redemption in a more cosmological Neoplatonic mode of the return to the Creator. There are no typological figures, such as we see in C. S. Lewis' Aslan, but a systematic incarnational model, more akin to that of Athanasius in his *De Incarnatione Verbi Dei*. The incarnation for Athanasius opened up the potential for deifying humans, and with them nature, in a kind of restoration of paradise, through a process of becoming one with uncreated divine energies experienced in creation.[98]

Eriugena's further description of this 'twofold' return is said to correspond to biblical ideas of general resurrection (*generaliter resurgere*) and special transformation (*specialitar immutari*):

> All of us men, without exception shall rise again in spiritual bodies and in the integrity of our natural goods, and we shall return into the ancient state which was ours in the beginning; but not all of us shall be changed into the glory of deification, which transcends all nature and Paradise itself, [. . .] for in the one is signified the restoration of nature, in the other, the deification of the saints.[99]

That there are two segregated or differentiated *teloi* after the manner of the return, the central point for Eriugena is that the general return is part of nature (and hence universal). This resolution of human nature back to God exposes certain flaws in his idealistic interpretations, and at 5.877a–b he acknowledges that Augustine and Boethius both objected to the notion that the human body could be transmuted into soul, and in turn that soul can be transmuted into God. At 5.878a he glosses over these, by citing Ambrose at length. For Eriugena, the substance of physical nature will perish: it will change into something better,

> so the change of human nature into God is not to be thought of as a perishing of the substance but as a miraculous and

---

97. Ratzinger, *Jesus of Nazareth: Part 2*, 55–56.
98. Ware, *Orthodox*, 22.
99. *Periphyseon*, 5.579b–c.

ineffable Return into that former condition which it had lost by its transgression.[100]

At 5.982c, he further cites that, "God dwells nowhere but in the nature of men and angels, to whom alone it is given to contemplate the Truth." God is literally 'no where,' but human nature is the place of his lighting or his *theophania*. Human nature, however, is on a par with angelic nature in that both are the place of God's appearing. Eriugena believes it was as a human that God chose to appear to *both* angels and men, thus giving human nature an eschatological privilege: they are not two different intellectual ways of looking at the divine being, as "in my Father's house are many mansions."[101] In the halls of this house all men will possess mansions when they return into their causes, whether their time on earth was spent well or ill.

4.2 Eriugena's Defence of Freedom

Given my hypothesis, that Tolkien was influenced by a number of Neoplatonist philosophers, alongside Anglo-Saxon texts—and to a considerable degree, by Eriugena—then to further support this claim, that human nature as 'being and gift' is temporally free within the eternal providence of God in Tolkien, I must close the circle as regards what shall be demonstrated in chapter 5: that Eriugena's own views on free will and determinism coincide with those of both Augustine and Boethius. In this respect, Tolkien's use of the Christian Neoplatonists speaks, as it were, with one voice, but in different accents. Given that human freedom is the *condicio sine qua non* within the participatory relationship between humanity and divinity, then freedom becomes therefore the 'accidental' ethical focus of humanity's essential giftedness. The earlier work of Eriugena—*Treatise on Divine Predestination*—is largely Augustinian, and early Augustine at that. The later *Periphyseon* brings human freedom *qua* freedom in terms of nature into a more mystical sphere, whereby the ontological relations between God's freedom and human nature become blurred, and resist the philosophical strictures propounded by Augustine and Boethius.

The background to the debate originates in Augustine's *De Libero Arbitrio* (c.AD 395), wherein his argument—colored by his opposition to the Pelagians—overemphasized the total human dependence on God's grace, thus appearing to support a hard determinist viewpoint.[102] In *De lib*

---

100. Moran, *John Scottus Eriugena*, 181–84, gives a more detailed exposition of this process of deification.

101. *Periphyseon*, 5.982c.

102. Whereas Augustine's later anti-Pelagian treatises lost the more optimistic

Arb 2.20.54, Augustine argued that human will can choose higher or lower things. Our weakened fallen natures tend to the low things: pleasures of the body rather than the soul. Later in *De lib Arb* 3.1.1, Augustine is unsure whether or not this tendency towards lower things is natural—like a stone falling—and hence, inevitable, or whether it is voluntary. He argues for both, in that our characters form in such a way that following pleasure becomes natural, though voluntary.[103] The dispute into which Eriugena was drawn originated in Gottschalk's interpretation of Augustine, which led him to promote a 'two-fold' or double-predestination—*gemina praedestinatio*—and borrowing a phrase from the *Sentences of Isidore* (2.6.1): *predestines ad vitam* and *ad mortem*. In Gottschalk's analysis, God's mind or will is immutable, and has been decided since before creation. Strictly speaking, and according to Gottschalk, the dammed are not predestined to sin but only to punishment, because God foresees their sin.[104] The rebel priest-monk Gottschalk had been severely censured by a synod at Mainz in 848 and again at a synod at Quierzy a year later. This resulted in his imprisonment in the abbey of Hautvillers, until his death in 868.[105] Eriugena was 'called in' to refute the errors of Gottschalk, and as the latter claimed to use Augustine as his authority, then Eriugena would use Augustine's teaching in his refutation. Eriugena placed reason (*ratio*) on an equal footing with the time-honoured authorities (*auctoritates*) of Scripture and the Fathers, and his dialectical method in the first chapter was received with a sense of

---

vista of the *De Libero Arbitrio*, they confirmed the position, for the most part implicit in his earlier work, that human will required constant divine assistance. See Kaufer, *Augustinian Piety*, 19.

103. His later writings became more extreme in the view that humans were dependent entirely on God's grace for every action and decision and, in this sense, some are predestined by God's will to be saved, whilst others are predestined to be damned. In this case, the individual has no power to save himself, since his nature is flawed. By the time Augustine completed *De Civitate Dei* in 427, he came even more emphatically to insist upon the conclusion that original sin is both universally debilitating and insuperable without the aid of unmerited grace (14.1). Furthermore, there is a predestination at work that is as rigorous as the foreknowledge by which God knows its results (14.11). Here too Augustine insists that we are morally culpable for the sinful choices that the will makes (14.3). So damaging are the effects of original sin, that the human will is free only to sin. Thus, the human race is comprised of a *massa damnata* (21.12), out of which God, in a manner inscrutable to us (22.28), has predestined a small number to be saved (21.12), and to whom he has extended a grace without which it is impossible for the will not to sin.

104. All men are thus 'free'; the elect are free from serious sins, the damned are free from virtue. The elect are slaves of *caritas*; the damned are slaves of *cupiditas*. Rist, *Augustine on Free Will*, 439–440.

105. Eriugena, *On Divine Predestination*, x.

wonder by his first readers, but this balance of reason and authority was to be greatly elaborated in *The Periphyseon*.[106]

In opposing Gottschalk's deterministic (and fatalistic) theology, Eriugena's patron—King Charles the Bald—had been persuaded that Gottschalk had in effect disseminated a doctrine which threatened to undermine the authentic Christian humanism of the Carolingian kingdom, by upsetting the delicate balance between the divine wisdom and the possibility for men to follow the path of justice.[107] My discussion on *Beowulf* above demonstrates that Eriugena was writing at a time of great change and expansion of Christian ideas in Europe, and he was not going to allow the fatalism of the (recent) pagan past to gain a foothold. Avital Wohlman notes in his introduction to the English translation that, in rising to his commissioned task Eriugena was clear and precise: Gottschalk was wrong, for no-one can hold to double-predestination. Given that God is eternal, we cannot say that He foresees or predetermines. Beyond that, to think that God foresees sin and punishment is illogical: evil does not exist, being a pure absence, so one cannot know it. To think that God has prepared hell from the beginning of time for human beings is a pitiful anthropomorphism.[108] Wohlman gives an excellent introduction to the context and content of this lesser-known work of Eriugena, and sums up the enduring contribution of 'John the Scot' in his greater work—*The Periphyseon*—as 'courage.' This virtue, he asserts, constitutes

> the never-ending task of breaking every idol, exposing every false identification, to return to the place of one's true identity, the 'non-being' par excellence, to live in an 'unknowing' analogous to the 'unknowing' of God. For John the Scot, human freedom and beatitude come only at this price.[109]

Eriugena's refutation is summarized as follows. God made all that he made of His own will, and out of no necessity, and it is vain to imagine that necessity is either in that will or prior to it. Whatever we understand concerning the divine will we must necessarily understand in the same way of His predestination also. If all necessity is excluded from this divine will, it is also excluded from His predestination.[110] In a typically Augustinian turn, he continues on the subject of the 'good,' as it is in the nature of all

106. Ibid.
107. Ibid., xxiii.
108. Ibid., xxv.
109. Ibid., xxix.
110. Ibid., 1.1.

things that they appear to be good because they derive from the highest good. However, this experience might also be as a punishment, and as such is said to be evil although they are by nature good. God's just punishment of 'evil-doers' is a kind of predestination, but one arising from His essential nature and substance.[111] The postulate that 'effects resemble their causes' is used as an extension to the argument. Reason forbids that one and the same cause can produce different and mutually opposed effects, yet if there are two predestinations in God, then God would be the architect and cause of both being and non-being (i.e., virtue and life/sin and death). This is illogical for Eriugena, as the two are mutually opposed. If God is the cause of all that truly 'is,' and also the cause of things which 'are not' (i.e., non-being), then God must have a dual nature. But God is said to be a unity and simple, and cannot therefore be the source of two predestinations.[112] God cannot be both the highest essence and not be the cause of those things only that derive from him. God is the highest essence, and is therefore the cause of those things which derive from him. By contradiction, however, sin, death, unhappiness, etc., are not from God, and he is not the cause of them. Sin and its effect, death, to which unhappiness is conjoined, are not (i.e., no thing). God is the cause of things that truly 'are,' and not the cause of things that 'are not.' This is a privation theory remarkably similar to that of Augustine, and its application to predestination seeks to demonstrate that God can only be the cause of those things that are, and are coherent with the nature of God's divine simplicity, free of any composition or number.[113]

Eriugena accuses the Gottschalkian heresy as a mid-point between two other mutually opposing heresies: Pelagianism, and the one that contradicts it; one that disparages the freedom of grace, and one which condemns freedom of choice.[114] He takes up similar themes to Boethius in Book 5 of his *Consolations*, supporting both free choice and just judgment of the world: free choice must not be defended in such a way that good works are attributed to it without the grace of God, nor must grace be so defended that evil deeds may be habitually performed.[115] There cannot at the same time exist free choice and the gift of grace, juxtaposed with the necessity of predestination, the necessary cause compelling and the voluntary cause effecting.[116]

111. Ibid., 2.5.
112. Ibid., 3.2.
113. Ibid., 3.3.
114. Ibid., 4.1. This heresy is, for Eriugena, caused by the subtle craft and beguilement of the devil (4.4).
115. Ibid., 4.3.
116. Ibid., 4.4.

Returning to the assertion of true predestination emanating from the nature of God, Eriugena reasons that free and rational human 'being' is so because it could better enjoy its own highest good and contemplation of its Creator. That humans have the 'gift' of freedom of the will, and using it dutifully and humbly towards their Creator, humanity can better live justly and happily.[117] That rational life was bound not to have been made otherwise than voluntary, since by the will of God which is the cause of all things, it was created in his own image and likeness.[118] Otherwise, how would the divine will, the highest reason of the universe and unrestricted by any necessity, make the human will to his own image and likeness if he did not create its own substance a free and rational will also? Here Eriugena can be seen to be dependent upon Augustine's *De Lib Arbitrio*, 3.15.42.

In chapter 5, Eriugena quotes liberally from this work in his refutation that God predestines humans to either good or evil. For Augustine, God is just in punishing sins because, whilst he does not compel or perform those actions which he knows will take place, he has foreknowledge of the actions. In a similar manner, God neither by foreknowledge nor by predestination compels anyone to live righteously.[119] There is no compelling cause in God which precedes a human will which by force compels it, though unwilling towards either good or sinful actions. The freedom of the will is true freedom, yet after the choice to sin, it is so vitiated that its punishment impedes it from either willing to live righteously, or should it so will, from doing so.[120] We can see then, that in Eriugena's earlier exposition of freedom his dependency upon Augustine (see especially chapters 12–14) has led him to assert forcefully that, in Gottschalk's naive misuse of the self-same Augustinian texts, God can neither compel nor predestine humans to sin or good acts of virtue, to eternal life or damnation. He may prepare them for beatitude, by an act of grace (Ch. 11), and that foreknowledge as seen in the Scriptures is to be equated with predestination, but only in the sense of divine election, which cannot be a double-predestination as of from a nature of opposites, or contrariety.[121] Those people that instead 'appear' to be destined to a life of sin, punishment, and torment, are so because they have not been chosen as God's elect for a life as a 'child of God.'[122] In this sense the three terms sonship, election, and predestination are equal in meaning.

117. Ibid., 4.5.
118. Ibid., and Genesis 1:26–27.
119. *Div Pre*, 4.5.
120. Ibid.
121. *Div Pre*, 13.3.
122. Ibid., 13.3.

In his more mature work—*The Periphyseon*—Eriugena proceeds to demonstrate that there is no predestination towards evil.[123] In the strictest sense, God could not be said to know evil at all, and his argument is based on the metaphysical presence that God is *una substantia*, and his method is more self-consciously dialectical and rationalistic, than simply a refutation of Gottschalk's misuse of Augustinian texts. God is *summa essentia*,[124] and is the opposite of non-being.[125] But evil is also non-being (a privation), and therefore God does not know evil, and could therefore not predestine people to evil. Eriugena's intention was to solve the apparent contradictions in Augustine's own account, and thus trump Gottschalk's intellectual shortcomings. God is a nature who is all good; therefore, he can in no sense be said to entertain the knowledge of evil. God is One: His being is His knowing, and His knowing is His acting. It is in this sense for Eriugena, that God could be said to predestine—*scire hoc est destinare*. His knowing causes things and thus destines them, but since God is good, God's foreknowledge (*praescientia*) can only be good in itself, and does not predestine the human will at all. Furthermore, God's knowledge is eternal, and the concept of God 'predetermining' in a temporal sense cannot rightly be attributed to Him. For Eriugena, the only sense in which we could speak of predestination is in the sense that God must be God. There can be no double-predestination or two destinations, or one divided into two parts. When we speak about God we cannot use literal (univocal) language, because God is incorporeal: God is existence (*esse*).[126] Evil, by contrast, does not exist.[127] There can be no 'death of the soul' due to God's foreknowledge, as Eriugena accuses Gottschalk of teaching: God cannot predestine anyone to death, since God is life and the source of life in all living things.

There are some noteworthy points in Eriugena's approach in relation to our wider discussion on freedom, determinism, and/or chance. First, his argument is based on careful metaphysics and dialectical reasoning about the nature of God, the good, and evil. Secondly, his argument (in his own estimation) is said to be superior to that of Gottschalk because of his more thorough understanding of the liberal arts—so important in the Carolingian view. Thirdly, Eriugena's position is extremely optimistic, in that salvation is available to all. The world is a place which gives opportunity

---

123. Section 4.3 (below) deals with freedom of the will in Eriugena's human anthropology, and provides a necessary addition to his earlier arguments in the *Treatise on Divine Predestination*.

124. *Periphyseon*, 366b, 414c, 416b.

125. Ibid., 365c.

126. Ibid., 390c.

127. Ibid., 394c.

for human nature to perfect itself. Even when our flawed judgment fails us, grace is available. Finally, Eriugena's God does not merely not know evil, he did not create hell. Human sinfulness is responsible for creating its own hell. In this we see Eriugena working as a skilful dialectician, but also a learned and subtle interpreter of Augustine, with traces of Origen and Gregory of Nyssa.[128]

4.3 Alfred Siewers' Celtic Otherworld Interpretation of Tolkien's 'Strange Beauty'

Alfred Siewers is a scholar whose primary interest in literature is ecological and philosophical, but in writing of Tolkien's mythology, he makes a link with Eriugena such that, in creating a mythology whose primary outlook is 'anti-modernist' and essentially 'Green,' "Tolkien's fantasy replicates a pattern of ecologically centred narrative design from the early Middle Ages, described as 'overlay landscapes.'"[129] These provide a way of "incorporating Christianity into ancestral beliefs and legends about places in the natural landscape," where in a monotheistic worldview the real earth may be imbibed with Otherworld realities. This, for Siewers, is a demonstration of how Maximus and Eriugena "fully articulated the cosmology of the overlay-landscape patterns approach to nature. [. . .] Maximus's writings undergirded what became the dogma of Christ's two natures [. . .] on the significance of Creation. As he put it, 'The one logos is many logoi, and the many logoi are one.'"[130] Siewers claims that the contemporary edge of Tolkien's retro-medieval modern fantasy strangely mirrors its medieval inspiration, and cites the particular cases of Tom Bombadil and Goldberry, Weathertop, the Old Forest, and Radagast the Brown, as a demonstration of the interface between immortal realms interlaced with the everyday world of physical experience.[131] Siewers highlights the occasions when in Tolkien's narrative he echoes this deeper dimensionality to landscape, layering natural and spiritual forces, history and place, reminiscent of the early medieval Welsh tale *Mabinogion* and the Irish *Táin Bó Cuailnge*.

---

128. Moran, *John Scottus Eriugena*, 32–33.

129. Siewers, *Cosmic-Christian Ecology*, 140.

130. Ibid., 148, quoting Maximus' *Ambigua* 22.2: "God—who is truly none of the things that exist, and who, properly speaking, *is all things*, and at the same time beyond them—is present in the logos of each thing in itself, and *in all* the logoi together, according to which *all things* exist."

131. Ibid., 141–42.

It was early Celtic 'Otherworld' texts, according to Siewers, that helped Tolkien develop his pattern of an eco-centric Middle-earth, portraying the natural world as a central character beyond human control and interests, and it was through this scholarship that he gained an awareness of a more cosmically-oriented Christianity. Here 'Otherworld' denotes a dimension of life and being beyond the immediate confines of time and space: a sense of the overlapping landscapes of the immanent (from the perspective of our senses) and the immaterial (from the perspective of eternity). Siewers defines the Otherworld as,

> a type of overlay or multiplex landscape that integrates aspects of spiritual, imaginative, and natural realms of human life and the physical environment, including wilderness and animals, and that permits shape-shifting as well as transport through time and space.[132]

Tolkien alludes to this Otherworld dimensionality when discussing the burial customs in the Danish pagan origins of the *Beowulf* poem:

> the account in Beowulf is even at first glance seen to be of complex origin. It is not merely a piece of mythology, or symbolic ritual (cf the Sea–burial), not merely the necessary complement to his mysterious arrival in a boat, although the Old English poetic account is plainly tinged with mystery and glimpses of the Otherworld.[133]

Furthermore, Siewers postulates that it was Eriugena's influence which explains how Tolkien's fantasy could stretch beyond his own Augustinian Catholicism, to embrace the imaginations of a wide range of religious and secular beliefs, and this has a parallel in how Eriugena departs markedly from Neoplatonist writes such as Augustine, Maximus, and Dionysius. Siewers fails, however, to provide any hard evidence of Tolkien's reading of, and dependency upon Eriugena, beyond his interests in literature and philosophy of late antiquity and the early medieval period.[134]

It has been shown in section 2.2 how structured music, from its Pythagorean origins and incorporated into Christian Neoplatonist philosophical modes of creation, attempts an account of the manner of how the finite, temporal, and divisible creation, may participate in the eternal, infinite, and indivisible (Form of the Good/God). The language of these key scholars—beauty, proportion, harmony, symmetry—may at first reading

---

132. Siewers, *Strange Beauty*, 5.
133. *Bodleian SC–MSS* A31 folio15/1 (also quoted above in section 3.2.1)
134. Siewers, *Cosmic-Christian Ecology*, 141–42.

appear abstract and indeed distant from human experience. Furthermore, such precise linguistic formulae may be assessed as being inadequate or even irrelevant, when dealing with the participation between these realms of reality and the world of becoming. Given the harmonious analogies of a Pythagorean structured universe, which appear to be characteristic in all these Neoplatonic developments, in subjects which defy a clearly defined outward form or structure—such as we encounter in overlay and evolving landscapes, and the phenomena of shape-shifting—these analogies break down. What we now understand to be Tolkien's presentation of a harmonious but changing world, we view from the Otherworld lens of Eriugena a cosmos which is not too easily defined in temporal and spacial existence. Siewers' use of Eriugena's dialectical approach of ontology/meontology, highlighted by early Irish sea legend, challenges the precision of other forms of the Neoplatonic cosmogonic world, ordered as it is by mathematical and musical ratios. If the Graeco-Latin traditions of late Antiquity and early medievalism appear too systematic and closely defined, then the philosophy of Eriugena—alongside the Western tradition—has indeed proven fruitful in my quest in making clearer judgments on Tolkien's co-creative genius, in respect of life as 'being and gift.'

For example, Siewers recounts how in the early Irish story *Immram Brain* the Irish ruler Bran mac Febail embarks upon a voyage, in which he encounters the sea and many of its creatures constituting an Otherworld, and that their home "conjoins this multidimensional archipelago of elements and beings that ultimately makes it an Otherworld as well."[135] When encountering the sea, Bran encounters also a "doubly enfolded landscape."[136] In contradistinction to what is simply 'natural,' Siewers explains the sea as both a watery plain that also encompasses a parallel reality, or perhaps a paradisiacal spiritual dimension encompassing the sea, where in a world without sin or crime all is fair and youthful, a world where nature's laws are suspended:

> A pleasant game, most delightful,
> They play in fair contention,
> Men and gentle women under a bush,
> Without sin, without crime.
> Along the top of a wood has floated
> Your coracle across ridges,

---

135. Siewers, *Strange Beauty*, 1.
136. Ibid., 3.

There is a beautiful wood with fruit
Under the prow of your little boat.[137]

This landscape has connections to a larger network of nature or Celtic Otherworld narratives, to biblical traditions, and even to analogies in later Welsh narratives and French traditions of the Holy Grail. Siewers adds that, "textually, the Otherworld constitutes a multidimensional trope, a multiform of oral and literary sources probably shaped in part by performance."[138] This literary evolution may be seen in the two minstrel sections in *Beowulf* (lines 883–914 and 1070–1158). These 'poems-within-our-poem' are, according to Heaney, "central to the historical and the imaginative world of the poem," and cause a temporary shift in the space/time continuity of the poem: they take us to another dimension, yet not unrelated to where the action breaks off and continues.[139]

Carl Phelpstead's study in the influence of Welsh and other Celtic sources on Tolkien's mythology draws our attention to Tolkien's well-documented love of both Wales and Ireland. He highlights, however, Tolkien's antipathy towards the Old Irish language groups, alongside his love of the Welsh language, and cites Tolkien's differing attitudes to both as being diametrically opposed.[140] Phelpstead cites evidence that Tolkien both studied and owned copies of the *Mabinogion,* from which Tolkien quotes in his O'Donnel Lecture given at Oxford on the 21st October 1955, entitled *English and Welsh*.[141] There are unpublished translations of the text in the Bodleian Library Special Collections, containing marginal notes, but these deal more with matters of translation than influences on his work.[142] Phelpstead points to a number of possible influences from the *Mabinogion* on Tolkien's own mythology, including the One Ring, elves, and dragons, but, like Siewers, can offer no dependency theory. He does acknowledge, however, that in the case of the elves, their Celtic linguistic origins are English, and not Irish or Welsh: "the *Engle* (i.e., the English) have the true tradition of the fairies, of whom the *Iras* and the *Wéalas* (the Irish and the Welsh) tell garbled things."[143] The textual influences upon Tolkien do not rest solely in Anglo-Saxon sources, however, but are multi-layered, and

137. Quoted in Ibid.
138. Siewers, *Strange Beauty,* 4.
139. Heaney, *Beowulf,* xiv.
140. Phelpstead, *Tolkien and Wales,* 25–26; Carpenter, *Letters,* 289.
141. Tolkien, *Monsters,* 172–73.
142. Phelpstead, *Tolkien and Wales,* 60–61; Bodleian SC-MS A18/1, folios 135r–153r, 149v.
143. Tolkien, *Book of Lost Tales 2,* 290.

contain traces of medieval works from the three literary traditions of England, Ireland, and Wales.[144] This is further evidenced in the text of the Irish lay containing *The Death of St Brendan* being contained in Tolkien's *Notion Club Papers (Part Two)*.[145] It is undeniable that this text, written in 1946 and two years after the completion of *The Two Towers*, had a profound effect on the final section of *LOTR*. We read in Lines 41–48 words which resonate with descriptions of Tolkien's Middle-earth topography, the land and geographical features of Mordor:

> We turned away, and we left astern
> the rumbling and the gloom;
> then the smoking cloud asunder broke,
> and we saw that Tower of Doom:
> on its ashen head was a crown of red,
> where fires flames and fell.
> Tall as a column in High heaven's hall,
>   its feet were deep as Hell.

It is difficult not to read these words, without imagining Frodo and Sam, skirting the inner borders of Mordor in the chapter, *The Land of Shadow*.[146]

There is a later version of this lay, entitled *Imram* (meaning 'sailing,' or 'voyage'), in the same text, and Christopher Tolkien's notes bear witness to three other untitled versions. This final text, like the former, displays a curious amalgam in a voyage of continuous but seemingly over-layered landscapes, as Brendan and his companions journey towards their place of final rest—Ireland.[147] The text speaks of clearly defined geographical places (Galway, the River Shannon, Lough Derg), but at times the descriptions are less precise and almost mystical. The sea voyage lasts for "a year and a day," and a further "forty days and ten" (lines 25–28): the latter being a biblical metaphor for a long time, and ten more besides. The passage of time is indefinite, as "It seemed to us then as in a dream that time had passed away" (lines 77–78), and voices that were neither those of men nor angels, "but maybe there is a third fair kindred in the world yet lingers beyond the foundered

---

144. Phelpstead, *Tolkien and Wales*, 64–65.
145. Tolkien, *Sauron Defeated*, 261–64.
146. Here we read that, "Orodruin was still belching forth a great fume that, mounted higher and higher, until it reached a region above the wind and spread in an immeasurable roof, whose central pillar rose out of the shadows beyond their view." *LOTR*, 955.
147. Tolkien, *Sauron Defeated*, 296–99.

land" (lines 91–94), a possible metaphor for the race of Elves. The narrator tells the audience that there are other things to learn "things out of mind" (line 123), but they are not to be known from mortals. But what is easily passed over, is a speculative link to the mystical imagery used by Eriugena, as we observe twice a reference to "a Cloud, a Tree, a Star" (lines 24; 99–100). The White Tree, linked to those in paradise (lines 69–70), has overtones of the White Tree of Gondor, and the standard of the king (Appendix D). In Tolkien's text, the Star prefigures the "unseen bridge that on arches runs to coasts that no man knows" (lines 107–8); its presence in the sky presages "the parting of the ways, a light on the edge of the Outer Night beyond the Door of Days" (lines 102–3). Tolkien simplifies the juxtaposed real world and Otherworld, but the use of tree and cloud in both the Irish and Tolkien's text has parallels with the mysterious language of Eriugena, in terms of the Tree of Life and Clouds of Theophanies, which link the earth with the fully realized life in the return to God, and participation in his divine presence. The clouds offer an apocalyptic mood, linked as they are with how the "saints are to be snatched up into the air and brought before Christ: they are a conveyance to the ultimate Otherworld."[148]

Bernard McGinn identifies two further uses of this motif, and rather than reading Eriugena as promoting an immanent rapture, proposes that the clouds are theophanies—an indirect manifestation of God. They can be viewed as "those occurring in history (e.g., the three kinds of contemplation realized in Elijah, Moses, and Christ), or beyond it, that is, the intelligible clouds of contemplation in which the saints will enjoy the divine presence in heaven."[149] I have shown that for Eriugena, *theosis* is a particular privilege beyond the general return of the whole creature into its causes at the end of the world. The Tree of Life motif has connections with both the state of paradise and the Adamic impulse to eat the forbidden fruit, and a complete participation and assimilation in the person of Jesus: "Now the tree of Life is Christ and its fruit is the blessed life and eternal peace in the contemplation of the Truth; for that is what is meant by deification."[150] Whilst these themes are not developed in Tolkien, their naming of them points us to a parallel in meaning and intention, alongside the borrowed traditions of Irish and Welsh sea motifs. Indeed, it is these sea motifs—oceans of divinity—which most readily highlights the Otherworld trope within Siewers' reading of Eriugena. These archipelagic social networks (below) are stylized

---

148. *Periphyseon*, 5.998B–1000A, reflecting St Paul's early eschatology in 1 Thessalonians 4:17.

149. McGinn, "Eriugena Confronts the End," 17

150. *Periphyseon*, 979b. Here he quotes directly from Augustine.

by Eriugena, in that his philosophical method is perceived as a journey out into the hostile waters in which

> tortuous digressions [...] obscure doctrines [...] the dangers of the currents of unfamiliar teaching, ever in immediate danger of shipwreck in the obscurity of the subtlest intellects, which like concealed rocks may suddenly split our vessel.[151]

For Eriugena, this journey into truth is powered (literally) by reason, a Latin term used to gloss the Greek *logos,* which, as we are reminded by Siewers, "played a large role in the iconographic doctrines of the divine Logos thickening into icon in the Incarnation, and in the cosmological writings of Maximus the Confessor that influenced Eriugena as translator and writer."[152] The journey itself, therefore consists of overlaying meanings for Eriugena, and highlights the multi-faceted approach to his whole philosophy.

At the commencement of Book Four of *The Periphyseon,* Eriugena identifies the sea with Divinity through energies of the primordial causes expressed as theophanies and visible effects in a redeemed sense of earth. So therefore, we have in Tolkien's *Imram,* the *Nauigatio,* and the *Imram Brain,* cosmic ideas which demonstrate overlay landscapes that defy the temporal constraints of time and space, and are at the same time gateways or portals to the heavenly realm of paradise. O'Loughlin asserts that the eighth-century text of the *Nauigatio Sancti Brendani* was an attempt to set out a monastic spirituality on the basis of the annual cycle of the liturgy, in order that monks might be fit for a life in paradise. The tale presents this desired end—the *terra repromissionis sanctorum*—as a place of which Brendan has already had a foretaste (cf. Heb 11:9). The key features of this 'land,' where the normal experience and restrictions of time and space no longer apply, is derived from Revelation 21–22.[153] The *Nauigatio* presents the actual world and worship within it, temporal and imperfect, and the journey is based in three islands. The first (as in Tolkien) is the physical Ireland, the second is also physical, but populated by perfect monks—the *insula deliciarum*—reflecting the ideal of monastic conditions. The third island is separated from ordinary space by a veil of fog—a dense cloud—and does not share time with the physical creation, because this island is not of this world, and is located at the "portals of paradise." Sailing from one island to the other is a metaphor for the teleological nature of the monastic life, and the distinction between this world and the world to come is said

---

151. Ibid., 743d–744a.
152. Siewers, "Desert Islands," 49.
153. O'Loughlin, *Imagery of the New Jerusalem,* 257.

to be that between a sacrament and its reality.[154] The progression is marked by the fact that the 'more holy' sanctifies the 'less holy': the first two islands are presented as places as well as states, whereas the third belongs to the new creation when the world has passed away (Rev 21:1). O'Loughlin cites no direct evidence that Eriugena was familiar with the *Nauigatio*, though it would certainly have been known to those who formed his initial readership. Therefore, he concludes with assurance that it was a factor (alongside other contemporary texts) "within the religious culture in which he taught and wrote" in forming his ideas of the New Jerusalem.[155] It may logically be inferred that by association, the philosophy around which Eriugena derived his understanding of the earth in relation to paradise is equally informed by this text (and others similar).

Given, therefore, that both Tolkien and Eriugena had access to the same texts (and/or literary traditions), which in turn demonstrate similarities in their respective philosophies on creation, demonstrating similar categories of ontology/meontology, it adds credence to the thesis of Alfred Siewers—though he has not made this link—that Tolkien was by a similar association influenced by Eriugena. If it were not so, then the similarities between Tolkien's and Eriugena's alleged use of Welsh and Irish texts seem harder to account for if we were not asserting some degree of dependence. I have demonstrated, using the case study in chapter 3, how these ontological ambiguities, evident in Eriugena's works, are present also in Tolkien's relation of human nature to the divine, and how they enrich his use of other borrowed traditions.

The similarities between these early Irish medieval sources and the cosmology and co-creation of Tolkien have inspired Siewers to postulate that it is *The Periphyseon* that culminates early Irish sea writings on nature from the standpoint of intellectual history: "The cosmic landscape symbolism of *The Peryphiseon* more than its philosophy [. . .] extends a place region analogous in qualities to the Irish sea Otherworld onto a creation-wide scale."[156] The text, for Siewers, illustrates views of nature implicit in the Otherworld trope, in ways relevant to current environmental philosophy. The *Periphyseon's* symbolizing of nature—its sea of divinity and clouds of theophany, its cosmic tree uniting paradise and earth, its fourfold textual iconography of a cosmic landscape—remains inseparable for understanding larger cultural contexts of the naturally mysterious Otherworld trope.

---

154. Ibid., 258.
155. Ibid., 259.
156. Siewers, *Strange Beauty*, 67.

Siewers cites Eriugena's definition of nature as including being and non-being, as having the foundational role in discussing the Otherworld's own philosophical and empirical contexts. In these contexts, non-being, "meaning that which is not readily apparent or instrumentally at hand, yet omnipresent both as mysterious essence and part of dynamic process," provides a working definition for 'spiritual' in relation to nature.[157] For Siewers, the Otherworld, like Middle-earth:

> this double-folded experience of landscape, distinct from Scholastic and Modern approaches to understanding nature, helped to shape a dynamic, quasi-ecological sense of region that resisted delusions of being able to possess the world, while blurring boundaries between human and non-human, body and idea.[158]

It may be inferred that this Eriuganian 'lack of certainty' may have informed and inspired Tolkien's examples of shape-shifting in the *Tale of Tinúviel*. In his *Periphyseon*, Eriugena described an analogous emanation of power in place, through what he called the "secret folds of nature" that were also called 'theophanies.' These were, in effect, the energies of God, or the 'primordial causes.' In Eriugena, the divine essence is always a mystery, but God is experienced in these theophanies or emanations, running constantly through the physical creation, "both transfigurative of and interactive with human imagination and the world, simultaneously transcendent and immanent."[159] We see something of this Otherworldview in the sub-creation of Arda—Middle-earth, as it becomes a reality from a 'mind-music-vision-reality' procession, originating in the thought of the One—Eru Ilúvatar—a co-creative process shared with his Ainur, via what is akin to a Neoplatonic metaphysics of music. However, for Eriugena, the immanent/transcendent dialectical language of God via these theophanies points always to the participatory relationship between God and his created effects, even if at times the language becomes dangerously pantheistic.

In support of his hypothesis, Siewers is able to assert that, "in this hyper-dimension of environment as process, figured as an alternate mode of non-temporality touching earth but energized by the divine, we find philosophical and ascetic analogues to the Otherworld."[160] So together with nature traditions and old gods lingering in stories, such as *Beowulf*, the Christian contexts helped shape a literary landscape "in-between subject

157. Ibid., 6.
158. Ibid.
159. Ibid.
160. Ibid.

and object, in ongoing empathetic if sometimes dangerous engagement with spiritual forces melding in Creation."[161] Eriugena's problem, when speaking of the uniting of God with creatures, is reflexive in terms of uniting all the hierarchies of nature, and includes the *exitus* and *reditus* of the cosmos. This dialectical unity of finite and infinite, divine and created nature, is *universalis natura* or *to pan* (*universitas*).[162] This latter term, however, is used also as the unity of created nature, and the interlocutor—Nutritor—speaks of the term *universitas* being unable to be grasped in one way only, but must be admitted to have multiplicity of meanings.[163] As with all of Eriugena's central concepts, there is a dialectical flux in the meaning of the term *universitas*. It is therefore grasped by a *multiplex theoria*, "the anarchic multiple contemplation of the human mind. *Universitas* does not mean being but signifies the dialectical interplay of being *and* non-being."[164]

The fourfold division of nature represents a cycle/dialectic which is both synchronic and diachronic, transcendent and immanent, in multiple temporalities. This 'fourfold' forms a type of iconographic landscape—or *multiplex theoria*—akin in textualized visual effect to the art of early monastic manuscripts, such as the *Book of Kells*.[165] This early ninth century Irish manuscript exhibits what could be called a stereographic effect, as there is a visual overlay in what the materiality of the Gospel is (i.e., a manuscript), and the thing of which it speaks (i.e., the *Logos*—Christ figure). In the illuminated manuscripts, the opening words of a Gospel are singled out for special decorative treatment. However, beyond the words themselves, and in this case the *In Principio*, St John himself is in the portrait, holding aloft a Gospelbook that bears a lozenge on its front cover. It is known that the lozenge motif was an early Christian symbol, found on early Christian lamps, perhaps denoting the Light of the World, but in other early art the lozenge is also linked to St John's Gospel, and can be reasonably identified as a symbol of the *logos* on that account.[166] In the Johannine Frontispiece in the *Book of Kells*, we see the lozenge symbol of the Word superimposed (or over-layered) upon the actual book containing the words of the Gospel. Boundaries overlap between words and images (Appendix E). This is seen particularly in the Chi-Rho figure from the incipit, or beginning of the eighteenth verse of Matthew chapter 1.

161. Siewers, *Strange Beauty*, 16.
162. *Periphyseon*, 2.528b–2.529c.
163. Ibid., 3.621a. Moran, *John Scottus Eriugena*, 258–60.
164. Moran, *John Scottus Eriugena*, 259.
165. Siewers, *Strange Beauty*, 76.
166. Richardson, "Themes in Eriugena's Writings," 275.

The text reads: 'XPI autem generatio.'[167] It is significant that this latter image, demonstrating the iconographic letters of 'Christ,' bear the mark of several lozenges, and occur immediately prior to the text speaking of Jesus' generation in the womb of Mary by the Holy Spirit, further emphasizing the link between the lozenge motif and the incarnate Word.

In Eriugenian terms, these textual images are a representation of the primordial causes, the *logoi* or divine energies are both in the spatial landscape of physical creation as theophanies, while already shaping it. Siewers further postulates that in the cosmic-landscape tropes of the sea, Eriugena's topology implies an earthly landscape that "resists spatial universalisms of what became normative European space."[168] Eriugena's schema is said to 'up-end' the conventional hierarchies that privilege a transcendent concept of either God or human subjectivity above nature. This kind of participatory ontology is one method whereby Eriugena renders uncertain the analogical relationship between God and the material world. Thus, prior to defining his fourfold division in nature, he writes:

> God, who Himself is incomprehensible, is after a certain mode comprehended in the creature, while the creature itself by an ineffable miracle is changed into God [. . .] Divine Nature, although it creates all things and cannot be created by anything, is in an admirable manner created in all things which take their being from it.[169]

The context of this particular analysis of nature begins by describing how iron—whilst being plunged into fire—is both separate and distinct from it will, if it remains in the fire, entirely resemble the heat source, whilst substantially remaining distinct. Whilst becoming molten it loses its shape and form, and reason dictates that the iron and fire are still distinct in their essential properties.[170] It is in this context that Siewers describes how Eriugena's landscape tropes, within the narrative of the *Periphyseon*, highlight an environmental language of philosophy:

> the mutual reciprocal cosmic process of kenosis and theosis [. . .] enfolding all Creation via the divinized human, and vice versa, in a participatory and transformative "language" [. . .] involves a

---

167. "Now the birth of Jesus Christ took place in this way. When his mother Mary had been betrothed to Joseph, before they came together she was found to be with child of the Holy Spirit."
168. Siewers, *Strange Beauty*, 76.
169. *Periphyseon*, 2.451b, 2.454c.
170. Ibid., 2.451b.

dynamically iconographic overlay inscription or topography, in which image is privileged more than phonetic writing.[171]

Given the example of *The Book of Kells*, by highlighting text as some aspect of the divine, then the embodiment of religious texts engages with physical meaning: word becomes reality—*Eä*, and it becomes reality not in isolation from the Divine, but via the 'theophanies' (primordial causes or divine energies) emanating into and transforming the world continually in what Siewers calls a 'process narrative.' This is not to imply a process theology, but to stress that this process of *becoming*—this transformation—takes place continually through the mutually reciprocal desire of humans, and the divine energies or grace. I have highlighted that in Tolkien's creation myth this reciprocal act of creation qua 'becoming' is a mutual process shared between quasi-divine agents (Valar) and humans, and not by the elves in Tolkien's own creation myth.[172]

Siewers develops his Eriugenian theme in that humans engaged with the relational *logoi* in this cosmic discourse become divinized with the non-human landscape: the *logoi* being the hidden causes of Eriugena's nature—the secret folds of the cosmos—the essence of created beings in the sense of his term "primordial causes." They are realized in their relation to God, which also establishes them in union with divine energies, because their relation is neither direct nor objectified.[173] In this sense, human being in the *imago Dei* (Gen 1:26–27) is the imaging forth of the divine,

> yet it is in a relationship external to God's mysterious essence as absolute Other, which apophatically is beyond-nothingness to the creature even as the creature is created by the divine '*ex nihilo*.'[174]

If at times Eriugena blurs the distinction between the Creator and the created—causes and their effects—then for Siewers this becomes understandable in a philosophical milieu that is not Scholastic, but participatory-iconographic, rooted in the geography and story-telling of the early Irish Sea archipalego. It is only in this context that Siewers postulates an environmental reading of Eriugena, even if at times this context is discounted in favour of earlier patristic views. Lossky claims that Eriugena's theological system is "a curious amalgam of Eastern and Western elements, a transposition of the doctrines of the Greek fathers upon a basis of Augustinian

---

171. Siewers, *Strange Beauty*, 77.
172. Tolkien, *Silmarillion*, 47.
173. See Lossky, *Mystical Theology*, 98–99.
174. Siewers, *Strange Beauty*, 77.

thought."[175] We might also say that Tolkien's theological project is a similar "curious amalgam," incorporating elements also of Eriugena's distinct mystical theology.[176] It is in this sense that Eriugena's focus on Nature as participatory-icon (in his fourfold schema) becomes understandable within his Hiberno-Latin background, in a tradition concerned with the 'naturalness' as well as the mystery of miracles.

In fusing together the physical and symbolic in "identity-with-difference,"[177] Siewers holds that Eriugena's treatise on mature nature offers both a metonymical and synecdochical parallel to the function of iconography: they (icons) resist totalizing possession or control, "and potentially realize a dynamic relational flow of energy between language and a natural world that still remains essentially a mystery."[178] In the case of *The Book of Kells*, above, the words of the gospel narrative instantiate *the* Word incarnate via iconographic textual symbols: there is a self-same directional flow between the symbol and that symbolized, and language becomes the metonymical figure of heaven and (Middle-)earth's reality. Within the third mode we find "the things which partly are still hidden in their causes, partly are manifest: their effects, of which in particular the fabric of this world is woven."[179] Eriugena later adds:

> All things which are in place (because everywhere they are seen to be enclosed in things greater than themselves) can be called places, although none of them is strictly speaking a place but is contained within the place (of its) proper nature, and although we see that it is by μετανομια (that is, by transference of name) that those things which are contained are called after the things which contain them [. . .] they are not contained by them in such a way that without them they could not subsist within their nature's limits.[180]

In this, Eriugena extends the Aristotelian notion of place as always being associated with being 'in' something, to a more elemental view. Everything in place is in a sense contained, but are within their own 'natural limits' in a manner that is paradoxically not containment. This 'metonomia' links language and symbol/icon, and in this reading of Eriugena—and by a similar association, Tolkien—one could embody an ecological sense of interchangeable yet

175. Lossky, *Mystical Theology*, 96.
176. Siewers, *Strange Beauty*, 78, and Lossky, *Mystical Theology*, 96.
177. See *Periphyseon*, 2.451b, above.
178. Siewers, *Strange Beauty*, 78.
179. *Periphyseon*, 1.445b.
180. Ibid., 1.480b.

different flow of energy. In metonymy a word is, in effect, a name related to the physical in image: it simultaneously draws attention to bodily or environmental connections of language, and to the difference between symbolic language and that symbolized.

The energized earth becomes a fluid textuality, and this can be said of Tolkien's representation of Arda in the First Age: it is subject to change—for good or ill—and yet the omniscience of Ilúvatar, and his being able and willing to 'utilise' the creative and/or destructive works of his creation, remains a mystery by his almost complete transcendence. If such a deity is at odds with Tolkien's own Catholic vision and artistry, then it may be held that *if* he was aware of *The Periphyseon*, and read it in the manner proposed by Siewers, then his own sub-creation displays that same "fluid textuality," precisely because the divine energies—via the Valar—pervade them. Siewers posits that Eriugena's approach to creation and place offers a potential ecological apophatic turn from outside a constructed mainstream Western past, rather than a 'retro-medievalism,' having a Scholasticism, "whose monumental ecclesiology grew from Augustinian Original Sin."[181] Eriugena's approach is less concerned with historical events, as in Augustine's literal reading of the Genesis text, and instead offers a dialectical relationship between divine energies within creation, and materiality itself. Given Siewers' interpretation of Eriugena, as both influenced and independent from Augustine, then we also see in Tolkien, whose own departure from this Augustinian tract was both original and deliberate, though he could never be said to be entirely free from it.[182] Eriugena links a fluid metonymy to an experience of the divine energies in nature. They are complex and varied, and unsystematic. Sometimes they involve image-relations, such as his landscape tropes of the Tree of Life and the Sea with Clouds, but in either case they speak of the primordial causes manifest in the theophanies infusing creation.[183] As I have demonstrated, these ethereal concepts are contained in (albeit) obscure texts of Tolkien, and it is therefore not unreasonable to read his use of language similar to Eriugena as having similar meaning. In Tolkien's *legendarium* these primordial causes 'infusing creation' are personified as Valar—immanent demigods.

Eriugena had a tendency to speak of God's ideas, or their emanating theophanies in nature (following Augustine), as created and more substantive of creatures than the dynamic sense in which they are described in

---

181. Siewers, *Strange Beauty*, 77.

182. This would be the position taken by Milbank, *Chesterton and Tolkien*, 71, and we shall see that Tolkien's use of Augustinian theodicy is far more creative than it would appear so upon first reading.

183. Siewers, *Strange Beauty*, 80.

Eastern patristics. He represents the divine ideas as creatures, the first created principles by means of which God creates the universe. Together with the Eastern theologians, he puts the ideas outside the divine essence, but at the same time he wants to maintain with Augustine their substantive character, and so they become the first created essences.[184] However, whether or not one considers these (Augustinian) theophanies or primordial causes subsisting in creation as created or uncreated, depends upon the perspective from which one views them: "In one way the things that were made through Him are under Him; in another way the things that He is are in Him."[185] In other words, from a temporal perspective, they might appear to be created manifestations, but from a more transcendent perspective they could be considered uncreated. In either case they are eternal—a mystery—and from the human standpoint, in flux. The real essence in the world lies in inconceivable relationships and movements connecting with divine energies: any direct relationship of creation with God in an objective linear sense is not possible: "an iconographic engagement of energies constitutes the interaction."[186] It is this higher and more transcendent sense of participation that both Eriugena and Tolkien recognize created being in relation to the Creator, as far as both writers are able. I have already asserted that in the case of Tolkien, this sense of participation is more developed, if one reads his works from the Thomist perspective of Jacques Maritain, alongside Tolkien's professional studies and readings of the Middle English poem, "Pearl."

Furthermore, in Eriugena's cosmology of miracles, the divine energies (or primordial causes) interweave the essence and the phenomenon of a thing upon the dynamically folded surfaces of creation, and it is in such a sense that Eriugena places his symbolic (or iconographic) landscape tropes. It is in a 'third world' of human being (physical environment) and non-being (dynamic theophany) as defined from the human perspective, that we observe "a mediation shaping landscape but resisting objectification of self."[187] In Eriugena's treatise on nature, human beings grow in the fold between theophany and physicality. He develops an anti-cogito, contrary to that of Descartes with its Augustinian roots: "I think therefore I know not what I am, except by participation in the larger context."[188] In his *Homily on the Prologue to the Gospel of St John,* Eriugena asks his hearers

---

184. Lossky, *Mystical Theology*, 96. Eriugena did not grasp the distinction between the essence and the energies, and was therefore unable to identify the ideas with God's creative acts of will.

185. *Periphyseon,* 2.640c–d.

186. Siewers, *Strange Beauty,* 82.

187. Ibid., 83.

188. Ibid.

to "observe the forms and beauties of sensible things, and comprehend the Word of God in them. [. . .] You are not a substantive light, but only participate in the self-subsisting light."[189] Later in the *Homily*, Eriugena explicates the Gospel statement that "the true Light that lights every man was coming into the world" (John 1:9), explaining that this refers to "those who, by spiritual regeneration through grace that is given in baptism, enter the visible world."[190] Thus, for Eriugena, the hiddenness of the Otherworld is always already here in our landscape, as human beings experience the world. Being and non-being entwine in the landscape of human life, in cosmic experiential and participatory language that is iconographic. This explains the causality (and freedom) of human space that is and is not our own. Such landscapes encompass nature in both senses of the English term—essence and physical environment—but in both cases relationally, because of its embrace of the hidden.

Siewers summarizes the genius of *The Periphyseon*, from his particular reading of Irish and Welsh lore and legend:

> More than anything else the Periphyseon arguably sought to shape textually a restoration of Eden-like wonder on earth, a wonder relating to realizing the significance of larger contexts of life is the sparkle of divine energies in nature, and of desert-style listening and obedience in obligation to them as part of being human.[191]

This Otherworld 'iconography-in-text,' which Siewers identifies in the early Irish and Welsh narrative traditions, could just as well apply to Tolkien's own sub-creative narrative, as they share borrowed traditions. Therefore, in the sense that it relates both to our own world, it has a participatory integrity all of its own. The creatures we read of in the First Age of Middle-earth exist in so far as they participate in something beyond themselves (as do the Ainur in relation to the One—Ilúvatar, and equally creation in relation to the Ainur). From the (Middle-)earthly perspective then, this is not immediately apparent, but as Siewers reads Eriugena—and by association, Tolkien—it all depends on perspective.

---

189. Quoted in Bamford, *Voice of the Eagle*, 86–87.

190. Ibid., 88–89, 93, 101. This refers to those which are said 'to be' within the fifth mode of being.

191. Siewers, *Strange Beauty*, 84.

Evil it will not see, for evil lies
not in God's picture but in crooked eyes,
not in the source but in malicious choice,
and not in sound but in the tuneless voice.[1]

---

1. Tolkien, *Mythopoeia*, in *Tree and Leaf,* 90.

5

A Diversion towards Mutability and the Possibility of Evil

5.1 Life as Gift and Variety: Augustine's Optimistic Neoplatonism

There is a repeated assertion in Augustine's works that all in creation, by the divine omnipotence of God, is good: even those rational creatures which lapse towards evil acts and dominance of others, demonstrate their goodness by making rational choices 'evilly', tending towards some kind of distorted view of order. Tolkien's created beings are the product of the mind of a God who creates *ex nihilo*, but not in the absolute sense of repletion and *id ipsum* that we see in Augustine. It has been observed that this task is shared with 'higher' created beings who, in turn, mould Middle-earth from within their own individual and free creative will. If Tolkien departs from Augustine here, it is more in the *modus operandi* of creation, than its essential theology. Intelligent and aesthetic weaving of musical thematics demonstrates a degree of independence in Tolkien's art, as well as tending toward a Neoplatonic view of universal balance and priority. This, however, is not entirely devoid of Augustinian influence, as we have seen God's creative plenitude expressed in terms of the ordering of perfection and procession of speech.[1]

The Greek philosophers denied that the world was created out of nothing (*creatio ex nihilo*) asserting instead that 'Out of nothing, nothing comes' (*ex nihilo nihil fit*).[2] Augustine rejected the early Neoplatonic

---

1. *De lib arb*, 3.9.24–25; 3.15.42–43.

2. David R. Griffin, "Creation out of Nothing," 119, 137. In line with others, Griffin refutes the assumption that the doctrine of *creatio ex nihilo* is to be read automatically from biblical texts, and that this assumption creates an insoluble problem of evil for theists. There is insufficient scope to incorporate an analysis of his version of process

theory of necessary emanation, as proposed by Plotinus, based on Plato's cosmogony, and held to the Christian doctrine of *creatio ex nihilo* as willed by God from eternity. This distinction (emanation/creation) is presented in clear juxtaposition by Alfons Puigarnau, whereby the incompatibility of Platonist emanationism and Christian providentialism has its root in the distinction between the Platonist conception of the One, and the Judaeo-Christian concept of a personal God. In Plotinian cosmogony, the maker is in fact powerful, but does not manage to maintain a complete transcendence over the material. In defending emanation, the One eliminates transcendence, and consequently, providence; with God (in Augustinian terms), transcendence is compatible with providence.[3] The world and time thus had a definite beginning.[4] But what God wills to create is determined by what God's intelligence has determined to be good. God's intellect is the primary motive to create. From Neoplatonism, however, both Augustine and Boethius derived their conception of God as timeless and unchanging. God is not only eternal, having no beginning, nor end, but he is without time, no past or future, but just an eternal 'now.'[5] In this eternal 'now,' God sees all the past, present, future of the world that His will and intelligence has created. According to Augustine, eternity is motionless, has no succession; everything is present at once, and there is no past nor future. Time was created by God out of nothing, *ex nihilo*.[6]

---

theology, but it is sufficient to say that an attempt to solve the problem of evil by this kind of theology is to have surrendered the basic premises of Judaeo-Christian monotheism. The philosophy and theology of Augustine and his Latin successors stands on this revealed monotheism.

3. Puigarnau, *Creation and Freedom*, 245–7; *Enneads*, 5,5,9. See also Mann, *Augustine on Evil*, 41–42.

4. The view that God is Creator of the universe/world out of nothing is Hebrew rather than Greek, and is the interpretation of the story of creation given in the book of Genesis. "In the beginning God created the heavens and the earth" (Gen. 1:1). The Nicene Creed of AD 325 states that God is the "maker of all things visible and invisible" and the Council of Chalcedon, after reaffirming what previous earlier creeds had said, identified God as "Ruler of all, the maker of heaven and earth and of all things seen and unseen." *CCC*, 337. Such is the position of the Catholic Church today (also *De Gen. c. Man.* 1.2.4).

5. *Sermo* 52.6,.6: and *Sermo* 117.3.5, quoted in the *CCC*, para 230: "Even when he reveals himself, God remains a mystery beyond words : 'If you understood him, it would not be God.'" This is supported in Boethius' *Consolations* Book 5, and his idea of God's eternity.

6. For a very good summary of Augustine's view on time and eternity, as distinct from that of Plotinus, see Knuuttila, "Time and Creation in Augustine," 109–11. Quoting from *Conf.* 11.14, he links the concept of created time to the soul's reflection on past events and anticipation of the future. In so doing, Augustine focuses on a psychological account of time.

For Augustine, the doctrine of *creatio ex nihilo* entails the notion of divine immutability as a corollary.[7] Creaturely existence can have no prior claim to God's activity without locking God into a real relationship to his creation. Hence, the relation of divine cause to created effect cannot be dialectical, as this would compromise God's transcendence and immutability and, ultimately, his status as Creator.[8] God's causality of temporal effects cannot in any way be thought to effect a change in God's own agency, or a compromise of God's simplicity. Creation must be seen as sheer gratuity (from the viewpoint of creatures), even though it is, paradoxically, internally reciprocal (from the concept of the Trinity). Augustine's persistent rebuttal of Pelagianism—that grace cannot originate with us—simply transposes this logic into the category of sanctification: human merit cannot be antecedent to the activity of grace without similarly rendering the divine act finite and reactive.[9] In this, God's transcendence and goodness are both safeguarded. It is this plenitude, giving being in an act of sheer delight, that in fact constitutes the ontological difference, and constitutes it for the first time in Judaism and Christianity: for this delight, this generosity, knows no opposite, not even non-being.[10] For Augustine, a man participates in God when his 'unlikeness' is taken away, when he is no longer wandering, as Augustine himself had done, 'in a region of unlikeness.' Adoption is God's action in removing all unlikeness and allowing us to participate in God's divinity.[11]

5.2 Evil as The 'Embodiment of Non-Being' from the Perspective of Being

A key assertion in Augustine's theology of creation is that all created things are intrinsically good, because they are 'engraced' within the creation of a good God. In rejecting Manichaeism's materialistic dualism, and given that his Christian belief required him to think of God as (or being) a non-corporeal being, Augustine then had to rethink the problem afresh. Jane Chance summarizes these contrasting beliefs and conflicts of belief, and that the distinctions cannot be underestimated in formulating Augustine's approach

---

7. Michael Hanby, *Augustine and Modernity*, 83.
8. *Conf*, 12.15.
9. *Conf*, 12.7; 13.2; *Enneads*, 6.9.9.
10. Hanby, *Augustine and Modernity*, 84; Rist, *Augustine: Ancient Thought Baptised*, 260. We have seen in chapter 4 how this concept of meontology is taken to an extreme position in Eriugena's Periphyseon, where being and non-being coincide in God.
11. *Conf*, 12.7; *De Trin*, 4.2.4.

to the problem of evil. The nature of God and matter, its origins and goodness, chart the locus of Augustine's intellectual ascent towards God in Book 2 of *De libero arbitrio*.[12] If God creates out of the fullness of God's goodness, then God will not create a thing unless he knows it as good.[13] God did not create out of any necessity, nor to perfect any deficiency in himself.[14] Good works (things) are created by a good God.[15] Therefore, if every creature is good, insofar as it exists, how then is there evil? Mann formulates Augustine's response as follows:

First, whilst every creature is good, some are better than others. Insofar as corporeal things exist at all, God has bestowed upon them some degree of measure. No creature is evil, in spite of the fact that some are worse (or less good) than others. When asked why this *privatio* of good occurs, firstly it must be observed that it is a natural tendency for creatures towards mutability and corruption, having been created *ex nihilo*. Secondly, we are subject to 'perspectival prejudices,' failing to see how local privations (and especially those which affect us) contribute to the good of the whole. To desire that finite beings would not pass away, is to wish that they were something other than they are. Thirdly, God owes nothing to anything or anyone. Anything that exists owes its entire existence to God.[16] Evil is sometimes predicated of the choices and actions of creatures possessing reason. Sin is not a desire for naturally evil things, for there are no naturally evil things that could serve as objects of sinful desires.[17] Augustine is fond of describing sin as the will's turning away from God, a culpable rejection of the infinite bounty God offers, in favour of infinitely inferior fare.[18]

Augustine had to reconcile his previously held beliefs on Manichaeanism, that God could be affected by evil, with the (Catholic) Christian view

---

12. Chance, *Mythology of Power*, 73–75.
13. *Conf*, 13.2; 13.4; *Civ Dei*, 11.21.
14. *Conf*, 13.4.
15. *Civ Dei*, 11.21.
16. Mann, *Augustine on Evil*, 43–44.

17. *De nat. boni c. Man,* 36: "evil is to use a good evilly." CCC 398: "In that sin man preferred himself to God and by that very act scorned him. He chose himself over and against God, against the requirements of his creaturely status and therefore against his own good. Constituted in a state of holiness, man was destined to be fully divinized by God in glory. Seduced by the devil, he wanted 'to be like God,' but 'without God, before God, and not in accordance with God.'"

18. Mann, *Augustine on Evil*, 46: "Described as the free rejection of an infinite good, however, the sin is not just culpable. It is staggeringly irrational; from a cost benefit viewpoint, the worse deal imaginable." A genuinely free will necessarily carries with it the liability to sin. But without the freedom of choice, with its built-in liability, humans would lack the capacity to choose and live rightly.

that the root of the matter lay with humanity.[19] If God was the origin of evil, then its presence in the world would be intolerable to the minds of his rational creatures, for it would make God weak, who himself could not resist evil. Only on the hypothesis that God gave intelligent creatures so supreme a freedom that they choose to turn away from him could God's good creation be seen to be capable of evil: "by becoming man and dying, God demonstrated in a grand paradox a strength in weakness which reverses the effect of evil on human nature."[20] Evans summarizes the logical entailment of these steps, being irresistible to Augustine once he was a Christian and understood their implications: First, evil was nothing.[21] Secondly, he (man) could both will evil and not will good, and that evil was the absence of good.[22] Thirdly, if God is the source of all that is good, and all that exists is good, then Augustine himself can be the source only of what does not exist—evil.[23] Fourthly, only by the grace of God can he do good.[24] Fifthly, the fear of evil is itself evil, and the more the thing feared is nothing, the more evil is the fear of it, because evil itself is a nothing.[25] Finally, he knew the absurdity of being afraid of something which is not there.[26]

It is in this respect that Augustine's Christian Platonism is said to be optimistic: it gives an account of an orderly world, where God is always in benevolent control of his creation, watching over its welfare, unchanging and kind. It is also a system designed to accommodate the problem of evil, to show how by the exercise of providence God contains evil and makes it impossible for it, in the last analysis, to do harm.[27] Indeed, he foresaw evil and planned to make the best of it. Before his conversion, Augustine admits that he had the utmost difficulty in envisioning God except in terms of something corporeal, perhaps infused into the world in some way, or diffused beyond it.[28] Augustine was much influenced here by Aristotle's *Categories*, when they were just becoming available in Latin. Evans notes that Aristotle's account of 'Being' was so convincing to the young Augustine,

---

19. Evans, *Augustine on Evil*, 5; *Conf*, 7.3.4.
20. Evans, *Augustine on Evil*, 5.
21. *Conf*, 3.7.12; 7.3.4–4.6: "I did not know that evil has no existence except as a privation of good, down to that level which is altogether without being."
22. Ibid., 7.3.4.
23. Ibid., 7.5.7.
24. Ibid., 2.7.15.
25. Ibid., 6.5.7.
26. Ibid., 7.5.7.
27. Evans, *Augustine on Evil*, 32.
28. *Conf*, 7.1.1.

that he thought that whatever existed, even God, must be capable of being described in terms of ten categories. In so doing, he was using the wrong sort of reasoning and model of perception, so that he could not rise above the conceptual limitations imposed by his own bodily state.[29] Thinking of God as some sort of body (*corporeaum aliquid*), somehow penetrating the whole mass of the world, which is a huge lump, Plotinus' own attempts to speak of the mode of God's presence everywhere—omnipresence—show that he has exploited his conceptual resources to the limit, and yet he has been obliged to talk about God in the language of physical location:

> Imagine a place where he is not, and it will be clear that he is in another place; at once he is contained, and there is an end to his placelessness. God must somehow be instantaneously present everywhere, [. . .] nothing containing and nothing left void; for we cannot think of God here and something else there, nor of all God gathered at one spot.[30]

Augustine's own attempts reflect the same difficulty, in that when he tried to banish the thought of physical space from his mind, he could put 'nothing' in its place; even when he tried to conceive of 'nothing,' Augustine could describe it to himself only as the 'space' from which something had been removed:

> If a body is removed from a place, and the place remains empty of every body, then we have nothing. Nothing is an empty space (locus inanis), a spacious nothing (spatiosum nihil), and it is conceivable only in terms of the bodily substance which surrounds it, and which defines it.[31]

The only way out which presented itself involved abandoning the corporeal view of things which had seemed such safe ground. 'Nothingness' must be something different from the *spatiosum nihil*, the empty space Augustine had already rejected as a possibility.[32] If there can be a 'contrary' to substance, or essence, then perhaps it is here that we shall find nothing, non-substance, non-being. If all that exists is good, it follows that what is deprived

---

29. Ibid., 4.16.28. Evans, *Augustine on Evil*, 33.
30. *Conf*, 7.1.1; 7.3.5; *Enneads*, 5.5.9.
31. *Conf*, 7.1.1.

32. Plotinus discusses the possibility of there being a 'contrary' to a substance in the unique case of the Highest Being: "the contrariety does not depend upon quality or upon the existence of a distinct genus of beings, but upon the utmost difference, clash in content, clash in effect." *Enneads*, 1.8.6.

of goodness is deprived of existence.³³ Even corrupt things are good, for if there were no good in them, there would be nothing there to be corrupted. If it were possible to deprive things of all goodness, they would no longer exist. Evil, therefore, begins to look like a taking away, a privation, a tendency to nothingness, rather than a *locus inanis*, a pocket of nothingness in a good world. Once Augustine arrived at this possibility, he saw that he need no longer attempt an understanding of how evil can have a bodily place in the universe that is simultaneously filled with the divine Being. Eleanor Stump explains this concept lucidly :

> 'Privation' here is a technical term of (medieval) logic and indicates one particular kind of opposition; its correlative is possession. A privation is the absence of some characteristic in a thing that naturally possesses that characteristic. Blindness is a privation of sight in Samson, but not in an inanimate object, because, unlike Samson, the inanimate object does not naturally possess sight. For these reasons, evil is not simply nothing on Augustine's views, as he is sometimes believed to have maintained. Rather, it is a lack or deficiency of some sort of being in something in which that sort of being is natural.³⁴

Talking about evil is not like talking about things, about what constitutes the world as things that are: it is talking about a 'process,' and therefore about something that happens *to* the things in the world. Sorting out the language of evil is an indispensable part of sorting out the language of God, for beneath the problem of evil lies the problem of God.³⁵ Book 7 of the *Confessions* says much about the nature of evil in both human and divine perspectives. Time and again, Augustine writes of learning to 'see' afresh, to attempt to see as God sees. Here Augustine is talking about the capacity simultaneously to grasp the nature of evil as the perversion of my own capacity to see or know, and to become open in love and knowledge to the reality of God.³⁶ He acknowledges that "for you [God], evil is just not there at all," and he goes on to repeat the same assertion for creation as a whole.³⁷ There simply is no such *thing* as evil, and not just because it doesn't exist from God's standpoint alone, but because it cannot exist: evil is not a *substantia*. There is no thing for God to see, though God is *aware* of the states of affairs that we call evil. To see evil as privation is to see it as

---

33. *Conf*, 7.12.
34. Evans, *Augustine on Evil*, 35; Stump, *Wandering in Darkness*, 384.
35. *Civ Dei*, 11.9.
36. Williams, *Insubstantial Evil*, 107.
37. *Conf*, 7.3.

something that affects my own perception of what is good for me: if evil is the absence of good, it is precisely that misreading of the world which skews my desires. Williams notes that

> to read the world accurately (in its relation to God the Creator) is also to repent [...,] that accurate reading of the world arises from the renewal of my own creaturely relation to God, my own shift into a relation to God that worthily represents what God truly is, and that thus overcomes the evil which is constituted by imperfect, corrupt or nonsensical pictures of the divine.[38]

Terry Eagleton drives this point home forcefully, quoting from Augustine's own pleasure in stealing fruit as a young man, and taking pleasure in the very sin of theft itself,

> I had no motive for my wickedness except wickedness itself. It was foul and I loved it. I loved the self-destruction, I loved my fall, not the object for which I had fallen, but my fall itself.[39]

Williams' reading of Augustine, makes no competitive distinction between the perspectives of God and humanity. The point of view of a creature, considering itself *in* itself, is not a neutral *locus standi*, but is an illustration of what evil is: "an account of the good of a creature abstracted from its place in the universe overall as ordered and loved by God."[40]

The point of view of God is not a perspective to be considered alongside others (just as the creation of this universe is not to be considered alongside the creation of any other 'counterfactual' universe). God's relation to creatures is not analogous to relations between creatures, in terms of 'use' or 'enjoyment.' 'Use' here implies the furtherance of the user's ends that makes them instrumental for another's good. 'Enjoyment' is finding one's fulfilment in concentrating one's action, vision, and energy on some reality outside oneself. This could never be said of Augustine's developing notion of God.[41] God has no need of anything to further the divine purposes, for God is wholly self-sufficient, necessarily and eternally possessed of bliss.[42] The only sense, according to Augustine, in which God 'uses' creatures is so to make them instrumental in their *own* fulfilment.[43]

---

38. Williams, *Insubstantial Evil*, 108.
39. Eagleton, *On Evil*, 111; cf. *Conf*, 2.4.9.
40. Williams, *Insubstantial Evil*, 108.
41. *De DocChr*, 1.1.4.
42. Williams, *Insubstantial Evil*, 108.
43. *De DocChr*, 1.1.32: God makes use of us for the sake of the exercise of God's own *bonitas*, which is the ground of our existence, so the divine use of us is always to that

The creature's perspective simply *is* defined by God's creative purpose, but that divine purpose is to maximise all possible fulfilment for the creature, since the good, the joy, the flourishing of the creature could never be in any way a threat to the divine bliss.

John Milbank's analysis of Augustine makes clear the notion that privation denies evil being located in any reality, power, or being whatsoever. It is impossibly instigated by will alone. Evil is neither caused by freedom, since freedom—as free—causes only the Good. Nor is finitude proffered as a credible excuse since, for Augustine, there is nothing defective in finitude as such. Rather, what is defective is the prevention of finite things from reaching their own proper finite share of perfection. Thus, for the Augustinian tradition, evil is radically without cause. In this way privation theory offers not an explanation of and for evil, but instead rigorously remains with its inexplicability, for 'explanation' can pertain only to existence, and here evil is not seen as something in existence. Since in this sense evil is so problematic, then it defies *problema*, and the need for either theodicy or ontodicy, "is regarded for this reason as not even explicable in principle, not even explicable for God."[44] No defence of God is required for the existence of 'no thing,' and returning to Tolkien, Ilúvatar cannot be culpable for the disordered pride of Melkor, nor Sauron, since they are both good and free—in a worldview where goodness apparently pervades all things. As inherited evil was held to have impaired our finitude, there was *in us* a causal bias towards evil (via original sin). Since grace renews our will, our evil decision to refuse grace is as groundless and causeless as Adam's original sin. For this reason, according to Augustine, the origin of evil must be passed over as "darkness and silence,"[45]

> as if there were a dreadful apophasis of evil that parodied the apophasis of the Divine. Because if evil is uncaused, there is indeed a sense in which it possesses us like an anti-cause proceeding from a Satanic black hole.[46]

Without a participatory mediation between a partially good finite, and an absolutely good infinite, the finite good will only arise through concealment of Being with which it is essentially in conflict:

---

divine end which is *our* blessedness.

44. Milbank, Being Reconciled, 18.

45. *Civ. Dei*, 12.7: "To try to discover the causes of such defection [. . .] is like trying to see darkness or to hear silence."

46. Milbank, Being Reconciled, 18.

To be, in the strict sense, is to be unvarying, immune to change, naturally eternal. Since being admits of no change, what ever is more 'true' is more 'simple' [. . .] the worst human beings become, the less simple they become; in Augustine's language, the less simple they are, the less they are.[47]

In Tolkien's language, such beings pass into 'shadow.'

What now follows is an assessment as to the extent to which Tolkien deviates from this aspect of privation, and never entirely escapes from the accusation of dualism. Such instances, whilst they give shape and drama to the whole, never outweigh the overshadowing influences of Augustine's Neoplatonic doctrine of privation and aesthetics.

5.3 The Good and Grotesque as Expressions of *Omnis Natura Bonum Est*

Whilst for Augustine, evil is a lack, a deficiency, and falling away from its own proper order, many of the grotesque figures of Tolkien's fiction are evil and truly monstrous, and yet are spared by the forces of good, so that they go on to be the cause of their own downfall. Both in their original fearful monstrosity and power, as well as in the way that power draws upon itself its own destruction, they witness to the good. The consistent theme of mercy is partly an awareness and reverential attitude to life as 'being and gift,' itself constituted as a good thing. In Tolkien's Middle-earth life is never taken cheaply, and always mourned (e.g., after battle of the four armies in *The Hobbit*); the morally upright characters in Tolkien's works are always unwilling to take life lightly or assert power over it.[48] Gollum was spared on separate occasions by Bilbo, Gandalf, Frodo and Faramir, as were Grima Wormtongue and Saruman by both (King) Theoden and the Ent, Treebeard. They had ample opportunity to redeem themselves, but refused repeatedly. After the destruction of the Shire, Frodo offers mercy to both Saruman and Wormtongue, but in refusing, the latter slits open Saruman's throat, and is himself killed by hobbit arrows. Alison Milbank posits that Tolkien has an Augustinian attitude to evil as a privation, and not a positive force in itself; that he presents evil human characters as physically warped and grotesque in the manner of

---

47. Rist, *Augustine : Ancient Thought Baptised*, 258–60.

48. We see this especially in the death and funerary customs of the dwarf-king Thorin Oakenshield (*The Hobbit*, 267) and Boromir (*LOTR*, 347). Aragorn's pact with the dead of Dunharrow—the Oathbreakers—is as much to release their souls from bondage, as it is to enlist their help in the battle with Mordor.

medieval devils.[49] Since human embodiment is a positive thing in itself, then evil must be a warping of that nature.

Examples are numerous. Upon Gandalf's exorcising the prolonged influence of Wormtongue upon Theoden King, Grima becomes ever more monstrous. He hisses, sprawls, and is thrust down on his belly like the judgement of the serpent in the Genesis myth;[50] The Lieutenant of Barad-dur, entering into a false parley with Aragorn, has the visage of a slavering mouth, as a wild beast.[51] The Ring-wraiths were once men of virtue and kingly or political substance, who had fallen. This grotesque presentation is a way of marking a fall from humanity, but achieves its evil aspects only by a bestiality that would be good in a wild beast or snake, but inappropriate in a man.[52]

The most problematic 'grotesque' within Tolkien's 'bestiary' is the spider Shelob, and her ancient ancestor, Ungoliant. In a particularly dark episode in *The Simarillion*, Melkor wounds the Two Trees of Valinor (above), whereupon Ungoliant "set her black beak to their wounds, till they were drained; and the poison of Death that was in her went into their tissues and withered them, root, branch, and leaf; and they died."[53] This chapter is fittingly called The Darkening of Valinor, and is a watershed for evil's influence on created being. The beauty of Middle-earth is for ever marred and deprived of the beauty and life of the two trees, and what they represent. Ungoliant is a creature who is entirely nihilistic and absorbing of all life around her.[54] Here Milbank raises the problem of ontology, that both Augustine and Aquinas were so keen to defend that all created matter is good. To categorise Ungoliant (and Shelob) in such a light is to contradict their lack of potential, as their very lives are murder and destruction:

> In Middle-earth, then, both good and evil function as external powers and as inner impulses from the psyche. It is perhaps fair to say that while the balances are maintained, we are on the whole more conscious of evil as an objective power and of good as a subjective impulse [. . .;] this lack of symmetry is moreover part of a basic denial of security throughout LOTR [. . .;] the benevolent powers offer no guarantees.[55]

---

49. Milbank, *Chesterton and Tolkien*, 71.
50. Tolkien, *LOTR*, 541–43, (cf. Gen 3:16).
51. Ibid., 872.
52. Milbank, *Chesterton and Tolkien*, 72.
53. Tolkien, *The Silmarillion*, 88–89.
54. Ibid., 94: "Dost thou desire the whole world for thy belly?"
55. Shippey, *Road to Middle Earth*, 174. See also Milbank, *Chesterton and Tolkien*,

Tolkien differentiates between what is created being, and what is corrupted and remodelled pre-existing real beings. The former is intrinsically good, but subject to free will and rejection of the good; the latter are products, evil beings manufactured as a mockery of 'the children of God.' Orcs were initially elves who

> by slow arts of cruelty were corrupted and enslaved; and thus did Melkor breed the hideous race of the Orcs in envy and mockery of the elves [. . .] and naught that had life of its own, nor the semblance of life could ever Melkor make since his rebellion [. . .] in the beginning.[56]

Tolkien seems here to be wrestling with a world made before he had worked out all the ontological implications of his choices, but his intentions are clear: he aims to hold fast to orthodox Christian accounts of evil, following Augustine (and Aquinas), in that creation is wholly good, and to existence itself as a good, which is not lost even if one becomes a Satan (or a Sauron). Any defence against the total depravation of all orcs is a clear tribute to the (religious) subtlety of Tolkien's craft. Tolkien clarifies this point in his own *Letters*. Trolls and orcs were not created by Morgoth, but that "he made them in counterfeit of certain creatures pre-existing." There is a wide gulf between creation by evil and corrupting what is ontologically good, being the free and rational creature of a good Creator. In Tolkien's world, orcs are "fundamentally a race of 'rational incarnate' creatures, though horribly corrupted, if no more so than many Men to be met today."[57] Furthermore, in defending the status of free will of both angelic and substantial creatures, he also defends the realities that creating beings manufacture or distort. Therefore, in the case of orcs, they are "part of the world, which is God's and ultimately good."[58]

In a posthumously published text, Tolkien alludes to the breeding of orcs to be the common belief of the Eldar. In point of fact, Tolkien shrouds their origin in a mystery contained within the dissonance of music created by Melkor, in that:

> Evil is fissiparous. But itself barren. Melkor could not 'beget,' or have any spouse. [. . .] Out of the *discords* of the Music—sc. Not directly out of either of the themes, Eru's or Melkor's, but of their dissonance with regard to one another—evil things appeared in

---

75–76.

56. Tolkien, *Silmarillion*, 58.
57. Carpenter, *Letters*, 190.
58. Ibid., 195.

Arda, which did not descend from any direct plan or vision of Melkor. They were *not* 'his children'; and therefore, since all evil hates, hated him too. The progeniture of things was corrupted. Hence Orcs? Part of the Elf-Man idea had gone wrong.[59]

It would appear that in this metaphysical section, Tolkien himself is unclear as to the origins of the orcs. This account is frustratingly incomplete, but Christopher Tolkien's notes acknowledge the significance of this passage, in that "this is the most comprehensive account that my father wrote of how, in his later years, he had come to 'interpret' the nature of Evil in his mythology."[60] Here it would appear that Tolkien is influenced by Pseudo-Dionysius, in that "Evil *qua* evil cannot produce and cannot sustain anything, cannot make or preserve anything."[61] His intention was, with respect to orcs, to be consonant with a Christian metaphysics of evil, though he felt under no obligation to fit in with formalized Christian theology.[62] Milbank observes that whilst they are full of malice and self-seeking, they also have

> a zany, quite comic discourse, showing the energy of being. [. . .] Shagrat and Gorbag are much more grotesquely presented than the orcs who capture Merry and Pippin, [. . .] as if the forces of evil become not just more powerful but also more strikingly visible as evil, the nearer they get to their source and stronghold.[63]

The complex case of orcs is integrated with the immanent being of Morgoth, the Vala Melkor who entered Middle-earth in order to corrupt and subjugate it. Tolkien's metaphysics of evil reside in a being who is "the greatest power under Eru (sc. The greatest created power)."[64] He could not be controlled or constrained by all the Valar combined, until he had become separated from his 'agents' (orcs, balrogs, etc.) into whom he had imputed, "power of recuperation and multiplication. So that they will gather again without further specific orders."[65] Part of his creative power has gone out into making an independent evil growth out of his control. This is highly significant, and consistent with how we have seen Tolkien's created beings

---

59. Tolkien, *Morgoth's Ring*, 405–6.
60. Ibid., 406.
61. *DivNom*, 729B.
62. Carpenter, *Letters*, 355. Here we read also that orcs are not evil in origin, even if they appear—as do some humans—as irredeemable.
63. Milbank, *Chesterton and Tolkien*, 76.
64. Tolkien, *Morgoth's Ring*, 390. This text, entitled "Melkor with Morgoth" was found amongst a newspaper dated April 1959, but may be dated as early as the summer of 1955.
65. Ibid., 391.

co-create and set free things other than themselves: in the case of the Valar, causing delight and wonder (cf. the creation of the dwarves); in the case of Morgoth, causing fear, mistrust, and ultimate domination. Indeed, as Morgoth, "when Melkor was confronted by the existence of other inhabitants of Arda, with other wills and intelligences, he was enraged by the mere fact of their existence, and his only notion of dealing with them was by physical force, or the fear of it."[66] Melkor's descent into materiality is accompanied by a diminution of being, consistent with a lapsarian understanding of evil, which we have seen as privative. Under the gaze of the Vala Manwë, "Both are amazed [. . .] to perceive the *decrease* in Melkor as a *person*; Melkor to perceive this also from his own point of view."[67] He is given a chance to repent, and kneels before Manwë in mock repentance, but in his decision to reject the path of true repentance—and begin the path back to his primeval nature—"he becomes much wickeder, and more foolish."[68] He is taken back to Valinor in chains, but full of trickery and malice. In this weakened state he is himself subject to the assembled Valar, and bides his time.

The spiders, Ungoliant and Shelob, however, do not fit easily into this optimistic Augustinian worldview. Their form of life *is* nihilistic, and their positive use of darkness as a means of assault implies not darkness so much, as "Unlight, in which things seemed to be no more."[69] This is not simply extending the apophatic to an extreme, but a negation of the possibility of any goodness whatsoever. In being confronted with Galadriel's phial of light, despite her initial wariness and reticence to attack, Shelob ultimately overpowers Frodo, who is left for dead.[70] The dualism here suggests a Manichaean universe of competing and equal forces of light and darkness, to which Augustine was ultimately opposed. We see this dualism also expressed between Melkor and Manwë, who strive for the possession of Arda (Middle-earth). Arda is fashioned not as God originally designs, but is subject to the competing forces and creative minds of the Ainur in terms of beauty or dysfunction.[71] Augustine speaks of evil as a "wounding of good," or as an infection, whose status is only accidental,

---

66. Ibid., 395.
67. Ibid., 391.
68. Ibid. There is another parallel to the *DivNom* 729C here, in that "Total deprivation means total powerlessness. A partial capacity, however, has some power, not in that it is a deprivation but in that it is not a total deprivation."
69. Tolkien, *Silmarillion*, 86.
70. Tolkien, *LOTR*, 757–58.
71. Tolkien, *The Silmarillion*, 21–22.

> For what is that which we call evil but the absence of good? In the bodies of animals, disease and wounds mean nothing but the absence of health; for when a cure is effected, that does not mean that the evils which were present—namely, the diseases and wounds—go away from the body and dwell elsewhere: they altogether cease to exist.[72]

Here Augustine uses the term 'substance' in its philosophical sense of 'substantial being,' whereas Ungoliant and Shelob seem to wound and infect their victims in a manner that is more metaphysically substantive, it is a sort of positive negativity.[73] There is strange comfort here for Gollum (or Smeagol) who, because of the sheer extent of Shelob's omnivorous darkness, she "walked through all the ways of his weariness beside him, cutting him off from light and from regret."[74] The ugliness of orcs may remind one of the loss of beauty, but the way in which Shelob negates difference itself stops Gollum from the pain and awareness of his lost self.[75] In one sense, Shelob is only grotesque if light is shone upon her; otherwise she lives in a world where there can be no individuation, no being, and no contrast to make possible the juxtaposition of the grotesque mode, and in this respect she is difficult to reconcile Augustine's premise that *omnis natura bonum est*.

Augustine's own reading of the problem does sift the evil from the good, but it also puts them close up against (or adjacent to) each other, in a grotesque contradiction, which is then shown to be correct in so far as a wicked man *is* an 'evil good':

> Nothing, then, can be evil except something which is good. And although this, when stated, seems to be a contradiction, yet the strictness of reasoning leaves us no escape from the conclusion. [. . .] Now, if a man is a good thing because he is a being, what is an evil man but an evil good? Yet, when we accurately distinguish these two things, we find that it is not because he is a man that he is an evil, or because he is wicked that he is a good; but that he is a good because he is a man, and an evil because he is wicked.[76]

---

72. *Enchr*, 3.11. Pseudo-Dionysius similarly sums up evil's metaphysical 'nature': "Good comes from the one universal Cause, and evil originates in numerous partial deficiencies. God knows evil under the form of good, and with him the causes of evil things are the capacities which can produce good." *DivNom*, 729C.
73. Milbank, *Chesterton and Tolkien*, 77.
74. Tolkien, *LOTR*, 750–51.
75. Milbank, *Chesterton and Tolkien*, 77.
76. *Enchr*, 4:13.

This paradox is true in a fallen world, where a man might choose to be evil (but the initial choice is itself irrational for Augustine).

5.4 A Critique of Augustine's 'Free-will' and 'Aesthetic' Theodicies

In section 2.3, I highlighted that the independent and free rebellion of Melkor to weave into the Great Music his own discordant notes resulted ultimately in the marring and destruction of the great lights and trees of Valinor. Their subsequent destructive malice in the First Age of Middle-earth did not go unpunished, but mercy was shown, and it would appear that Tolkien is creating a mythology whereby good and evil can coincide. Ilúvatar remains aloof and unconcerned, and the free peoples of Middle-earth are left to fend for themselves, with an apparent attitude of fatalism, that good and evil are inevitably a part of life's experience. The manner in which Tolkien writes lends itself to what became known as an aesthetic theodicy, that there is some benefit to humanity, as created being, in the juxtaposition of these two realities. If Tolkien is to escape the charge of dualism—the kind that Augustine was eager to refute in his writings against the Manichaeans—then this approach to his attempt at theodicy needs careful evaluation. It is assumed, in the first instance, that Tolkien's 'theodicy' (if it be one) is informed by Augustine's writings, over and above his portrayal of evil as a privation.

Three recent contributions by Eleonore Stump and Hohyun Sohn have challenged the modern concept of theodicy. In her later work, Stump supposes that Augustine's chief concern was an attempt to explain the ontology of evil, and not to create a theodicy as such.[77] Nothing about this position of Augustine's constitutes a solution to the problem of suffering, nor did Augustine or any later medieval philosophers suppose it did.[78] Augustine is also known for his suggestion that the evil permitted by God contributes to the beauty and goodness of the whole universe, just as a dark patch may contribute to the lightness and beauty of a painting. One may interpret this suggestion on Augustine's part as an attempt at theodicy, too. However, to

77. Stump, "Augustine on Free Will," 124. She notes also that even amongst scholars who are careful to make explicit what they mean by 'free will' still don't agree much about the nature of Augustine's theory of free will. In this earlier work, she challenges the commonly accepted libertarian approach to Augustine's theology of free will, and suggests strongly (but not definitely) that Augustine's teaching on free will rests on compatibilist premises. The libertarian claims are constantly modified here to accommodate Augustine's own developments. See especially 130–35.

78. Stump, *Wandering in Darkness*, 384.

take this suggestion of Augustine's as an attempted theodicy is to suppose that, for Augustine, the answer to the question 'why does God allow suffering?' is that suffering has an aesthetic value for God. Hohn's critique differs from Stump's in that his chief objection is the disproportionate suffering of an eternity in hell, for sins committed in a temporal and finite arena (that is life). That a just God could create a world where heaven and hell together highlight God's providential care for the world, and that this cosmic order of justice is brought about by the condemnation of sinners, the proving of the just, and the perfecting of the blessed, is not tenable:

> Any punishment that is infinitely prolonged would be excessive and ugly, and intolerable to God [. . .] and that no sin committed in time deserves an eternal punishment in hell: the beauty of hell is refuted.[79]

Stump rejects both of these 'pseudo-theodicies'—free-will and Aesthetic—sometimes mistakenly attributed to Augustine, because neither of them is compatible with the claim that God would allow a human person to suffer only if through that suffering alone God can provide an outweighing benefit that goes primarily to the sufferer.[80] Furthermore, those who interpret Augustine's aesthetic suggestion as a kind of theodicy have misidentified the question to which his suggestion was meant to be an answer. For Augustine, God's original plan for the world was that the world have in it only good and not evil. I have shown above that evil is first introduced into a good world created by a good God through the misuse of free will on the part of the creatures created good by God.

God permits the misuse of free will and all the suffering consequent on it; but the world as God permits it to be is not the world as God originally planned it. The world as it is now is therefore a result of God's Plan B, not his Plan A. Stump distinguishes God's 'antecedent will' from God's 'consequent will.' God's antecedent will is what God would have willed if everything in the world had been up to him alone. God's consequent will is what God actually does will, given what God's creatures will.[81] In the circumstances of post-fall human life, with human misuse of free will, God's consequent will includes allowing human suffering in some cases. An obvious flaw in this critique is that God's consequent will may represent a defeat for God, a sadness, a deficiency of some sort, in the fact that God's consequent will is different from his antecedent will: that God's Plan A for the world had to be

---

79. Hohn, "The Beauty of Hell? 47–57, 57
80. Stump, *Wandering in Darkness*, 384.
81. Ibid., 385.

replaced by God's Plan B. This is the question/problem to which Augustine's aesthetic 'theodicy' is directed. The universe that results from God's Plan B has suffering in it; but it has great compensatory beauty in it as well, a beauty that would not have been actualized as it is known without the suffering. Plan B therefore is not a defeat. God is able to make a world with suffering in it even more beautiful than the world would have been had there been neither moral evil nor suffering. The point for Augustine is precisely that Plan B is a triumph for God, not a defeat (and we see this in Iluvatar's acquittal of Melkor).[82] Moral evil is not like pain: it is not morally permissible to cause moral evil as a means to some good. In fact, God does not cause *any* moral evil. He only allows moral evil to be introduced into the world by the free choices of creatures. And so, in Augustine's account, God allows moral evil and its consequences in the sense that with his consequent will he permits it to occur; but God does not cause it or will its existence with his antecedent will. To claim that this world, even with its evil and suffering, is more beautiful than the world would have been without evil and suffering is therefore *not* to explain the morally sufficient reason for God to allow evil. It is one thing to ask why God's allowing moral wrongdoing and suffering does not constitute a defeat for God. It is another thing entirely to ask why God would allow moral wrongdoing and suffering in the first place. It is only the first question that is at issue in Augustine's suggestion about the aesthetics of the post-fall world: the second question was taken up in Boethius' *Consolations,* which considers the freedom and chance in the affairs of men, alongside God's providential ordering of the world.

The source of all things is the light and truth of the divine—unconstrained, immaterial, and invulnerable. As such, the divine is in no way compromised or in competition with agencies of finitude (which are by nature constrained and vulnerable). In what is not divine, there must be a plurality of agencies, displaying a variety of freedom or self-determination. Therefore, what to an unreflective observer may look like 'evil'—the aesthetically disagreeable, the contingently annoying—is no more than a particular arrangement of action and constraint, degrees of instability and vulnerability, liable to variation as it inextricably interacts within the circumstances arising out of mental functioning. Whilst Augustine has now come to realize that corruptibility is not *ipso facto* incompatible with good in some measure, he sees this in the whole plenitude of creation. Harmony and beauty may not be evident at every level of existence, and there are the 'lower reaches' of creation, which are nonetheless *conveniens* (fitting)

---

82. Ibid., 386.

within the whole.⁸³ Williams identifies the characteristic problem of the human agent in two ways: First, it is the subordination of spirit to trivial and finite desires. Secondly, it is the confidence of created spirit that it is able by its own immanent action to free itself from this subordination. The solution is reconnecting the finite mind with infinite agency—the loving wisdom of God. The opening of that 'reconnection' depends entirely upon the initiative of God in Jesus Christ.⁸⁴

Williams, like Stump and Hohn, rejects a description of Augustine's project as 'aesthetic,' as privileging a divine 'point of view.' In defending the privative account of evil, Williams—following Evans—rules out any statement of the cause or source of evil that treats it in a "spatialised way."⁸⁵ Similarly, and by association, it is essential that God and the created mind are simultaneously 'despatialized.' If God, the most fundamental form of activity there is, cannot be thought of as occupying a territory, and the human spirit or mind reflects this primary activity in its own non-territorial character, then that which interrupts the relation of the creature to its Creator—evil—must belong to the same frame of reference.⁸⁶ Augustine is attempting to place the origin of evil within the interactions of human history, and not in a classification of substances—a single medium of extension. The aesthetic model of theodicy cannot, therefore be reduced to the idea of a resolution by appeal to a divine perspective, which (when eternity implies timelessness) sees all creation in a single simultaneous moment, and being (personally) unconnected with the subjectivity of created beings.⁸⁷

Not all beings in the universe are destined to live for ever. For the merely animate, as opposed to the spiritual creature, continued existence is not properly desirable beyond their allotted span. In God's eyes, it is good that they perish when they do. Likewise, it is good that a spiritual creature, however depraved—even a Melkor or Sauron—should continue in being, so as to go on exhibiting the specific kind of good associated with spiritual existence. John Hick characterizes this approach as "aesthetic rather than ethical": God is perceived more as the "Artist enjoying the products of his creative activity [. . .] than the Person seeking to bring about personal relations with created persons."⁸⁸ In so far as this is a theodicy governed

---

83. Williams, *Insubstantial Evil*, 109; *Conf*, 7.12, 7.13 and 7.16.

84. *Conf*, 7.18.

85. Williams, *Insubstantial evil*, 110. His indebtedness to Gillian Evans' text, *Augustine on Evil*, is clearly stated in note 3, 122.

86. Ibid.

87. Ibid.

88. Hick, *Evil and the God of Love*, 59.

by aesthetic criteria, it fails to do justice to the personal: the justification lies in the eye of the divine beholder, the one subject to whom the whole system is present or visible. Williams, like Stump, argues that a theodicy which privileges the observer's standpoint is "theologically and spiritually vacuous"; that "anaesthetics of evil" is not, in any sense, a philosophical or theological answer to the problem.[89]

Hick's objection to an alleged aesthetic theodicy lies in his more fundamental objection to Augustine's use of Plotinus, in that he is said to Christianize the Neoplatonic emanationism underlying this principle of plenitude:

> God acts deliberately to form a universe, and He acts in terms of the principle of plenitude, considering it better to produce all possible forms of being, lower as well as higher, poorer as well as richer, all contributing to a wonderful harmony and beauty in His sight, than to produce only a society of blessed angels.[90]

All that Augustine would appear to achieve here is to substitute God's creative will for the automatic 'radiating' of being from the One. But why should God act by any such principle? If creation's form is directed or dictated by some kind of principle, then we have lost sight of the freedom of God's will to act with finite persons, whose own freedom mirrors that of God. The love of God is being conceived in metaphysical rather than personal terms.[91] Augustine testifies to the totality of beings as better than the higher elements alone, and of the principle that things must be unequal for there to be any particular things at all.[92] What Augustine neglects to present, in a clear and systematic statement is that God creates the maximum possible variety of creatures, and that the universe is a system of interdependent agencies, wherein by God's creative providence each thing is what it is, in virtue of where it stands in that universal order. Thus, "things further down the scale that contribute to the good of things higher up, find their own good in so doing."[93] The principle that Augustine is elaborating is not strictly one of plenitude alone, but also one of interdependence. We see this in Tolkien's 'Music of the Ainur,' where in unison they sing their Song of Creation, bringing all things into being—as extensions of the mind of Ilúvatar. They do not occur at the same time (dwarves follow men, who

---

89. Williams, *Insubstantial Evil*, 107.
90. Hick, *Evil and the God of Love*, 83.
91. Ibid.
92. *Conf*, 7.13 and *Civ Dei*, 11.22.
93. Williams, *Insubstantial Evil*, 114.

in turn follow elves), but in procession, but nevertheless there was wonder in the revelation of Arda.[94]

The aesthetic vision is never absent from this principle. Augustine remarks about the importance of the eyebrow to the well-proportioned face; a world containing sin can still as a whole be beautiful, as is a picture with dark patches and contrast.[95] The darkness of sin in itself is terrible, but yet the entire universe does not, because of it, cease to reflect the order of God's wisdom. The ultimate punishment of sin, in manifesting God's just laws, balances the order of the whole. Sin is not in some way good, when seen against a sufficiently large backdrop: what is good, is the procession of the universe which, in God's providence, includes in its final reckoning the manifestation of the gravity of sin, and the triumph of God's rectifying action. Augustine postulates that once God chooses to make a world that is both temporal and interdependent, the logic of that free determination requires variety, and the "oscillations of circumstances" as agents act upon each other, never at any point attaining perfect balance within the world's history. Williams finds here a compatibility with *De Civitate Dei* 11.23, that without human sin, the world would have been full "only with good natures." The accusation that ascribes evil only to 'lower' elements in creation is a mistake—a failure to see how they fit into the good of 'higher' levels of organisation, and so into the good of the whole.[96] In Tolkien's own terms Melkor, being the *greatest* of the Ainur, was the one to fall, thus negating this particular misreading of Augustine.

---

94. Tolkien, *The Silmarillion*, 18.
95. *Civ Dei*, 11.22.
96. Williams, *Insubstantial Evil*, 115

"All human beings desire to know," and truth is the proper object of this desire. Everyday life shows how concerned each of us is to discover for ourselves, beyond mere opinions, how things really are.[1]

---

1. John Paul II, *Fides et Ratio*, para 25; *cf.* Aristotle's *Metaphysics*, I, 1

6

Concluding Comments: There and Back Again

This book arises out of a genuine desire and will to know 'what is,' what things are in relation to God, their source and origin and that to which all things will eventually return. The fantasy and metaphysical writings of J. R. R. Tolkien offer a wide-ranging account of what life is, as 'being and gift.' The conclusion of my investigation considers the significance of the work in terms of its engagement with Tolkien's entire *corpus*, published and unpublished, and in relation to that stated in *The Prolegomenon*.

Tolkien and the Neoplatonists in Dialogue

I demonstrated in chapter 2 that the emergent Christian Neoplatonism of late Antiquity and early medievalism, in respect of its theology and philosophy of creation and fall, arising as it does out of a doctrine of God, is a primary influence upon the philosophical framework of Tolkien's Middle-earth *legendarium*, (largely) giving an account of nature as essentially good in its unique giftedness, and evil as privative. There is no escaping here Tolkien's desire to answer, or at least face up to, the human condition of fallenness, in the face of the beauty and originality of creation, however one envisages its manner of origin. This is consistent with Augustine's assertion that all in creation, by the divine omnipotence of God, is good. Even those rational creatures which lapse towards evil acts and dominance of others, demonstrate their goodness by making rational choices 'evilly,' tending towards some kind of distorted view of order. Tolkien's created beings are the product of the mind of a God who creates *ex nihilo*, but not in the absolute sense of repletion and *id ipsum* that we see in Augustine. This task is shared with higher (or prior) created angelic beings, who in turn mould Middle-earth (Arda) from within their own individual creative will. Intelligent and aesthetic weaving of musical thematics—both consonant and discordant—demonstrates a degree of independence and freedom in Tolkien's art, as well as tending towards a Boethian view of universal balance and priority.

I have demonstrated that a corrective in favor of Aquinas' more positive philosophy of 'being as gift' is a better reading out of the *musica universalis* tradition of the early medieval period. Maritain's aesthetics, inspired as they are by a more theological reading of Neo-Thomism, have inspired Tolkien's own aesthetics of beauty and goodness, being rooted in this Catholic understanding of how being has a radical giftedness in creation. David Jones' development of Maritain suggests that all art has a symbolic and/or sacramental element which points beyond itself and is participatory in something more than itself. For Jones (and Tolkien), this is the superabundant creativity in God, which is imputed as human creativity and freedom.

Tolkien and the Dialectic of Freedom and Doom

In the final two parts of chapter 3, I identified significant philosophical links to what precedes them, in that the return is brought about by a participatory relationship between (perfect) God and (fallen) humanity. Within the dual allegories of *Pearl* and *Leaf by Niggle* we observe Tolkien's use of Old and Middle English inspiration, melding together the fantasy and the real; the sacramental and the material worlds colliding in their respective natures. Life as a gift is a non-negotiable aspect of being within the Neoplatonic outlook of Tolkien's sources.

For Eriugena, we see it is a going forth into materiality, for the procession of God into all things as created effects means that all things have the one primordial cause, the same beginning, and ultimately will have the same end. In the procession from God, the nothingness from which all things are created is actually God's self, because there can be nothing coeternal and coexisting with God. This 'nothing' becomes 'something' through the creative process, in that the unknowable reveals itself through creation, and in so doing becomes something that both itself and created effects can know. Creation has 'being' both coeternal and coessential with God. For perfect human nature, beings are essentially free. Eriugena does not dissolve or splinter the integrity of human nature: our descent into materiality merely cloaks and hides our true nature from our own understanding. Human nature is a whole and a unity. The late medieval 'overlay landscapes' occasionally and deliberately confuse the distinction between these two worlds—or 'spots of time'—eternity and temporality, in which life is situated. Tolkien was aware of this from his studies and translations of *Beowulf*, and acknowledges it in several parts of his own *legendarium*. The interplay between the cosmic and the particular, that which is tangible and historical, and that which properly belongs to myth, is demonstrated out of his readings of *Beowulf*.

The Neoplatonic Boethian legacy written into Tolkien's mythology presents beings who are free in their own moral agency and also within the timelessness of God. Providence is the divine reason itself, the unfolding of temporal events as this is present to the vision of the divine mind. Fate is the same unfolding of events as it is worked out in time, as we perceive it in the temporal world. Hence, Lúthien can plead for Beren's life, and can be transformed in her own ontological status by both her own free agency in time, and by the compliant will of the god, Mandos. Beings are not simply materiality, and yet in the more precise (and orthodox) Thomist view, in the metaphysics of participation, the principle nevertheless remains: being is always in relation to something prior to itself on a cosmological scale, and its true nature or essence can only be known to the extent in which it participates in its origin.

The freedom, which is possessed by God in His essential nature, is mediated by this participation, and therefore what is known by God and acted upon as providence, is represented as true human freedom within the enfoldments of God's order, fate, and providence. My defence of a (Latin) Boethian philosophy of 'being as free,' in respect of Tolkien's philosophy—as opposed to a more deterministic Alfredian (Anglo-Saxon) outlook, focused on divine power—is entirely consistent with the participatory notion of 'being as gift,' and with the developed tale *Of Beren and Lúthien*. Tolkien's re-paganized world can hold such creatures who see their fates as uncertain because he writes against a backdrop of Christian incarnational and sacramental certainties, as did the writer of *Beowulf* and *Pearl*. Tolkien's use of borrowed traditions from Old and (to a lesser extent) Middle English sources demonstrates a broad Augustinian-Boethian Neoplatonism, but will be seen to be sufficiently original and creative around the concepts of 'Otherworld' landscapes. In these layered texts we encounter a world peopled by free moral agents, but also a rich and diverse world of aesthetic beauty, each aspect of which has its corresponding shadow existence.

Life and Being as a Fusion of Timelesness and Sensuality

Chapter 4 developed further my argument that, for Tolkien and the Neoplatonists, life and being subsist only within the larger context of participation in the One. Whilst the more mystical Neoplatonism of Eriugena diverges from the musical themes of Augustine, Boethius, and Aquinas, he nevertheless stresses the teleological nature of created being, alongside his participatory ontology with God. Alfred Siewers' analysis makes bold claims of how the Irish and Welsh sea legends provided a backdrop for Tolkien's own participatory ontology, in terms of an ecocentric cosmos. Given that both Eriugena and Tolkien were aware of, and used these pre-Scholastic texts, then my claim that Tolkien's philosophy of being displays a striking similarity to that of Eriugena, is suggestive of some degree of dependency. However, this cannot be established from any testimony or reference in any of Tolkien's letters or published works. From his professional studies, therefore, we are now able to understand at certain turns in his *Tale of Tinúviel* narrative Tolkien's independence from the Graeco-Latin trajectory of Neoplatonism expounded in the previous chapters. In the Eriugenian worldview, the *ordo* or 'doom' of a thing's materiality is governed by the mind, and need not simply be a consistent or fixed outward form: thus giving rise for Tolkien to develop an intriguing phenomenon of shape-shifting and a world in flux—a protean formal cause, lacking any formal certainty.

In the absence of hard evidence of Tolkien's dependency upon Eriugena, here I may have to concede that he relies also on European tales for such concepts. However, there is sufficient evidence for a philosophical foundation for the phenomenon, independent of these Northern sources. The freedom of the will as defended by Eriugena originates in the nature of God, mediated by participation and gift. His earlier work (*On Divine Predestination*) reflects a keen Augustinian anthropology of this will as gift, whilst his later *Periphyseon* is more mystical in its dialectical method.

The recapitulation of Eriugena's dialectical approach to the *exitus*—*reditus*, of both perfect and fallen human nature, provides a necessary foothold in understanding what Tolkien considered human nature 'to be.' What we truly know of ourselves in our undifferentiated state of being, is hidden to us as a result of the fall which, and in Eriugena's allegorical terms, is a voluntary lapse from blessedness and eternity (which is timelessness) into corporeality, temporality, and sensuality. For Eriugena, human nature is a kind of 'realized mutability,' whose nature is still a unity and subsists in eternal close proximity to the Creator. The *reditus* is not so much a loss of 'self,' but a full realization of what it would mean to be 'human nature' had we not sinned. Unlike Augustine and Aquinas, nothing is 'super-added' to human nature, but a transformation—a *theosis*—takes place to effect this return.

Within the hierarchy of created being, I have shown that arising out of the Neoplatonic 'familial' identity, humanity has a unique status amongst other 'non-human' animals, with our attendant faculties of reason and emotional intelligence. This is stated in co-operative relational identity to the divine—being made in God's image and likeness, and our journey towards final redemption (or *theosis*). The Orthodox tradition, with its emphasis upon this *theosis*, reaffirms that our primal vocation is to participate in the divine life itself: God has brought us from 'non-being into being,' for more than mere biological existence. Indeed, one is a person only insofar as one reflects the 'being in communion' of the three persons of the Holy Trinity. Here the notion of personhood is not to be confused with the modern notion of 'individual.'[1] This sense of participation is emphasized in the *Offertory Prayers* of the priest in the Roman Rite of the Mass: "By the mystery of this water and wine, may we come to share in the divinity of Christ, who humbled himself to share in our humanity."[2] *Theosis* is therefore a two-way exchange—the former is only possible via the latter: participation in God via the humility of the incarnate Word. In its Pauline sense, Pseudo-Dionysius relates this participation to the pre-existent *persona* of Jesus, in that:

> Every being and all the ages derive their existence from the Pre-existent. All eternity and time are from him. The Pre-existent is the source and is the cause of all eternity, of time and every kind of being. Everything participates in him and none among beings fall away. "He is before all things and in him all things hold together."[3]

Tolkien's *Tale of Tinúviel* is a love story cast from this Neoplatonist mould, in a particular manner, and crafted to the needs of a skilled storyteller. Beren—as man—is both free and loved, capable of love and virtue. His contingent existence and essential (mutable and mortal) nature would be reduced to puppetry if his dignity were for a moment compromised by instrumental and/or deterministic influences. His free choices—like those of Lúthien—are key in allowing him to 'test his mettle,' and forge his own relationships based on honour and love for another. That he is able to do so lies in an extension of the Platonic concept of participation, but one which requires a more mystical approach, and one which does

1. 2 Peter 1:4; Breck, "The Sacredness and Sanctity of Human Life," 46–47.
2. *Roman Missal*, 564.
3. *Div Nom*, 5.820A; *cf.* Colossians 1:17.

not privilege ontological certainties based on narrow categories of being. After his "second death," Beren is joined for ever to the fate of Lúthien, "and their paths lead together beyond the confines of the world."[4] Their return is assured, but is not identified in *The Silmarillion* text. What is most real about us is cloaked via our descent into materiality; what is now most real in Beren and Lúthien is fully actualized beyond our grasp. If Siewers is correct in his assertion that Tolkien utilized Eriugena's *Periphyseon* in his environmental presentation of Middle-earth, then that self-same work can be seen to account for the fluidity of being/non-being in Tolkien's ontology/meontology in *The Tale of Tinúviel*. I have presented in a redacted form, therefore, a carefully crafted narrative, independent but related to the more classical strands of the Neoplatonist tradition, but one which displays sufficient originality which would have resonated with Tolkien's interest in both North European and Celtic writings.

Tolkien's Metaphysics of Evil's Lack of Being

In chapter 5, I shifted the focus of my investigation from material identity, participating in God's goodness and beauty, towards the possible models of mutability: ideas which Tolkien would have known, given his interest and use of Neoplatonic models of creation. That some good things are better than others, raises the possibility that the principle of plenitude appears to compromise a corrupt rational creature in favor of an aesthetic corporeal entity. For Augustine, this is quite the opposite, and he uses a variety of examples to assert his point.[5] No creature, then, is evil, in spite of the fact that some are 'worse' than others.[6] The word 'evil,' when predicated of creatures, refers to a privation, that absence of goodness where goodness might have been present.[7] Tolkien's sense of pity of 'evil things,' alongside his (English) sense of fair play and chance of reform, has as its ethical basis the intrinsic goodness of finitude, and life is never totally devoid of its original giftedness, as a creature of God. This is expressed in Aquinas' Platonic metaphysics of participation. Whilst these themes are broadly represented in Tolkien's account of 'being,' they are not the whole of the

---

4. Tolkien, *Silmarillion*, 225.

5. Mann, *Augustine on Evil*, 44, cites Augustine's assertion that corrupted gold is better than uncorrupted silver, meaning that the rational spirit corrupted by an evil will is still better than an uncorrupted irrational spirit, and that any spirit, no matter how corrupted, is better than any uncorrupted body (cf *De nat. boni c. Mani*, 5).

6. *De nat. boni c. Mani*, 14.

7. *Conf*, 3.7.12.

matter. Late Antiquity and early medievalism bear several significant departures from this Augustinian approach—even if it is difficult to verify in certainty of documentation and/or source. In this sense, Ungoliant is the most problematic and demonstrates strains of Manichaeism juxtaposed with his otherwise Christian Neoplatonic framework. The coexistence of evil and good is represented in both *schemata* by way of an aesthetic understanding of the problem, as in Augustine also.

In making the connection between the aesthetic concept of evil, between Augustine and Tolkien, the analysis of Sohn, Stump, Williams, and Hick are persuasive in that this may be an unsatisfactory solution to the *problem,* when viewed either from the purely human or purely divine perspective. Following Williams' reading of Augustine, I have shown that the principle of plenitude ought not to stress so much the virtue of 'variety,' but in this plenitude the interdependence of created beings—something equally present in Tolkien's account of the *musica universalis* tradition. Consonance and dissonance, woven together, bring forth life via the music-vision-reality procession, not despite, but taking into account, the competing wills of the Ainur as immanent Valar. Here God is presented as having a limited omniscience of *how* things will work themselves out, but a complete omnipotence in *that* things will work out for good or ill. The Children of Ilúvatar—elves and men—are brought forth out of the 'secret folds' of God's benevolent nature, and the Ainur share in participation, but without full knowledge of the actualization of Middle-earth.

It is a fact of life in the Middle-earth of the First Age and beyond, that the lives of elves and men are bound together in a common purpose: a participatory struggle against evil and its effects. From the standpoint of the individual, great suffering amidst heroic deeds ensue, and yet from the vista of the whole might be seen to contribute to the good of all.

Opportunities for Further Development

Given the limitations and scope of this investigation, there are several significant areas for further research and development. The response of David Jones to Jacques Maritain's theological Neo-Thomism shifts the focus of created art beyond the work of poetry or art *per se*, and introduces a symbolic and sacramental aspect to created things. As Tolkien's writings suggest a participatory goodness in created being, then by association the material elements within creation suggest a higher giftedness—a mediatory grace. This, according to Craig Bernthal's recent study, is written through Tolkien's entire published *corpus*. Given Tolkien's 'high' view of sacramentality in life and creation, then an extension study to section 2.5 would open up his works alongside a deeper scrutiny of his Neo-Thomistic ideas of God's immanence in materiality.[8]

A further opportunity for development lies in the more obscure texts of Tolkien's posthumously published works, and how they reflect a metaphysics broadly consonant with the Platonic and Aristotelian tradition, but aligned directly to neither one exclusively. Tolkien's mysticism has been highlighted in light of the influence of the Irish Sea legends linked to Eriugena. Given the overlaying of textual icons in the works of both Tolkien and Eriugena—highlighted in the work of Alfred Siewers—their respective approaches to environmental integrity is open to further investigation.

In tribute, the last word lies with the subject in whose work this thesis stands—J. R. R. Tolkien—and sums up his own project, alongside the many (unnamed) sources from which he worked:

> But in God's kingdom the presence of the greatest does not depress the small. redeemed Man is still man. Story, fantasy, still go on, and should go on. The Evangelium has not abrogated legends; it has hallowed them, especially the 'happy ending.' The Christian has still to work, with mind as well as body, to suffer, hope, and die; but now he may perceive that all his bents and faculties have a purpose, which can be redeemed.[9]

---

8. Bernthal, *Tolkien's Sacramental Vision*.
9. *Tree and Leaf*, 73.

Appendix A
Michelangelo's Statues in the Accademia, Florence

Fig. 1: The Young Slave

Fig. 2: The *Awakening Slave*

APPENDIX A: MICHELANGELO'S STATUES IN THE ACCADEMIA 245

Fig. 3: The Atlas Slave

246 APPENDIX A: MICHELANGELO'S STATUES IN THE ACCADEMIA

Fig. 4: David, front elevation

Fig 5: David, rear elevation

Fig 6: David, left elevation

APPENDIX A: MICHELANGELO'S STATUES IN THE ACCADEMIA 249

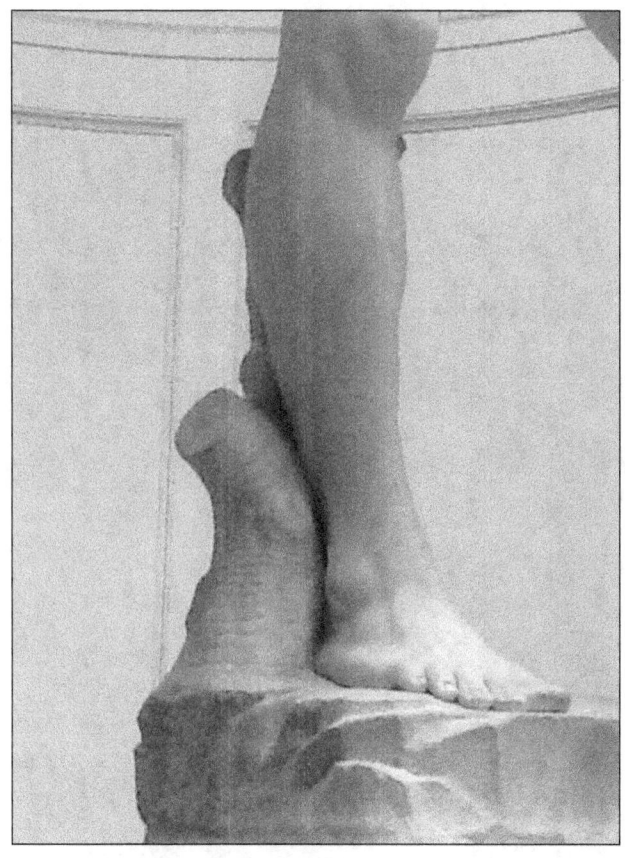

Fig 7: David, detail

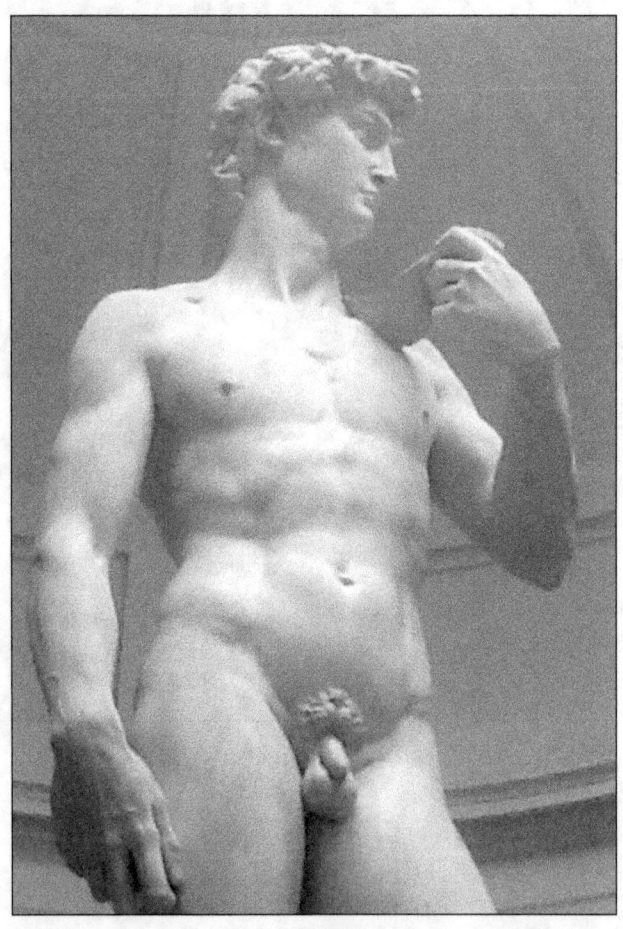

Fig 8: David, close-up

Appendix B

A Synopsis of *The Tale of Tinúviel,* or *Of Beren and Lúthien*

(*The Silmarillion,* pages 194–225)

Barahir, the father of Beren was resisting the dark Valar, Morgoth, whose whereabouts were revealed under torture of one of his kinsmen, Gorlim. The host were slain, all except Beren, who journeys to the scene after a visit of the spectre of the now murdered Gorlim. In his rage he slays the orc captain, and severs his father's hand, thus retaining the ring of his kingship.

After an extensive killing spree, and being pursued by Morgoth's army, Beren flees south over the mountains of Gorgoroth, and into the forbidden land of Doriath, ruled by the elf-king Thingol. It was in the glades of Doriath that he first saw Lúthien Tinúviel dance. She was immortal, and of mixed race: her father being an elf, but her mother a Maia—a 'semi-divine' being, like Sauron and Gandalf. Lúthien was the fairest of all Elves and Men, and her song was that of a nightingale, which is also a pseudonym for Tinúviel. Beren falls hopelessly in love with her, but they are betrayed and brought under her protection to her father, Thingol. He is enraged that a mortal should think thus about his (immortal) daughter, but she pleads for him, as he asks for her hand in marriage. As Beren explains the fate of his people, Thingol takes pity, and spares him. He is set a seemingly impossible task before he can marry her: the return of a precious jewel—a Silmaril—from the crown of Morgoth, which resides in his secret lair, Angband.

Beren accepts the task, and sets off south, whereupon Lúthien remains silent in song, as the shadows lengthen. He is taken captive again, and taken to king Finrod Felegund. The sons of Fëanor—Celegorm and Curufin—who have a lasting claim on the Silmarils, plot to kill Felegund when they hear of his support for Beren. Felegund, Beren and ten other elves set out on their quest, slaying orcs, and disguising themselves as the servants of Sauron. Supernaturally, Sauron becomes aware of them, and contests with Felegund in song, and prevails, laying bare their disguises and, being thrown into a cave, they await their evil fate. One by one they were devoured by a werewolf. When only Beren and Felegund remain, Lúthien supernaturally perceives their plight, but is locked in a tower to prevent her helping Beren. Through various enchantments she escapes. She is taken captive by Celegorm and Curufin, but is saved by the dog, Huan, but meanwhile Felegund is killed by the werewolf. Lúthien passes onto Sauron's Isle, by use of her song, and upon hearing it Beren replies. Desiring her as a prize for Morgoth, Sauron sends out wolves to capture her, but they are slain one by one by Huan. Finally, Sauron changes his form into a wolf and attacks the dog. In the struggle he changes again to a serpent, but is defeated. In a 'disembodied' form he is made to relinquish his Isle, and sent in the form of a vampire back to Morgoth. Lúthien throws down the gates of Sauron's Isle, and releases the captives—including Beren.

After burying Finrod Felegund, Beren, Lúthien and Huan make a winter journey back to Doriath, where they are attacked by the now exiled Celegorm and Curufin in the forest of Brethil. Beren and Huan prevail, but Beren is wounded by an arrow and treated by Lúthien. He then leaves her sleeping to continue his quest alone. His *Song of Parting* is heard by Lúthien, and she follows him, with the dog for company. In being reunited they journey towards Angband, having 'shapeshifted' into forms of fell bats, and Huan the visage of the now dead, Drauglin. Carcaroth the 'Red Maw' lies in wait. He is the most fearsome and powerful werewolf, tormented with Morgoth's hatred, but Lúthien reveals herself before him and performs a kind of exorcism on the werewolf. Because of her love for Beren, Lúthien has already forfeited her immortality, and they enter Morgoth's land unseen, and into his throne-room. There Lúthien sits before Morgoth and sings an enchanting song, lulling him to sleep and dreaming, as *"dark as the Outer Void where he once walked alone."* All Angband slept as Beren cut out a Silmaril from the crown of Morgoth. As he tried to cut out the others, a shard broke off his knife waking the Dark Lord. The three escaped without disguise to the gate, but were set upon by Carcaroth. As Beren held out the light of the Silmaril, the werewolf bit off his hand and ran away madly, driven to despair by the pure light of the jewel.

Beren is now fearfully wounded by the werewolf's venom, but Lúthien revives him with a song and they are borne aloft by eagles to the borders of Doriath. As they return to Thingol, they are given permission to marry, as Beren has the jewel in his hand - even if his hand is inside the wolf. Carcaroth brings fear to Doriath, and Beren—now recovered—sets off with a party to hunt him down. On finding him they lay in wait, and finally attack him. The werewolf and Huan are locked in mortal combat, and Carcharoth is killed. Sadly, Huan dies of his own wounds, and Beren sustains further serious injuries. The hand and jewel are cut from the belly of the werewolf. Both are incorrupt, but the hand disappears, leaving behind the Silmaril only.

His quest being over, Beren's doom is 'full-wrought'. He and the hound, Huan, are born aloft, and upon the greeting of Lúthien, he dies. His spirit remained in the Halls of Mandos—the place of judgment and parting—refusing to leave the world, until Lúthien came to say her last farewell. In having chosen mortality, eventually she dies and sings before Mandos. Her song moved him so deeply that he sought the will of the One (God), Ilúvatar, at whose bidding Manwë offered her two choices: to remain in Valimar, to dwell forever with the valar (gods) and being released of her suffering; or, to return to Middle-earth as a mortal with Beren, and suffer a second death. She chose the latter, thus eventually leaving the confines of the world. In so doing, the Two Kindreds of elves and men were forever joined.

Appendix C

Three Crosses in the Churchyard of Whalley Abbey, Lancashire

Fig. 9.

APPENDIX C: THREE CROSSES IN THE CHURCHYARD OF WHALLEY ABBEY

Fig. 10.

Fig. 11.

Fig. 12.
Detail relating to Fig. 10.

Appendix D

The Standard of the King of Gondor

Appendix E
Iconography In The *Book Of Kells*

Fig.14

St John the Evangelist holds aloft his Gospelbook, with
detail below of the 'lozenge' motif on its cover.

260 APPENDIX C: ICONOGRAPHY IN THE BOOK OF KELLS

Fig. 15

APPENDIX C: ICONOGRAPHY IN *THE BOOK OF KELLS* 261

Fig. 16

The Chi-Rho Monogram,
demonstrating the 'lozenge' motif at the intersection of the two
Greek letters, which serves as the incipit for the narrative of the life
of Christ and, in particular, his conception by the Holy Spirit.

Bibliography

Aeterni Patris: Encyclical of Pope Leo XIII on the Restoration of Christian Philosophy. http://w2.vatican.va/content/leo-xiii/en/encyclicals/documents/hf_l-xiii_enc_04081879_aeterni-patris.html.

Ainsworth, Harrison. *The Lancashire Witches.* 1849. Reprint, Nelson, UK: Gerrard, 1965.

Alton, David. *The Fellowship of the Ring: J. R. R. Tolkien, Catholicism and the Use of Allegory,* Text of a lecture given to the Catholic Society of the University of Bath and Bath Spa University College, on the 20th February 2003. http://www.ewtn.com/library/HUMANITY/J. R. R.TOLK.HTM.

The Anglo-Saxon Beowulf: The Scôp or Gleeman's Tale and the Fight at Finnesburg. Translated by Benjamin Thorpe. Oxford: James Wright, 1855.

The Anglo-Saxon Genesis. Translated by L. Mason. Burnham-on-Sea, UK: Llanerch, 1990.

The Apostolic Fathers. Translated by J. B. Lightfoot and J. R. Harmer, edited by Michael W. Holmes. 2nd ed. Grand Rapids: Baker, 1990.

Aquinas, Thomas. *On Being and Essence.* Translation and Notes by Armand Maurer. Toronto: Pontifical Institute of Mediaeval Studies, 1961.

———. *Quaestiones Disputatae De Potentia Dei.* Edited by Joseph Kenny OP. Westminster, MD: Newman, 1952. English Dominican Friars Online Edition. http://dhspriory.org/thomas/QDdePotentia.htm.

———. *Questiones Disputatae de Veritate.* Translated by R. W. Mulligan SJ et al. Chicago: Regnery, 1952-54. http://dhspriory.org/thomas/QDdeVer.htm.

———. *Summa Contra Gentiles.* Translated by Anton C. Pegis, edited by J. Kenny, OP. New York: Hanover House, 1955-57. http://dhspriory.org/thomas/ContraGentiles.htm.

———. *Summa Theologiae.* Translated by the Fathers of the English Dominican Province. Cincinatti, OH: Benziger, 1947. http://www.ccel.org/ccel/aquinas/summa.html.

———. *Super Boethium de Trinitate.* Translated by Rose E. Brennan (Q1-4, 1946) and Armand Maurer (Q5-6, 1953). http://www.dhspriory.org/thomas/BoethiusDeTr.htm#23.

Aristotle. *De Caelo I and II.* Edited and Translated by Stuart Leggatt. Warminster, UK: Aris and Phillips, 1995.

———. *Metaphysics I–XI*. Translated by Hugh Tredennick. Cambridge: Harvard University Press, 1936.
Augustine. *De Civitate Dei*. Translated by Henry Bettenson. London: Penguin, 2003.
———. *The Confessions*. Translated by Henry Chadwick. Oxford: Oxford University Press, 1991.
———. *De Doctrina Christiana. The Fathers of the Church, Volume 2: Saint Augustine*. Translated by John J. Gavigan, edited by Roy J. Deferrari. Washington, DC: Catholic University of America Press, 1950.
———. *De Genesi ad Litteram*. Translated and annotated by John H. Taylor, SJ. New York: Newman, 1982.
———. *De Genesi contra Manichaeos. Works of St Augustine, Part 1, Volume 13*. Edited by John E. Rotelle. New York: New City, 2001.
———. *De Libero Arbitrio*. Translated and edited by Peter King. Cambridge: Cambridge University Press, 2010.
———. *De Musica, The Fathers of the Church (A New Translation), Volume 4*. Translated by R. C. Taliaferro, edited by H. Dressler. Baltimore, MD: Catholic University of America Press, 1947.
———. *De Natura Boni contra Manichaeans. A Select Library of the Nicene and Post-Nicene Fathers of the Christian Church, Volume 4*. Translated by A. H. Newman, edited by P. Schaff, 351–365. Edinburgh: T. & T. Clark, 1887.
———. *De Trinitate. A Select Library of the Nicene and Post-Nicene Fathers of the Christian Church, Volume 3*. Translated by W. G. T. Shedd, edited by P. Schaff, 1–228. Edinburgh: T. & T. Clark, 1887.
———. *Enarationes in Psalmos, A Select Library of the Nicene and Post-Nicene Fathers of the Christian Church, Volume 8*. Translated by A. C. Coxe. Edited by P. Schaff. Edinburgh: T. & T. Clark, 1887.
———. *The Enchiridion. A Select Library of the Nicene and Post-Nicene Fathers of the Christian Church, Volume 3*. Translated by A. Outler, edited by P. Schaff, 237–276. Edinburgh: T. & T. Clark, 1883.
Basham, Gregory, and Eric Bronson, eds. *The Lord of the Rings and Philosophy: One Book to Rule Them All*. Chicago: Open Court, 2003.
Bates, Brian. *The Real Middle Earth: Magic and Mystery in the Dark Ages*. London: Sidgwick & Jackson, 2002.
Beowulf: A New Verse Translation. Translated by Seamus Heaney. London: Faber and Faber, 1999.
Bernthal, Craig. *Tolkien's Sacramental Vision: Discerning the Holy in Middle-Earth*. Kettering, OH: Second Spring, 2014.
Birzar, Bradley J. *J. R. R. Tolkien's Sanctifying Myth: Understanding Middle-earth*. Wilmington, DE: ISI, 2003.
Boethius. *The Consolations of Philosophy*. Translated by Patrick G. Walsh. Oxford: Oxford University Press, 1999
———. *Fundamentals of Music*. Translated by Calvin M. Bower and Claude V. Palisca. New Haven, CT: Yale University Press, 1989.
Bosworth, Joseph. *An Anglo-Saxon Dictionary*. Reprint, Oxford: Oxford University Press, 1976.
Bratman, David. "Gifted Amateurs: C. S. Lewis and the Inklings." In *C. S. Lewis: Apologist, Philosopher, and Theologian*, edited by D. L. Edwards, 279–332. Westport, CT: Greenwood, 2007.

Breck, John. "The Sacredness and Sanctity of Human Life." In *Theological Issues in Bioethics: An Introduction with Readings*, edited by Neil Messer, 45–49. London: Darton, Longman, and Todd, 1998.
Brennan, Brian. "Augustine's De Musica." *Vigiliae Christianae*, 42/3 (1988) 267–81.
Brett, Phillip. *Benjamin Britten: Peter Grimes*. Cambridge Opera Handbooks. Cambridge: Cambridge University Press, 1983.
Britten, Benjamin, and R. Ellis Roberts. *The Company of Heaven*, London: Faber Music, 1937.
Burrell, David. "Desire and the Semantics of God-talk: Beyond a 'Negative/Positive' Polarity." Talk delivered at The Aquinas Colloquium: 'Participation and Analogy', Blackfriars, Oxford, 3rd March 2012
———. *Knowing the Unknowable God: Ibn-Sina, Maimonides, Aquinas*. Notre Dame, IN: University of University of Notre Dame Press, 1986.
———. *Aquinas: God and Action*. London: Routledge, 1979.
Burrell, David, and Isabelle Moulin. "Albert, Aquinas, and Dionysius." In *Rethinking Dionysius the Areopagite*, edited by Sarah Coakley and Charles M. Stang, 103–19. Oxford: Wiley-Blackwell, 2009.
Caedmon's Metrical Paraphrase of the Parts of the Holy Scripture in Anglo-Saxon. Translated by Benjamin Thorpe. London: Society of Antiqueries of London, 1832.
Caldecott, Stratford. "Is Life a Transcendental?" *Radical Orthodoxy: Theology, Philosophy, Politics* 1.1&2 (2012) 188–200.
———. "Over the Chasm of Fire: Christian Heroism in *The Silmarillion* and *The Lord of the Rings*." In *Tolkien: A Celebration. Collected Writings on a Literary Legacy*, edited by Joseph Pearce, 17–33. London: Fount, 1999.
Carabine, Deirdre. *John Scottus Eriugena*. Oxford: Oxford University Press, 2000.
———. *The Unknown God—Negative Theology in the Platonic Tradition: Plato to Eriugena*. Louvain: Peeters, 1995.
Carpenter, Humphrey. *J. R. R. Tolkien: A Biography*. London: Allen and Unwin, 1977.
Casarella, Peter J. "Cusanus on Dionysius: The Turn to Speculative Theology." In *Rethinking Dionysius the Areopogite*, edited by Sarah Coakley and Charles M. Stang, 137–48. Oxford: Wiley-Blackwell, 2009.
Catechism of the Catholic Church. London: Geoffrey Chapman, 1994.
Chadwick, Henry. *The Consolations of Music, Logic, Theology and Philosophy*. Oxford: Clarendon, 1981.
Chance, Jane, and Alfred K. Siewers, eds. *Tolkien's Modern Middle Ages*. Basingstoke, UK: Palgrave Macmillan, 2009.
Chance, Jane, ed. *Tolkien and the Invention of Myth*. Lexington, KY: University of Kentucky Press, 2004.
———. *The Lord of the Rings: The Mythology of Power*. Lexington, KY: University of Kentucky Press, 2001.
Chesterton, Gilbert K. *The Coloured Lands*. Illustrated by the author, edited by Maisie Ward. London: Sheed and Ward, 1938.
Chism, Christine. "Middle-Earth, the Middle Ages, and the Aryan Nation: Myth and History in World War II." In *Tolkien the Medievalist*, edited by Jane Chance, 63–92. London: Routledge, 2003.
Clarke, George, and Daniel Timmons, eds. *J. R. R. Tolkien and His Literary Resonances: Views of Middle Earth*. Westport, CT: Greenwood, 2000.

1 Clement. In *The Apostolic Fathers*. Translated by J. B. Lightfoot and J. R. Harmer, edited by Michael W. Holmes, 2nd ed., 28–64. Grand Rapids: Baker, 1990.

Coakley, Sarah, and Charles M. Stang, eds. *Rethinking Dionysius the Areopogite*. Oxford: Wiley-Blackwell, 2009.

Coakley, Sarah, ed. *Religion and the Body*. Cambridge: Cambridge University Press, 1997.

Copleston, Frederick C. *Aquinas*. Harmondsworth, UK: Penguin, 1955.

Coulombe, C. A. "*The Lord of the Rings*—A Catholic View." In *Tolkien: A Celebration. Collected Writings on a Literary Legacy*, edited by Joseph Pearce, 53–66. London: Fount, 1999.

Curry, Patrick. *Defending Middle Earth, Tolkien: Myth & Modernity*. London: Harper Collins, 1997.

———. "Tolkien and His Critics: A Critique." In *Root and Branch: Approaches toward Understanding Tolkien*, edited by Thomas Honneger, 75–139. Zurich: Walking Tree, 2005.

Cusa, Nicholas. *Da Docta Ignoranta: Nicholas of Cusa on Learned Ignorance*. Translated by H. Lawrence Bond. New York: Paulist, 1977.

Dadosky, John D. "The Proof of Beauty: From Aesthetic Experience to the Beauty of God." *Analecta Hermeneutica* 2 (2010) 1–15.

Damphinais, Michael, Barry David, and Matthew Levering, eds. *Aquinas the Augustinian*. Washington, DC: Catholic University of America Press, 2007.

Davies, Brian. *Thomas Aquinas on God and Evil*. Oxford: Oxford University Press, 2011.

———. *The Thought of Thomas Aquinas*. Oxford: Clarendon, 1992.

Davis, Stephen T., ed. *Encountering Evil: Live Options in Theodicy*. Louisville, KY: Westminster John Knox, 2001.

Dawson, Christopher. "Introduction" to Jacques Maritain, *Religion and Culture*, No.1 of *Essays in Order*. London: Sheed and Ward, 1931.

Deely, John. *Medieval Philosophy Redefined: The Development of Cenoscopic Science, AD 354–1644 (From the Birth of Augustine to the Death of Poinsot)*. Scranton, PA: University of Scranton Press, 2010.

DeYoung, Rebecca, et al. *Aquinas' Ethics: Metaphysical Foundations, Moral Theory, and Theological Context*. Notre Dame, IN: University of Notre Dame Press, 2009.

The Divine Office: The Liturgy of the Hours According to the Roman Rite. London: Collins, 1974.

Dodaro, Robert, and George Lawless, eds. *Augustine and His Critics: Essays in Honour of Gerald Bonner*. London: Routledge, 2000.

Dubs, Kathleen E. "Providence, Fate and Chance: Boethian Philosophy in *Lord of the Rings*." In *Tolkien and the Invention of Myth*, edited by Jane Chance, 133–42. Lexington, KY: University of Kentucky Press, 2009.

Duclow, Donald F. *Masters of Learned Ignorance: Eriugena, Eckhart, Cusanus*. Aldershot, UK: Ashgate Variorum, 2006.

Eagleton, Terry. *On Evil*. New Haven, CT: Yale University Press, 2010.

The Earliest English Poems. Translated by Michael Alexander. Harmondsworth, UK: Penguin, 1966.

Eco, Umberto. *The Aesthetics of Thomas Aquinas*. Cambridge: Harvard University Press, 1988.

Eden, Bradford L., ed. *Middle Earth Minstrel: Essays on Music in Tolkien*. Jefferson, NC: McFarland, 2010.

———. "The 'Music of the Spheres': Relationships between Tolkien's *Silmarillion* and Medieval Cosmological and Religious Theory." In *Tolkien the Medievalist*, edited by Jane Chance, 183–93. London: Routledge, 2003.

Edwards, D. L., ed. *C. S. Lewis: Apologist, Philosopher, and Theologian*. Westport, CT: Greenwood, 2007.

Eliot, Thomas S. *The Complete Poems and Plays of T. S. Eliot*. London: Faber and Faber, 1969.

Eriugena, J-S. *Homily on the Prologue to the Gospel of John*. In *The Voice of the Eagle: The Heart of Celtic Christianity*, translated by Christopher Bamford. Barrington, MA: Lindisfarne, 2000.

———. *Periphyseon (The Division of Nature)*. Translated by I. P. Sheldon-Williams, revised by John J. O'Meara. Montréal: Bellarmin, 1987.

———. *Treatise on Divine Predestination*. Translated by Mary Brennan, with an introduction to the English Translation by Avital Wohlman. Notre Dame, IN: University of Notre Dame Press, 1989.

Evans, Peter. *The Music of Benjamin Britten*. Reprint, Oxford: Clarendon, 2002.

Evans, Gillian R. *Augustine on Evil*. Cambridge: Cambridge University Press, 1984.

Fallon, Robert. "Maritain's Poetic Knowledge in Stravinsky and Messiaen." In *Jacques Maritain and the Many Ways of Knowing*, edited by Douglas A. Ollivant, 284–302. Washington, DC: Catholic University of America Press, 2002.

Flieger, Verlyn. "J. R. R. Tolkien and the Matter of Britain." *Mythlore* 87 (2000) 47–58.

———. "Naming the Unnameable: The Neoplatonic 'One' in Tolkien's *Silmarillion*." In *Diakonia: Studies in Honor of Robert T. Meyer*, edited by Thomas Halton and Joseph P. Williman, 127–32. Washington, DC: The Catholic University of America Press, 1986.

———. *Splintered Light: Logos and Language in Tolkien's World*. Grand Rapids: Eerdmans, 1983.

Garth, John. *Tolkien and the Great War: The Threshold of Middle Earth*. London: Harper Collins, 2003.

Gray, William. *Fantasy, Myth and the Measure of Truth: Tales of Pullman, Lewis, Tolkien, MacDonald and Hoffman*. New York: Palgrave Macmillan, 2009.

Griffin, David R. "Creation Out of Nothing, Creation Out of Chaos, and the Problem of Evil." In *Encountering Evil: Live Options in Theodicy*, edited by Stephen T. Davis, 108–44. Louisville, KY: Westminster John Knox, 2001.

Halton, Thomas, and Joseph Williman, eds. *Diakonia: Studies in Honor of Robert T. Meyer*. Washington, DC: The Catholic University of America Press, 1986.

Hammond, Wayne G., and Christina Scull, eds. *Lord of the Rings 1954–2004: Scholarship in Honor of R. E. Blackwelder*. Milwaukee, WI: Marquette University Press, 2006.

Hanby, Michael. *Augustine and Modernity*. London: Routledge, 2003.

Hankey, Wayne J. "Reading Augustine through Dionysius." In *Aquinas the Augustinian*, edited by Michael Damphinais et al., 243–57. Washington, DC: Catholic University of America Press, 2007.

Hart, David B. *The Beauty of the Infinite: The Aesthetics of Christian Truth*. Grand Rapids: Eerdmans, 2004.

Herbert, David, ed. *The Operas of Benjamin Britten*. London: Hamish Hamilton, 1979.

Hibbs, Thomas. *Aquinas, Ethics, and Philosophy of Religion: Metaphysics and Practice*. Bloomington, IN: Indiana University Press, 2007.

Hick, John. *Evil and the God of Love*. London: Macmillan, 1966.

Hohn, Hohyun "The Beauty of Hell? Augustine's Aesthetic Theodicy and Its Critics." *Theology Today* 64 (2007) 47-57.
Holmes, John R. "Tolkien, 'Dustsceawung', and the Gnomic Tense: Is Timelessness Medieval or Victorian?" In *Tolkien's Modern Middle Ages*, edited by Jane Chance and Alfred K. Siewers, 43-58. Basingstoke, UK: Palgrave Macmillan, 2009.
The Holy Bible. Revised Standard Version. London: Collins, 1952.
Honneger, Thomas, ed. *Root and Branch: Approaches toward Understanding Tolkien*. Zurich: Walking Tree, 2005.
Houghton, John W. "Augustine in the Cottage of Lost Play: The Ainulindalë as Asterisk Cosmogony." In *Tolkien the Medievalist*, edited by Jane Chance, 171-82. London: Routledge, 2003.
Hudson, Benjamin, ed. *Studies in the Medieval Atlantic*. Basingstoke, UK: Palgrave Macmillan, 2012.
Jenson, Keith W. "Dissonance in the Divine Theme: The Issue of Free Will in Tolkien's Silmarillion." In *Middle Earth Minstrel: Essays on Music in Tolkien*, edited by Bradford L. Eden, 102-13. Jefferson, NC: McFarland, 2010.
The Jerusalem Bible. London: Darton, Longman & Todd, 1974.
John Paul II. *Fides et Ratio: On the Relationship between Faith and Reason*. London: Catholic Truth Society, 1998.
Jones, David. *Epoch and Artist: Selected Writings*. Edited by Harman Grisewood. London: Faber and Faber, 1959.
Kaufman, Peter I. *Augustinian Piety and Catholic Reform: Augustine, Colet, and Erasmus*. Macon, GA: Mercer University Press, 1982.
Knuuttila, Simo. "Time and Creation in Augustine." In *The Cambridge Companion to Augustine*, edited by Norman Kretzman and Eleanor Stump, 103-15. Cambridge: Cambridge University Press, 2001.
Kretzman, Norman, and Eleanor Stump, eds. *The Cambridge Companion to Augustine*. Cambridge: Cambridge University Press, 2001.
Laarhoven, Jan Van. "Thomas op Vaticanum II." In *De praktische Thomas. Thomas van Aquino: De consequenties van zijn theologie voor hedendaags gedrag*, 113-27. Theologie en samenleving, 10. Hilversum: Gooi en Sticht, 1987.
Le Guin, Ursula K. *The Language of the Night: Essays on Fantasy and Science Fiction*. London: Women's Press, 1989.
Leithart, Peter J. *Deep Comedy: Trinity, Tragedy and Hope in Western Literature*. Moscow, ID: Canon, 2011.
Lemna, Keith. "The Angels and Cosmic Liturgy: An Oratorian Angelology." *Nova et Vetera* (English ed.) 8.4 (2010) 901-21.
Lewis, Charles S. *The Literary Impact of The Authorised Version*. London: Athlone, 1950. http://www.biblicalstudies.org.uk/pdf/kjv_lewis.pdf.
Louth, Andrew. "The Body in Western Catholic Christianity." In *Religion and the Body*, edited by Sarah Coakley, 111-30. Cambridge: Cambridge University Press, 1997.
Lossky, Vladimir. *The Mystical Theology of the Eastern Church*. Cambridge: James Clarke, 1991.
Luling, Virginia. "An Anthropologist in Middle Earth." In *Proceedings of the J. R. R. Tolkien Centenary Conference*, edited by Patricia Reynolds and Glen Goodnight, 53-57. Milton Keynes, UK: Mythopoeic, 1995.
Luthi, Max. *The Fairytale as Art Form and Portrait of Man*. Translated by J. Erikson. Bloomington, IN: Indiana University Press, 1985.

McDermott, Timothy, ed. *Summa Theologiae: A Concise Translation*. London: Methuen, 1991.

McEvoy, James, and Michael Dunne, eds. *History and Eschatology in John Scottus Eriugena and His Time*. Leuven: Leuven University Press, 2002.

McGinn, Bernard. "Eriugena Confronts the End." In *History and Eschatology in John Scottus Eriugena and His Time*, edited by James McEvoy and Michael Dunne, 4–37. Leuven: Leuven University Press, 2002.

McIntosh, Jonathan. "Ainulindalë: Tolkien, St Thomas, and the Metaphysics of Music." In *Music in Middle-earth*, edited by Heidi Steimel and Friedhelm Schneidewind, 53–72. Zollikofen, Switzerland: Walking Tree, 2010.

———. "The Flame Imperishable: Tolkien, St Thomas and the Metaphysics of Faërie." PhD diss., University of Dallas, 2009.

McMahon, Robert. *Understanding the Medieval Meditative Ascent: Augustine, Anselm, Boethius and Dante*, Washington, DC: Catholic University of America Press, 2006.

Mann, William E. "Augustine on Evil and Original Sin." In *The Cambridge Companion to Augustine*, edited by Norman Kretzman and Eleanor Stump, 40–48. Cambridge: Cambridge University Press, 2001.

Marenbon, John. *Medieval Philosophy: An Historical and Philosophical Introduction*. London: Routledge, 2007.

Maritain, Jacques. *Art and Scholasticism and the Frontiers of Poetry*. Translated by J. W. Evans. New York: Scribner's Sons, 1962.

———. *Bergsonian Philosophy and Thomism*. Translated by J. Gordon Andison and Mabelle L. Andison. New York: Philosophical Library, 1955.

———. *Creative Intuition in Art and Poetry: The A. W. Mellon Lectures in the Fine Arts*. Washington, DC: The National Gallery of Art, 1952.

———. *Theonas: Conversations of a Sage*. Translated by F. J. Sheed. London: Sheed and Ward, 1923.

Matthews, David M. *Britten*. London: Hause, 2013.

Maurer, Armand. *About Beauty: A Thomistic Interpretation*. Houston, TX: Center for Thomistic Studies, 1983.

Maximus the Confessor. *The Ambigua: On Difficulties in the Church Fathers, Volume II*. Translated and edited by Nicholas Constas, Cambridge: Harvard University Press, 2014.

Messer, Neil, ed. *Theological Issues in Bioethics: An Introduction with Readings*. London: Darton, Longman, and Todd, 2002.

Mettepenningen, Jürgen. *Nouvelle Théologie—New Theology: Inheritor of Modern Thought, Precursor of Vatican II*. London: T. & T. Clark, 2010.

Milbank, Alison. *Chesterton and Tolkien as Theologians: The Fantasy of the Real*. London: T. & T. Clark, 2007.

Milbank, John, and Simon Oliver, eds. *The Radical Orthodoxy Reader*. London: Routledge, 2009.

Milbank, John, and Catherine Pickstock. *Truth in Aquinas*. London: Routledge, 2001.

Milbank, John, Catherine Pickstock, and Graham Ward, eds. *Radical Orthodoxy: A New Theology*. London: Routledge, 1999.

Miles, Jonathan. *Backgrounds to David Jones: A Study in Sources and Drifts*. Cardiff: University of Wales University Press, 1990.

McIntosh, Jonathan S. *The Flame Imperishable: Tolkien, St Thomas, and the Metaphysics of Faerie*. Kettering, OH: Angelico Press, 2017.

Montag, John. "Revelation: The False Legacy of Suarez." In *Radical Orthodoxy: A New Theology*, edited by John Milbank, Catherine Pickstock, and Graham Ward, 38–63. London: Routledge, 1999.

Moran, Dermot. *The Philosophy of John Scottus Eriugena: A Study of Idealism in the Middle Ages*. Cambridge: Cambridge University Press, 1989.

O'Connell, Robert J. *Augustine's Early Theory of Man*. Cambridge: Harvard University Press, 1968.

Oliver, Simon. "Introducing Radical Orthodoxy: From Participation to Late Modernity." In *The Radical Orthodoxy Reader*, edited by John Milbank and Simon Oliver, 3–27. London: Routledge, 2009.

———. *Philosophy, God and Motion*. London: Routledge, 2005.

———. "The Sweet Delight of Virtue and Grace in Aquinas' Ethics." *International Journal of Systematic Theology* 7.1 (2005) 52–71.

Ollivant, Douglas A., ed. *Jacques Maritain and the Many Ways of Knowing*. Washington, DC: Catholic University of America Press, 2002.

O'Loughlin, Tom. "Imagery of the New Jerusalem in the *Periphyseon* and Eriugena's Irish Background." In *History and Eschatology in John Scottus Eriugena and His Time*, edited by James McEvoy and Michael Dunne, 245–60. Leuven: Leuven University Press, 2002.

O'Meara, John J. *Studies in Augustine and Eriugena*. Washington, DC: Catholic University of America Press, 1992.

O'Meara, John J. *Eriugena*. Oxford: Clarendon, 1988.

O'Neill, Timothy R. *The Individuated Hobbit: Jung and the Archetypes of Middle Earth*. Boston: Houghton Mifflin, 1979.

O'Reilly, Kevin. *Aesthetic Perception: A Thomistic Perspective*. Dublin: Four Courts, 2007.

Otten, Willemien. *The Anthropology of Johannes Scottus Eriugena*. Leiden: Brill, 1991.

Payne, F. Anne. *King Alfred and Boethius: An Analysis of the Old English Version of the Consolations of Philosophy*. Madison, WI: University of Wisconsin Press, 1968.

Pearce, Joseph, ed. *Tolkien: A Celebration. Collected Writings on a Literary Legacy*. London: Fount, 1999.

Phelpstead, Carl. *Tolkien and Wales: Language, Literature and Identity*. Cardiff: University of Wales Press, 2011.

Plato. *Parmenides*, Translated by Samuel Scolnicov. Berkeley: University of California Press, 2003.

———. *Republic*. Translated by Desmond Lee. London: Penguin, 1974.

———. *Timaeus and Critias*. Translated by Desmond Lee. London: Penguin Classics, 1965.

Plotinus. *The Enneads*. Translated by Stephen MacKenna. London: Penguin, 1991.

Puigarnau, Alfons. "Creation and Freedom in Ancient Neoplatonism: A Road to the Middle Ages." Paper presented at the University of Leeds, during the International Congress on Medieval Theology. *Ars Brevis* (1998) 243–54. http://www.raco.cat/index.php/arsbrevis/article/viewFile/93818/142195.

Pseudo-Dionysius the Areopogite. *The Complete Works*. Translated by Colm Luibheid. New York: Paulist, 1987.

Purcell, Henry. *Ode on St Cecilia's Day 1692*. Edited by Peter Dennison. Bury St Edmunds, UK: Novello, 1975.

Rateliff, John. "And All the Days of Her Life Are Forgotten: *Lord of the Rings* as Mythic History." In *Lord of the Rings 1954–2004: Scholarship in Honour of R. E. Blackwelder*, edited by Wayne G. Hammond and Christina Scull, 67–100. Milwaukee, WI: Marquette University Press, 2006.

Ratzinger, Joseph. *Jesus of Nazareth: Part 2—Holy Week from the Entrance into Jerusalem to the Resurrection.* London: Catholic Truth Society, 2011.

———. *The Spirit of the Liturgy.* San Francisco: Ignatius, 2000.

Relihan, Joel C. *The Prisoner's Philosophy: Life and Death in Boethius's Consolation.* Notre Dame, IN: University of Notre Dame Press, 2006

Richardson, Hillary. "Themes in Eriugena's Writings and Early Irish Art." In *History and Eschatology in John Scottus Eriugena and His Time*, edited by James McEvoy and Michael Dunne, 261–82. Leuven: Leuven University Press, 2002.

Rist, John. *Augustine: Ancient Thought Baptised.* Cambridge: Cambridge University Press, 1996

———. "Augustine on Free Will and Predestination." *Journal of Theological Studies* 20.2 (1969) 420–47.

The Roman Missal. London: Catholic Truth Society, 2010.

Rorem, Paul. "The Early Latin Dionysius: Eriugena and Hugo of St Victor." In *Rethinking Dionysius the Areopogite*, edited by Sarah Coakley and Charles M. Stang, 71–84. Oxford: Wiley-Blackwell, 2009.

Rziha, John. *Perfecting Human Actions: St Thomas Aquinas on Human Participation in Eternal Law.* Washington, DC: Catholic University of America Press, 2009.

Sadie, Stanley, ed. *The New Grove Dictionary of Music and Musicians.* 2nd ed. London: Macmillan, 2011.

The Saga of the Völsungs: Together with Excerpts from the Nornageststháttr and Three Chapters from the Prose Edda. Translated by George K. Anderson. Newark, NJ: University of Delaware Press, 1982.

Sawyer, Frank. *The Rock: Christ, Church and the World in T. S. Eliot's 1934 Pageant: 'The Rock.'* 2011. http://srta.tirek.hu/data/attachments/2011/08/11/Eliot_-_The_Rock.pdf.

Shippey, Tom. *The Road to Middle Earth.* London: Harper Collins, 2005.

———. *J. R. R. Tolkien: Author of the Century.* London: Harper Collins, 2000.

Siewers, Alfred K. "Desert Islands: Europe's Atlantic Archipelago as Ascetic Landscape." In *Studies in the Medieval Atlantic*, edited by Benjamin Hudson, 35–63. Basingstoke, UK: Palgrave Macmillan, 2012.

———. *Strange Beauty: Ecocritical Approaches to Early Medieval Landscape.* Basingstoke, UK: Palgrave Macmillan, 2009.

———. "Tolkien's Cosmic-Christian: The Medieval Underpinnings." In *Tolkien's Modern Middle Ages*, edited by Jane Chance and Alfred K. Siewers, 139–53. Basingstoke, UK: Palgrave Macmillan, 2009.

Skögemann, Pia. *Where the Shadows Lie: A Jungian Interpretation of Tolkien's Lord of the Rings.* Wilmette, IL: Chiron, 2009.

Sohn, Hohyun. "The Beauty of Hell? Augustine's Aesthetic Theodicy and Its Critics." *Theology Today* 64 (2007) 47–57.

Spitzer, Leo. *Classical and Christian Ideas of World Harmony: Prolegomena to an Interpretation of the Word " Stimmung."* Baltimore, MD: John Hopkins University Press, 1963.

Steel, Carlos G. *The Changing Self: A Study on the Soul in Later Neoplatonism: Iamblicus, Damascius and Priscianus*. Brussels: Palais der Academien, 1978.
———. "The Return of the Body into the Soul." In *History and Eschatology in John Scottus Eriugena and His Time*, edited by James McEvoy and Michael Dunne, 581–609. Leuven: Leuven University Press, 2002.
Stevens, Jen. "From Catastrophe to Euchatastrophe: J. R. R. Tolkien's Transformation of Ovid's Mythic Pyramus and Thisbe into Beren and Luthien." In *Tolkien and the Invention of Myth*, edited by Jane Chance, 119–32. Lexington, KY: University of Kentucky Press, 2004.
Stone-Davis, Ferdia J. *Musical Beauty: Negotiating the Boundary between Subject and Object*. Eugene, OR: Cascade, 2011.
Stump, Eleanor. "Augustine on Free Will." In *The Cambridge Companion to Augustine*, edited by Norman Kretzman and Eleanor Stump, 124–47. Cambridge: Cambridge University Press, 2001.
———. *Wandering in Darkness: Narrative and the Problem of Suffering*. Oxford: Oxford University Press, 2010.
Te Velde, Rudi. *Aquinas on God: The Divine Science of the Summa Theologiae*. Aldershot, UK: Ashgate, 2006.
———. *Participation and Substantiality in Thomas Aquinas*. Leiden: Brill, 1995.
———. "Questions on Analogy/Analogia Entis." A paper delivered at the Aquinas Colloquium "Participation and Analogy," Blackfriars, Oxford, 3rd March 2012.
Tolkien, J. R. R. *Beowulf: A Translation and Commentary, together with Sellic Spell*. London: Harper Collins, 2014.
———. *The Book of Lost Tales: Part One*. London: Allen & Unwin, 1983.
———. *The Book of Lost Tales: Part Two*. London: Allen & Unwin, 1984.
———. *The Hobbit*. 3rd ed. London: Allen & Unwin, 1966.
———. *The Legend of Sigurd and Gudrun*. London: Harper Collins, 2009.
———. *The Letters of J. R. R. Tolkien*. Edited by Humphrey Carpenter. London: Harper Collins, 2006.
———. *The Lord of the Rings*. 3-vol. ed. London: Unwin, 1979.
———. *Morgoth's Ring: The History of Middle-Earth, Volume X*. London: Harper Collins, 1994.
———. *The Monsters and the Critics, and Other Essays*. London: Harper Collins, 2006.
———. *The Old English Exodus: Text, Translation & Commentary*. Oxford: Clarendon, 1982.
———. *Sauron Defeated: The History of Middle-Earth, Volume IX*. London: Harper Collins, 1992.
———. *The Silmarillion*. London: Unwin Paperbacks, 1979.
———. *Sir Gawain and the Green Knight* (including *Pearl* and *Sir Orfeo*). London: Harper Collins, 2006.
———. *The Tale of the Children of Hurin*. London: Harper Collins, 2007.
———. *Tree and Leaf* (including *On Fairy Stories, Mythopoeia, Leaf by Niggle*, and *The Homecoming of Beorhtnoth*). London: Harper Collins, 2001.
Trapani, John G. *Poetry, Beauty and Contemplation: The Complete Aesthetics of Jacques Maritain*. Washington, DC: Catholic University of America Press, 2011.
Treschow, Michael. "Wisdom's Land: King Alfred's Imagery in His Preface to His Translation of Augustine's SOLILOQUIES." In *Divine Creation in Ancient, Medieval and Early Modern Thought: Essays Presented to the Revd. Dr Robert D. Crouse*, edited by Michael Treschow et al., 257–82. Leiden: Brill, 2007.

Tóth, Beáta. "Life as an Analogical Concept." *Radical Orthodoxy: Theology, Philosophy, Politics* 1.1&2 (2012) 95–120.
Vatican Council II: The Conciliar and Post Conciliar Documents. Rev. ed. Northport, NY: Costello, 1988.
Ward, Graham. "Affect: Towards a Theology of Experience." *Radical Orthodoxy: Theology, Philosophy, Politics* 1.1&2 (2012) 55–80.
Ware, Kalistos. *The Orthodox Way*. Cretswood, NY: St Vladimir's Seminary, 1999.
Weinreich, Frank, and Thomas Honeger, eds. *Tolkien and Modernity*, 1. Zollikofen, Switzerland: Walking Tree, 2006.
West, Richard C. "Real World Myth in a Secondary World." In *Tolkien the Medievalist*, edited by Jane Chance, 259–67, London: Routledge, 2003.
Wilcox, Miranda. "Exilic Imaginings in the Seafarer and The Lord of the Rings." In *Tolkien the Medievalist*, edited by Jane Chance, 133–54, London: Routledge, 2003.
Williams, Rowan. *Grace and Necessity: Reflections on Art and Love*. London: Continuum, 2005.
———. "Insubstantial Evil." In *Augustine and His Critics: Essays in Honour of Gerald Bonner*, edited by Robert Dodaro and George Lawless, 105–23. London: Routledge, 2000.
Winterson, Jeanette. *Art Objects: Essays on Ecstacy and Effrontery*. London: Vintage, 1996.
Wood, Robert E. *Placing Aesthetics: Reflections on Philosophic Tradition*. Athens, IL: Ohio University Press, 1999.

www.ingramcontent.com/pod-product-compliance
Lightning Source LLC
Chambersburg PA
CBHW071239230426
43668CB00011B/1504